THE ROAD HALF TRAVELED

TRANSFORMATIONS IN HIGHER EDUCATION:
THE SCHOLARSHIP OF ENGAGEMENT

THE ROAD HALF TRAVELED

UNIVERSITY ENGAGEMENT AT A CROSSROADS

Rita Axelroth Hodges and Steve Dubb

Michigan State University Press • *East Lansing*

♾ The paper used in this publication meets the minimum requirements
of ANSI/NISO Z39.48-1992 (R 1997) (Permanence of Paper).

Michigan State University Press
East Lansing, Michigan 48823-5245

Printed and bound in the United States of America.

18 17 16 15 14 13 12 1 2 3 4 5 6 7 8 9 10

LIBRARY OF CONGRESS CATALOGING-IN-PUBLICATION DATA

Hodges, Rita Axelroth.
The road half traveled : university engagement at a crossroads / Rita Axelroth Hodges and Steve Dubb.
p. cm.—(Transformations in higher education: the scholarship of engagement)
Includes bibliographical references and index.
ISBN 978-1-61186-046-7 (pbk. : alk. paper) 1. Community and college—United States. I. Dubb, Steve. II. Title.
LC238.H63 2012
378.1'030973—dc23
2011050517

ISBN 978-1-61186-046-7 (Paper)
ISBN 978-1-60917-340-1 (E-book)

Cover design by Charlie Sharp, Sharp Des!gns, Lansing, MI.
Book design by Aptara

Michigan State University Press is a member of the Green Press Initiative and is committed to developing
and encouraging ecologically responsible publishing practices. For more information about the Green Press
Initiative and the use of recycled paper in book publishing, please visit www.greenpressinitiative.org.

Visit Michigan State University Press at www.msupress.org

Contents

Figures

Foreword

Charles Rutheiser

Several years ago, I was conducting ethnographic research in a neighborhood adjacent to a large urban university. While interviewing a community leader, I referred to the university as an "anchor institution." The woman looked puzzled for a moment then smiled. "I guess that's about right," she said, "an anchor is something that gets dropped on people's heads." She and her fellow residents had valid grounds for cynicism. As was the case in many other poor neighborhoods located next to large universities in cities around the country, relations between her community and the university had been marked by decades of conflict, tension, and mutual distrust. The institution was located in the community, but not of it, surrounded by walls and several other less tangible yet still formidable barriers. In many respects, the university was more oriented and tied to peer institutions in other cities and even other countries than to the neighborhood that stood, literally, across the street. The wealth of the university, symbolized by its state-of-the-art buildings bearing the names of prominent donors, stood in stark contrast to the many dilapidated and abandoned buildings in one of the poorest communities in the city.

Things have changed since that interview. The university referred to above has since committed itself to charting a much more engaged and positive relationship with the community residents. This development was, in part, inspired and guided by the examples of some of the colleges and universities profiled in this volume that, over the past decade, have sought to undo the historic disconnect between themselves and their surrounding communities and redefine what it means to be an anchor institution in more constructive and socially responsible ways.

Nationally, the increased interest of anchor institutions in local community and economic development has been driven by multiple factors. In some cases, the shift was sparked by the commitment of faculty, administrators, and university presidents to practice and value more engaged scholarship and community service. In other instances, increased crime prompted universities to recognize the limited effectiveness of creating secure, fortified enclaves amid seas of concentrated poverty. Still other university leaders realized that their ability to attract and retain both staff and students was closely tied to the stability and appeal of the neighborhoods surrounding their campuses. These internal dynamics within institutions of higher education have been bolstered by a growing recognition by governments, economic development experts, and philanthropies that universities and hospitals—often shorthanded as "eds and meds"—are not only the current major economic engines in many urban areas, but also offer some of the best prospects to catalyze future growth in an increasingly knowledge-based economy.

The renewed interest of anchor institutions in their surrounding communities has been manifest in different ways. As this study suggests, universities can play several different kinds of value-added roles—as leader, facilitator, convener, and investor in various forms of human capital and physical development. But it is just as important to note that, without what Hodges and Dubb describe as a clear "anchor institution mission" that intentionally and strategically deploys the economic, human, and intellectual capital of institutions to improve the long-term welfare of the communities in which they reside, the growth of universities by themselves will not necessarily improve circumstances for the people who live in distressed communities adjacent to these institutions and, indeed, could make conditions worse. In (alas, still far too) many places, the growth of universities and colleges has been driven by narrow institutional self-interest, with scant, if any, regard for the needs and interests of their neighbors. Still, a relatively small but increasing number of colleges and universities around the country have begun to adopt and implement more enlightened definitions of their institutional self-interest that recognizes, in varying degrees to be sure, the need to engage residents and other community actors and work with them for their mutual benefit.

The institutions profiled in this volume represent some of the most promising examples of how colleges and universities can work with communities to help create mutually advantageous "win-win" solutions that work for both the institutions *and* the communities in which they are located. While there have been many reports and articles on the role of universities as anchor institutions, the authors of this study have aimed to go beyond promotional "feel-good" pieces and anecdotal accounts to not only paint a picture of what these institutions have done, but ask how and to what extent their activities have affected low-income communities in both positive and negative ways. Finding that the effects of these activities have been promising, but often limited or mixed, in their benefit to the community, the authors make some suggestions about how these strategies can be refined and refocused for even greater positive impact.

Indeed, while much has been learned and accomplished, much more remains to be done. Despite the tireless labors of committed practitioners, the field of anchor institutions remains very much in a nascent state, with limited means to share information about what has worked (and what hasn't), about building the capacity of anchors to function as more responsible and responsive institutions, and about understanding the full and true impact of efforts to date. For example, we still know far too little about how and to what extent even the best efforts have improved outcomes for populations of low-income children and families.

Given the relatively small number of universities that have adopted an anchor institution mission as our authors have defined it, it might be very optimistic to say that the road has been "half traveled." At the very least, the half that remains gets a lot more challenging beyond this point, covering much steeper and perilous terrain, full of twists and turns, precipices and chasms, and no shortage of potential dead ends and rockslides. In fact, in some respects, the road ahead exists only as dotted lines on a map charting multiple possible rights of ways rather than a single, clear paved route. One of the major contributions of this volume is to identify what some of these pathways have been, what future pathways could look like, and what new kinds of planning, capacity-building, and trailblazing skills are needed—by both individual institutions and the field as a whole—to realize the promise and opportunities that anchor institutions hold.

Preface

We did not know it then, but the development of this book owes a considerable debt to a brief opening in our nation's politics, when it appeared that universities might be taken seriously as partners for rebuilding America's communities.

In the wake of President Barack Obama's election, a group of over one hundred activists known as the "urban and metropolitan policy caucus," led by attorney Rachel Godsil and community development consultant Paul Brophy, were asked by the incoming Obama administration to put together a series of recommendations for Shaun Donovan, then the president's nominee to lead the U.S. Department of Housing and Urban Development. After hearing a panel moderated by Ira Harkavy, founder and director of the Netter Center for Community Partnerships at the University of Pennsylvania and a leading national figure in the university engagement movement, Brophy was convinced that recommendations to the incoming secretary should also include a group that would advise on strategies for mobilizing "anchor institutions as partners in building successful communities and local economies." Harkavy chaired this new group, dubbed the Anchor Institutions Task Force, and, through a fortuitous chain of events, both of us were recruited, in mid-December, to spend the next two weeks in a mad dash to conduct research, compile comments and writings from about two dozen task force members (including university presidents and leading academics), organize the input we received, and synthesize the submissions into a coherent report. Together with Ira Harkavy, Joann Weeks, and Eleanor Sharpe (and working with editor Paul Brophy), we completed the task.

To no one's surprise, our recommendations, although well received by Obama administration officials, have resulted in, at best, minor modifications of policy. There is, indeed, a greater willingness to encourage participation of anchor institutions in government initiatives (including, notably, the Sustainable Communities Initiative, Choice Neighborhoods, and Promise Neighborhoods). Outside government, one can identify prominent philanthropic initiatives, most notably the Living Cities' Integration Initiative, which has a budget of $80 million and supports comprehensive efforts in five cities to leverage anchor institutions for community economic development. Still, quite frankly, we acknowledge that anchor institutions remain largely marginal to most community economic development policy.

But our time on the report to Secretary Donovan also formed an important crucible in our thinking about some of the critical questions that we would attempt to address in this book. First, we believed that it was important to bring together two, sometimes separate, tendencies within the university engagement movement—one of which focuses on partnerships (often seen as "soft" by detractors) and one of which focuses more on "brick and mortar" community economic development (sometimes seen as a distraction from universities' "core educational mission" by critics). Rather than think of this as an "either/or" choice, we sought to illustrate the full range of university activity since we believe both ends are important. For example, because the lifetime earnings differential between high school graduates and those who do not graduate exceeds $100,000, it is hardly sensible to act as if partnerships with public schools are of no economic importance. At the same time, we think a perspective that limits itself to faculty and student activity and fails to look at the corporate side of the university (e.g., purchasing, hiring, investment, and real estate) is missing an important half of the picture. And, further, such corporate investments play a vital role in helping the university create the community conditions in which its educational and research efforts may thrive. As we seek to demonstrate, when the corporate and academic sides of engagement are well aligned, the whole can be much greater than the sum of its parts.

Second, we sought to put forward a new language to frame a fresh way of thinking about the community economic development role of universities. While the term "anchor institution" has been widely used ever since it was popularized by Harvard business professor Michael Porter, the idea of an *anchor institution mission*, we believe, is new. The point, quite simply, is that universities are important community economic actors and, through the *conscious* and *strategic* application of their corporate and intellectual resources in a coordinated fashion for community economic benefit, universities can have a powerful and more beneficial impact on surrounding neighborhoods.

Third, we wanted to push the field to take community economic development outcomes more seriously—a long time goal of the Democracy Collaborative, which provided the institutional base for our research. As the report to Secretary Donovan illustrates, university partnership leaders can be proud of many achievements. But few universities have pursued poverty reduction in surrounding neighborhoods effectively. By highlighting some of the promising practices that are *beginning* to address such economic issues, we hope this study initiates a conversation about how universities can be more effective in truly benefiting the lives of people living in their surrounding communities.

Fourth, we sought to develop more specificity about what it means for a university to pursue an anchor institution mission. In the end, we came up with a typology of three different strategies. We label these (1) "facilitator" strategies, where the university supports a broad range of partnerships in many different neighborhoods; (2) "leadership" strategies, where the university applies significant resources on a select number of often adjacent low-income neighborhoods; and (3) "convener" strategies, where the university acts as part of a broader coalition and works with other groups in specific neighborhoods, but ones that might not be so close to the university campus.

We did not know when we started this work that we would end up with a typology of strategies. Indeed, our typology only emerged after reviewing the research results from our ten site visits. But we did initially seek to advance the discussion of university-community partnerships to think more clearly about both the *community development context* as well as an *anchor institution strategy*, and we hope the typology we have offered provides a useful step in that direction.

The last point worth emphasizing is that this book builds off of a report of the same title that we authored in 2010. When we began our research in early 2009, we envisioned writing a report that would highlight some best practices for university leaders, community development practitioners, policymakers, and the foundation community. We did not imagine that this work would end up being published as part of Michigan State University's series on Transformations in Higher Education. In revising the report for publication in this series, we made a number of changes to address the comments of two anonymous reviewers and, more broadly, to situate this work within the existing literature. One modification we made was to seek to develop in more depth and detail the rationale for the typology we developed, as well as highlight both the utility of that framework and its limitations. Another change we made was to add text in part 3 that better situates the "best practices" we highlight in that section within the context of the broader best-practices literature in the university engagement field. We also shifted the organization of the material—shortening the introduction and lengthening the conclusion, for example. We made a number of further additions and subtractions to refine concepts, update data, and so forth throughout the study. Lastly, we invited Charles Rutheiser of the Annie E. Casey Foundation to write a foreword to provide a current perspective on how philanthropy is viewing anchor institution strategies and community partnerships today.

We began this preface noting the brief period at the end of 2000 when it seemed a real policy opening was possible. It is not shocking that the policy window shut, but, at the same time, it is important to realize that much of the energy from that period continues to echo and has led to a growing anchor institution movement nationally. History shows us that change is often imperceptible, until it happens. When Jonathan Baldwin Turner—a former professor at Illinois College in Jacksonville, Illinois—gave a speech in 1850 calling for a "State University of the Industrial Class," it seemed relatively few listened. Twelve years later, President Abraham Lincoln signed the Land-Grant College Act into law. A "New Morrill Act" for the twenty-first century—as President Nancy Cantor of Syracuse University, among others, has called for—may yet be possible.

Introduction

Universities and colleges, which simultaneously constitute preeminent international, national, and local institutions, potentially represent by far the most powerful partners, "anchors," and creative catalysts for change and improvement in the quality of life in American cities and communities. For universities and colleges to fulfill their great potential and more effectively contribute to positive change in their communities, cities, and metropolitan areas, however, they will have to critically examine and change their organizational cultures and structures and embed civic engagement across all components of the institution.

—Ira Harkavy et al., "Anchor Institutions as Partners in Building Successful
Communities and Local Economies," in *Retooling HUD for a Catalytic Federal
Government*, edited by Paul Brophy and Rachel Godsll, 2009

Universities are place-based institutions anchored within their communities, and they are increasingly recognized as key contributors to urban and community development. (Here and throughout this book, we use the term *university* to refer broadly to all institutions of higher education.) Their economic impact can hardly be overstated. Nationwide, universities employ over two million full-time workers and another million part-time workers, as well as enroll more than 18 million students. In 2006 alone, the nation's universities purchased over $373 billion in goods and services—or more than 2 percent of the nation's gross domestic product.[1] Universities, of course, are much more than economic engines. They are first and foremost intellectual centers with enormous knowledge-producing and problem-solving abilities, and they have come to an increasing recognition that by helping to solve real-world problems as they are manifested locally, they can advance their core missions of research, teaching, and service.[2]

By definition, anchor institutions are tied to a certain location "by reason of mission, invested capital, or relationships to customers or employees."[3] To put it simply, anchor institutions cannot move. As a result, the well-being of the anchor institution is inextricably tied to the welfare of the community in which it is located. As the United States has shifted from a manufacturing to a service- and knowledge-based economy, the economic weight of these anchor institutions has grown. And, in nearly all urban and metropolitan areas, universities and hospitals are the largest such institutions. For example, a 1999 Brookings Institution paper by Harkavy and Zuckerman found that in each of the twenty largest cities in the United States, a higher education or medical institution was among the top ten private employers.[4]

In the last two decades, a number of universities, spurred by a variety of factors, have embraced their role as anchors in their communities. This realization has often been accompanied by substantial investments to help develop the neighborhoods surrounding their campuses, which is the major focus of this book. In some cases, such revitalization efforts have been spurred by urban deterioration and crime that have encroached directly onto the university campus. But there are also many broader factors encouraging universities to increase their community investment, including an intellectual movement that identifies "engaged scholarship" as contributing to the university's core mission; growing pressure to fill social service and infrastructure gaps that stem in part from the declining revenue base of state and local government; and, last but not least, universities' increasingly powerful role as economic institutions in their own right. Responding to these factors, universities have not only increasingly engaged their academic resources and developed strong partnership programs, but a number of universities have also leveraged their business or "corporate" practices (real estate development, procurement, endowment investment, hiring, and so forth) to help underwrite the costs of large community revitalization efforts. There are valuable lessons to be learned from the experience to date, but there is also a real danger that anchor institution strategies, unless implemented well, will fail to meet the challenge, as set forth in the Anchor Institutions Task Force report cited above, of improving the quality of life in American cities and communities.

In this work, unlike much of the literature, we have chosen to place greater emphasis on what we have labeled "corporate" practices and less emphasis on specific partnership programs. Because of this focus, we often end up highlighting university administrators while paying less attention to the contributions of faculty and students. We made this choice for a number of reasons. One is that we wanted to emphasize the central *economic* importance of universities in community economic development, quite independently from their academic resources. Whether for good or for ill, universities, simply by virtue of their size, have a considerable economic impact on their surrounding communities. We also wanted to examine more closely the relationship of the university as an *institution* to the community, rather than assess individual programs. To be sure, we highlight individual programs where appropriate, but our goal is to identify overall strategies and approaches that leverage universities' corporate resources, in combination with partnership programs and faculty and student efforts, to achieve community economic development objectives.

Two risks are worth highlighting, particularly when enlisting the corporate engagement of a university. One is that anchor institution strategies may improve the quality of life in target neighborhoods, but without markedly improving the welfare of longtime neighborhood residents—frequently low income and people of color—some of whom may move out of the neighborhoods due to increased rental values or rising property taxes. In short, absent provision up front to maintain mixed-income neighborhoods (through such means as inclusionary zoning, community land trusts, or other policy measures that promote mixed-income development), anchor institution strategies bear the risk of promoting, albeit without intending to, gentrification and less diverse communities.

A second, and perhaps more subtle, risk is to fail to maintain an appropriate balance institution-wide between technology transfer, economic clusters and related programs, on the one hand—and low-income neighborhood partnership work, on the other. Although the focus of this book is on anchor institution strategies that aim to improve the welfare of low-income communities, we find much to praise in university technology transfer programs. Nonetheless, there is a risk of "community engagement" being exclusively defined in such terms. If such unbalanced community investment were to occur, anchor institutions, by focusing their capital on jobs with educational requirements beyond the reach of most area residents, might inadvertently contribute to and deepen a growing U.S. class divide. As Congressional Budget Office data affirm, from 1979 to 2007 the share of U.S. after-tax income of the top 1 percent of Americans more than doubled, from 7.5 percent of total income to 17.1 percent, while the share going to the bottom 80 percent fell from 58 percent to 48 percent. A conscious decision to defy this trend requires universities to generate jobs and wealth specifically designated for community members at the lower end of the socioeconomic scale. In short, universities, in developing their strategies to improve the conditions in distressed communities, must recognize that they are often in the position of "swimming upstream."[5]

Building from this understanding, this study was designed to examine a cross-section of ten urban colleges and universities in an attempt to assess (1) the degree to which anchor-based development initiatives and partnership programs take into account critical issues of economic inclusion; (2) how such programs are organized, including goals and targets, the degree of community involvement in decision-making, and the establishment of internal incentives and metrics; and (3) promising practices that have the greatest chance to contribute to building individual and community wealth in distressed and underserved neighborhoods.[6]

It is our hope that, by understanding the successes and limitations of current efforts, anchor institutions can better ensure that the needs of longtime, particularly low-income, residents are built into the design of these initiatives from the beginning. Moreover, by providing valuable tools and practices to those implementing anchor strategies, we aim to help these institutions build on lessons already learned.

The ten institutions profiled here—and many others across the country—have demonstrated a variety of innovative ways universities can partner with their local communities, organizations, and government to *begin* to address problems of poverty, unemployment, inadequate schooling, affordable housing, crime, and other social issues. Taken together, these developments lead us to believe that we are on the verge of an important new vision of what might be possible if urban universities seek to *fully achieve their anchor institution mission*—that is, to *consciously and strategically apply their long-term, place-based economic power, in combination with their human and intellectual resources, to better the welfare of the communities in which they reside.*

The concept of an anchor institution mission is related to, yet distinct from, the broader concept of community engagement. Community engagement, understood in its broadest sense, involves universities interacting with the outside world in a "problem-solving" framework and can be applied to any scale of problems—be they local, regional, national, or even global; in some cases, the term gets further watered down to simply mean the provision of services. By contrast, an anchor institution mission implies a specific engagement of the institution with its surrounding community. To restate and emphasize the seemingly obvious, "place-based" economic power refers to the university's economic impact in its local geographic area. Pursuing an anchor institution mission, then, involves much more than building favorable town-gown relations or public relations; rather, it involves a strategic reorientation of the university mission to focus dedicated corporate and academic resources to assist in community economic development and local problem-solving work.

In the past two decades, a number of universities have taken significant steps toward adopting conscious, place-based anchor institution strategies. Nevertheless, even among the leaders, the road to fully achieving this anchor institution mission remains only half traveled. Through this publication, we hope to present both a challenge to the field—to realize this mission—as well as an illumination to policymakers, foundation officers, community partners, and practitioners of the potential of this emerging movement.

To begin our study, we examined a list of approximately twenty-five higher education institutions in urban locations that are nationally recognized for their community partnership and community development efforts. After careful review, ten of these institutions were selected to study in further detail. We included institutions diverse in size and locale, as well as a mix of private and public universities, in order to discover practices that could be implemented widely. More specifically, we intentionally selected at least one Ivy League research university, one land-grant institution, one historically black college, and one community college. Demonstrating their prominence in the field of study, nine of the ten colleges selected for this study were recognized by the President's 2008 Higher Education Community Service Honor Roll, many with distinction. Eight of these institutions qualified for the Carnegie Foundation for the Advancement of Teaching's new voluntary community engagement classification. Westfield State College president Evan S. Dobelle named five of these schools as being among the nation's top twenty-five "best neighbor" colleges and universities in 2009.

The ten colleges and universities selected for this study are Emory University, Indiana University–Purdue University Indianapolis, LeMoyne-Owen College, Miami Dade College, Portland State University, Syracuse University, University of Cincinnati, University of Minnesota, University of Pennsylvania, and Yale University.[7]

From May to October 2009, we conducted site visits to the selected ten institutions, spending two days on average at each location. At most locations, meetings included a mix of university faculty, staff, and administration, as well as representatives from community-based organizations, foundations, businesses, and local government.[8] Several follow-up interviews were also conducted by telephone. The focus for these visits was deconstructing the existing models of anchor-based and anchor-driven community development in a way that could inform practices going forward.

We briefly introduce these sites below in relation to their current anchor institution practices.

Emory University

Emory University is a private research university established in 1836 in Atlanta, Georgia, that enrolls approximately 7,000 undergraduates and 6,000 graduate students. Each year more than 200 courses in dozens of departments engage 4,000 students in community work as part of their course requirements. The Office of University-Community Partnerships has sustained strong relationships with local community organizations and has been effective in building nonprofit capacity. One key program is a twelve-month fellowship program that involves student teams working with nonprofit partners and is accompanied by group seminars and faculty support. As an anchor institution, Emory has been fairly modest in its resource commitment toward community economic development, but there is promise of more sustained, place-based initiatives ahead.

Indiana University–Purdue University Indianapolis

Indiana University–Purdue University Indianapolis (IUPUI) is a large, public institution established in 1969 that enrolls approximately 22,000 undergraduates and 8,000 graduate students each year. The institution prioritizes service-learning, community work-study, volunteering, and internships for its students that also provide benefits to community partners. For many years, IUPUI has sustained strong K-12 relationships based on the community school model, which is coordinated by its Office of Neighborhood Partnerships (ONP). The university is now a key partner in comprehensive revitalization of the Near Westside community through the Great Indy Neighborhoods Initiative. ONP and its umbrella organization, the Center for Service and Learning, receive strong support from university administration for such efforts; however, corporate investments have yet to be aligned with the Center's partnerships.

Lemoyne-Owen College

LeMoyne-Owen College is a private, historically black college and liberal arts institution in Memphis, Tennessee, that enrolls around 1,000 students. It was formed in 1968 through the merger of LeMoyne College (1862) and Owen College (1947). Service-learning and numerous other partnerships connect the campus to the community, although resources and capacity are limited—LeMoyne-Owen has faced grave fiscal challenges in recent years. Despite such challenges, the college has continued to attract significant federal funding to support the LeMoyne-Owen College Community Development Corporation, which it established in 1989 to institutionalize its commitment to the surrounding community. The CDC, which operates as a private, not-for-profit 501(c)3, is now a lead partner in revitalizing the

Soulsville community through workforce training, small business development, and increased homeownership. Establishing the CDC as an autonomous organization focused on community development has allowed LeMoyne-Owen College to focus on its primary mission of education, and more recently, rebuild its enrollment numbers.

Miami Dade College

Miami Dade College (MDC) enrolls over 170,000 students each year at its eight campuses in Miami-Dade County, Florida. MDC began as a community college in 1960, and in 2003 expanded to offer a four-year bachelor's degree program. The college has an open-door policy for enrollment, reflecting the administration's view that educational access is the largest contributor to economic development. The college provides many in-kind resources to residents and local nonprofits, particularly through educational programs, as well as an array of cultural programs for the broader community. The Center for Community Involvement oversees service-learning opportunities for 5,000 students each year, as well as one of the largest literacy tutoring programs in the nation. Several college programs provide workforce training and small business development in low-income areas, although little focus has been given to an institution-wide, place-based approach to community development.

Portland State University

Portland State University is the largest university in the state of Oregon, enrolling approximately 20,000 undergraduates and 8,000 graduate students. It was established in 1946 as a public institution to serve returning World War II veterans. In the 1990s, Portland State worked closely with city and business officials to redevelop the area immediately surrounding campus, primarily through real estate development. In recent years, it has consciously taken a broader approach to community engagement rather than focus on development of a specific neighborhood. Still, it has continued its collaboration with city partners, investing in transit and sustainable regional development. The Center for Academic Excellence oversees a large service-learning program as well as a senior capstone program, with significant academic resources dispersed throughout the region.

Syracuse University

Syracuse University is a private research university established in 1860 in Syracuse, New York, that enrolls 13,000 undergraduates and 6,000 graduate students. Its multifaceted engagement effort focuses on K-12 education, urban revitalization, and green development. The university is a lead partner in the Near West Side Initiative, an effort to rehabilitate and revitalize the Near West Side community through arts, culture, and technology. Syracuse is also the catalyst for a citywide initiative to create a signature strip of cutting-edge cultural development that connects University Hill with downtown Syracuse, known as the Connective Corridor. Through such initiatives, Syracuse has strategically leveraged its intellectual resources to stimulate redevelopment in its local community under the vision of

"Scholarship in Action." The corporate side of the university is also philosophically commit-ted to community economic development and continues to develop programs and policies to further support this effort.

University of Cincinnati

The University of Cincinnati is a public institution established in 1819 in Cincinnati, Ohio. It enrolls over 30,000 undergraduate students and 9,000 graduate students. Since 2003, it has been engaged in a partnership involving the area's largest anchor institutions (including three health organizations and the zoo) to create the Uptown Consortium, an anchor-based approach to community development. As of 2009, the trustees of the University of Cincin-nati alone have allocated nearly $150 million from the university's $833 million endowment to support community development—an investment that the administration views as "patient capital." Much of the development through the Consortium generally has been focused on real estate, although partners hope to address broader socioeconomic goals going forward. The university is also a leader in the Strive educational partnership and sev-eral other local school initiatives.

University of Minnesota, Twin Cities

The University of Minnesota, Twin Cities is a large, public research university and land-grant college established in 1851 in Minneapolis and St. Paul. It enrolls more than 33,000 under-graduates and 18,000 graduate students. In recent years, Minnesota has aimed to broaden its land-grant mission and more strategically align university resources with its urban, as well as rural, community. Within this agenda, Minnesota has given particular attention to community collaboration and capacity building, as well as institutional infrastructure to support engagement. In regards to urban engagement, the University Northside Partnership and the new Urban Research and Outreach/Engagement Center are key efforts focused on bringing stakeholders together to work on education, health, and economic development in North Minneapolis. The Office of Business and Community Economic Development over-sees significant efforts in minority contracting as well as small business development. A university-wide Office of Public Engagement facilitates the advancement of the community engagement agenda across the university's research, teaching, and outreach missions, although many partnership initiatives across the campus still remain diffuse and disconnected.

University of Pennsylvania

The University of Pennsylvania is an Ivy League, private research university in Philadelphia. Established in 1740, it enrolls approximately 10,000 undergraduates and 10,000 graduate students. It has made significant one-time and ongoing financial commitments to commu-nity development. Penn maintains the nation's largest and most successful university local purchasing program, and emphasizes economic inclusion practices in its contracting and hiring. The Netter Center for Community Partnerships leads a multifaceted approach that galvanizes resources to improve local schools, urban nutrition, and community development; this work has been sustained for over twenty years and across three different university presidents. Under the leadership of the Netter Center and the School of Education, the university has emphasized K-12 educational partnerships, as well as public health partnerships with Penn's professional schools.

Yale University

Yale University is an Ivy League, private research university established in 1701. Located in New Haven, Connecticut, it enrolls approximately 5,000 undergraduate and 7,000 graduate students. Yale has helped to dramatically improve safety in New Haven, with its largest contribution made through payments in lieu of taxes (PILOTs) to the city. Through Yale's Office of New Haven and State Affairs, Yale promotes four primary objectives: economic development (particularly supporting local biotech start-ups), community partnerships (especially with K-12 schools) and home ownership assistance, public safety, and downtown retail revitalization (the university owns 310,000 square feet of retail space, which it manages with an eye to promoting public safety and downtown redevelopment). Yale's employer-assisted housing program, one of the nation's largest, has financed the purchase of over 925 homes with an estimated combined value of $150 million. Yale also maintains partnerships with twenty New Haven public schools, with a focus on science education.

In part 1 of this book, we provide a consolidated history of university engagement with local communities. We make a case for the deep relationship between higher education and economic development, and the role that the federal government has played in influencing this connection over the last 150 years, beginning with the Morrill Act of 1862. We also discuss the growth of service-learning and the particular role that urban deterioration and crime played in spurring universities to act in more strategic ways and increasingly recognize their role as anchors in their communities. We present key questions as the work moves forward regarding institutionalization, accountability, and true impact on those most in need.

We then outline three general roles that universities assume in anchor-based community development—facilitator, leader, or convener—which emerged as patterns among the ten institutions studied. This framework, or distinction of university roles, allowed us to further deconstruct the various manifestations of anchor institution strategies among a diverse cross-section of cases.

Specifically, we found that at many of the large, public institutions, the university served as a *facilitator* in broad efforts for local and regional development. IUPUI, Miami Dade College, and Portland State provide examples of this approach. At these universities, educational opportunity, service-learning experiences, and in-kind resources are emphasized, due in large part to their limited financial resources. While they engage many community partners, there is little geographic or thematic focus of institution-wide investment. In other schools, we found the university serving as the *leader* in community development efforts, with a focus on revitalization of a particular neighborhood(s) that is often adjacent to campus and whose deteriorating conditions threatens the university's ability to maintain its rank or stature. Demonstrating this approach are Cincinnati, Penn, and Yale. These schools tend to dedicate significant institution-wide resources (i.e., academic, corporate, and human) toward comprehensive community development efforts, but while community stakeholders are regularly consulted, they often have only a moderate degree of control over the content of the "community partnership" decisions made. In the remaining schools, we found that the university was not as neutral or as focused as were those in the other roles, but instead served as a *convener*, working to forge coalitions with community stakeholders in a collaborative fashion. Examples of this approach are Emory, LeMoyne-Owen, Minnesota, and Syracuse. Largely free from direct threats of crime and deterioration (as seen near or on the borders of the *leaders'* campuses), these institutions have the opportunity to make more strategic investment choices. The common choice for these schools is to invest somewhat limited institutional resources, while leveraging significant external funding, toward economic development and capacity building of particularly challenged neighborhoods.

After introducing these three roles, we present a general overview of six major areas in which urban colleges and universities have frequently sought to work in partnership to improve the welfare of their surrounding communities. These areas include comprehensive neighborhood revitalization; community economic development through corporate investment; local capacity building; public education and health partnerships; academic engagement; and multi-anchor, city and regional partnerships. In addition, we discuss intricacies of this work including the challenges of creating an engaged community, establishing partnership programs and goals, institutionalizing an anchor vision, securing funding and leveraging resources, building a culture of economic inclusion, sustaining participatory planning and robust community relationships, and meeting the needs of low-income residents and neighborhoods who are partners in these efforts.

Part 2 delves into the stories of the ten profiled colleges and universities. We discuss the various and multifaceted strategies, as well as significant commitments of resources and time, to community development that these ten sites revealed. These efforts ranged from service-learning courses and community-based research, on the one hand, to local procurement and contracting policies, on the other, and from in-kind trainings and facilities, to millions of dollars invested in real estate development designed to achieve community development objectives.

In studying these ten universities, the goal was neither to praise nor find fault with existing efforts, but to move beyond promotion, public relations, and anecdotes to assess how these initiatives affect (positively and negatively) those most in need, and how such strategies can be focused for the greatest impact.

While we have designated each university as taking one of three general roles in its approach to community development—facilitator, leader, or convener—it is critical to note that we do not prescribe any one approach but rather seek to explore the promising practices at each of these institutions that have the greatest potential to contribute to improving the quality of life, as well as building individual and community wealth, in distressed and underserved neighborhoods.

Thus, in part 3, we highlight a number of "best practices" from the ten profiled institutions. By diving deeper into the experiences of these universities and their partners, including specific policies adopted and roadblocks faced, we hope to provide valuable tools for other universities implementing anchor-based community development strategies.

Part 4 then asks the question: *Provided a university acknowledges its role as an anchor, how does it achieve its anchor institution mission?* This section of the book discusses universities' roles in leveraging their resources for community development and analyzes the potential for higher education institutions to fully realize their mission as anchors. Drawing on the experience of the ten profiled institutions, as well as our own, we produce a vision of a comprehensive strategy linking promising practices for maximum impact and sustainability. Specifically, we discuss the role of university leaders, philanthropy, and policy in supporting an anchor institution mission.

For university leaders, we focus on the need for greater institution-wide investment and collaboration. In particular, we call for a more conscious linking of the corporate and academic sides of the university, to work with its community in democratic, mutually beneficial, and respectful partnerships. Further, we believe that adopting a strategic, place-based approach to community development can help ensure that existing institutional resources have much greater impact than if dispersed more broadly.

Foundations, we suggest, can encourage universities to pursue their anchor institution mission by using their convening power to bring practitioners together to develop a common voice, as well as promote comprehensive initiatives. In the case of the latter, a funders' group could lead a collaboration among multiple constituencies—anchor institutions, foundations, federal departments, and local government—to provide incentives and support to individual, or groups of, universities to fully realize their anchor institution mission.

We then discuss how public policy is needed to help move faculty and university administrators to make the kinds of changes needed to embed and sustain an anchor institution mission across all components of the institution. In particular, we argue that federal funding for higher education engagement should specifically leverage universities' economic power for community benefit. The federal government could also convene a multi-stakeholder group that would support cross-anchor institution collaborative efforts through a competitive grant program. Suggestions for future areas of research are also presented.

In short, for universities to realize an anchor institution mission, they and the foundations and government that support them must continue to move beyond rhetoric and take serious action. Moreover, to ensure this action benefits the university, the community generally, and low-income residents in particular, we argue that such initiatives be collaboratively planned, implemented, and evaluated.

There is no question that over the past few decades, and especially the last ten to fifteen years, there have been a number of important advances in university engagement. Nonetheless, a central question remains: will anchor institution strategies make a substantial difference in the economic well-being of low-income families and in the stabilization and revitalization of the neighborhoods in which they live?

What is ultimately required, we believe, is a much deeper level of institutional engagement, in which universities commit themselves to consciously and strategically applying their place-based economic power, in combination with their human and intellectual resources, to better the long-term welfare of the communities in which they reside in general, and the welfare of low-income residents in particular.

As the ten institutions profiled in this book demonstrate, a great deal has been learned and accomplished in recent years by anchor strategies. Building on this experience, as well as the nation's economic state of affairs, an unprecedented opportunity exists for urban universities to achieve a powerful fulfillment of their anchor institution role. It is our hope that this study will contribute to this important evolution as universities seek to embrace and advance their work to a new level of critical impact.

PART 1

The Past and Present of University Engagement

This nation faces significant societal challenges, and higher education must play a role in responding to them. [There is] widespread agreement that colleges and universities have civic and public purposes, including the preparation of an enlightened and productive citizenry and engaging in scholarship that both addresses pressing problems and holds a mirror to society to allow for self-reflection and self-correction. The question is how to achieve these aims.

—John Saltmarsh et al., *Democratic Engagement White Paper*, 2009

Brief History of Universities, Community Partnerships, and Economic Development

Universities, in addition to their central role in education, play a critical economic development role. Nowhere has the connection between higher education and economic development been more clearly drawn than in the United States. This link was made explicit in 1862 when Congress passed the Morrill Act, establishing a system of land-grant colleges by allocating federal land to the states to support the establishment of public universities in each state. As James Collier of Virginia Tech notes, while the Morrill Act certainly served to expand access to university education, its "primary goal was to solidify the American economic infrastructure in anticipation of the Civil War's outcome." Senator Justin Smith Morrill (R-VT) himself, in calling upon Congress to pass the Land-Grant Act, argued that land-grant colleges not only would provide education for the "sons of toil," but would also speed growth in agriculture, "the foundation of all present and future prosperity."[1]

Historically, community partnership work has not been as visible in U.S. higher education as economic development, but it too has deep historical roots.[2] On the university end, one of the most obvious areas is the development of cooperative extension. Cooperative extension, from its founding, has been a program that supports a university-linked system of information transmission from state "land-grant" colleges and universities to the populace through a network of professional "extension agents" who provide public and outreach services. Cooperative extension continues to this day. Presently, extension offices exist in every county in the United States and employ over 15,000 people. Although cooperative extension is often seen as only dealing with rural areas, its impact has been far broader. An early innovator was the state of Wisconsin, which initiated its statewide cooperative extension program under the leadership of famed progressive activist Governor Robert La Follette, years before the federal government passed the Smith-Lever Act of 1914, setting aside federal funding for cooperative extension programs in every state. For example, in 1908, Extension Division programs in Wisconsin were conducted for urban schoolchildren and adults in a public health effort aimed at preventing tuberculosis; the following year, Extension Division professors helped Milwaukee conduct an economic survey of the city, "including studies of industrial hygiene and education, working conditions, hospitals, municipal health and sanitation problems."[3]

On the community-initiated end, the settlement house movement of the late nineteenth and early twentieth centuries also was an early initiator of what today might be called university-community partnership work. In its most frequent form, a settlement house was a building in a poor community that was used as a community center. Settlement houses taught literacy and urban survival skills to immigrants and rural migrants and helped organize tenants to secure better housing. Although settlement houses started off campus, university students often lived in the facilities and frequently provided much of the settlement houses' staffing. Hull House, organized by Jane Addams in partnership with the University of Chicago, is one of the best known of these efforts. Addams, in particular, succeeded in getting prominent support for Hull House at the University of Chicago, among both the university administration and the faculty. It was also the University of Chicago's first president, William Rainey Harper, who declared that the university should be the "Messiah of the democracy, its to-be-expected deliverer." And of course it was as a faculty member at the University of Chicago where the philosopher John Dewey first developed his theories of "learning by doing" and experiential education.

For a variety of reasons, the prominence of university-community partnerships and university economic development activity declined in the first half of the twentieth century. The reasons are not hard to discern: agriculture, once the foundation of "all" prosperity (in Morrill's words) became less significant, as the United States became a primarily urban and metropolitan country and many land-grant colleges largely failed to shift the focus of their cooperative extension work to reflect the changing economy and growing urbanization. Also, the issues of rural-urban migration and immigration from abroad that had led to the settlement house movement in the first place subsided, as immigration laws restricted entry to the United States. Moreover, universities became increasingly linked to the federal government, especially through military research contracts, which made local community economic development activity relatively less important to universities.

But then circumstances changed again. The roots of today's generation of community-university partnerships can be traced to the late 1960s, when activist academics began to insert community work into university curricula. Robert Sigmon and William Ramsey of the Southern Regional Education Board coined the term "service-learning" in 1967 to describe the work of university students and faculty on a Tennessee Valley Authority project in East Tennessee conducted by Oak Ridge Associated Universities in partnership with tributary area organizations.[4]

As service-learning grew, it developed a strong antipoverty cast. Michael Lounsbury of Cornell University and Seth Pollack, director of the Service Learning Institute at California State University–Monterey Bay, write, "While the practitioners had different origins, they were united in the belief that students could be productive foot soldiers in the war on poverty." Federal funds helped promote this work through the National Student Volunteer Program (established in 1969 by President Richard Nixon and renamed the National Center for

Service-Learning in 1979) and the federal volunteer office, ACTION.[5] The election of Ronald Reagan as president in 1980 soon led to the end of federal support for these programs. Nonetheless, after this initial setback, service-learning in the 1980s rebounded, as advocates placed new emphasis on the academic benefits for college students, while deemphasizing activism. This shift was critical in gaining the bipartisan support that led President George H. W. Bush to sign a bill restoring federal funding to service-learning in 1990, legislation that was expanded when President Bill Clinton came to office in 1993. A decade later, service-learning had become ubiquitous, with the advocacy group Campus Compact estimating in 2004 that 98 percent of its 1,000-plus member campuses offered service-learning courses.[6]

Meanwhile, the federal government also played a key role in encouraging the reconnection of universities to local economic growth. Specifically, in 1980, Congress passed the Bayh-Dole Act, which helped bring about a large expansion of university local economic development activity by enabling universities to profit from their professors' discoveries. From 1980 to 2000, the number of patents issued to universities increased from an average of 250 a year to 3,000 a year. Many have criticized Bayh-Dole for commercializing the university, but there is no doubt about its extraordinary economic impact. A 1999 study of the Association of University Technology Managers found that university technology-transfer activities contributed $40 billion to the U.S. economy and helped support 270,000 jobs nationwide.[7]

In the 1990s, community partnership activity received a considerable boost, as a combination of factors led a number of universities to begin developing more broad-based strategies. One of these factors was the end of the Cold War, which brought with it at least the prospect of declining military contracts. In this environment, faculty members who could add value to the university in a different way gained more clout. More broadly, the end of the Cold War promised, at least for a time, the possibility that the university would become less focused on federal research attuned to national goals and more focused on local research attuned to meeting statewide or community goals. Modest federal support also helped spur university engagement initiatives, such as establishment of the Office of University Partnerships (OUP) at the U.S. Department of Housing and Urban Development in 1994. OUP grew to have an annual budget that peaked at slightly over $33 million. Additionally, roughly one-quarter of the Learn and Serve America program's budget (or about $10 million a year) supported university service-learning programs. The Department of Commerce also has a small University Centers program in the Economic Development Administration: average funding in the 2000s was about $6.5 million a year.[8]

More urgency, too, was given to the potential benefits of community partnerships when a national wave of urban crime, spurred in large measure by the spread of crack cocaine in the late 1980s, hit major U.S. cities. Meanwhile, federal funding for social service programs had been severely cut during the Reagan administration. Conditions in America's urban core grew more desperate. One indicator is the murder rate. For example, in New Haven, homicides nearly tripled, rising from twelve in 1985 to thirty-four in 1991. In Philadelphia, homicides also climbed rapidly, growing from 273 in 1985 to a peak of 503 in 1990. Nationally, the urban concentration of violent crime reached record levels: in 1991, the seven most populous cities in the United States alone accounted for more than one-fourth of all homicides nationwide.[9]

In response, a growing number of universities decided that they literally could not afford to ignore the deteriorating conditions surrounding their campuses without risking driving away the students and faculty on whom their stature ultimately depended. Two of the universities profiled here, Penn and Yale, are very explicit in acknowledging the critical role public safety issues (including specific instances of murder) played in how they developed their initiatives. In other cases, such as Cincinnati, general neighborhood deterioration and perception of crime spurred a similar university response.

Lee Benson, Ira Harkavy, and John Puckett of the University of Pennsylvania highlight (albeit more diplomatically) the importance of these factors in their book, *Dewey's Dream: Universities and Democracies in an Age of Education Reform*: "In the aftermath of the cold war, accelerating external and internal pressures forced research universities to recognize (very reluctantly) that they must—and could—function as moral/intellectual institutions simultaneously engaged in advancing universal knowledge, learning *and* improving the well-being of their local geographic communities (i.e. the local ecological systems that powerfully affect their own health and functioning)."[10] Although Benson and his colleagues refer specifically to research universities, this movement has taken hold in higher education institutions of all sizes and sorts. As a result, in the mid-1990s, community partnership centers began blossoming on a number of campuses across the country—centralized units that could galvanize and manage vast resources and programs being directed to the community. Partnership centers helped coordinate otherwise disparate community efforts, occasionally leading to comprehensive university engagement strategies.

Heading into the twenty-first century, a new and deeper understanding of the importance of the role of universities in community economic development began to emerge, leading many universities to greatly expand their community partnership efforts—this time, less out of a sense of crisis than out of an appreciation of the opportunity an anchor institution strategy provides. Many of the institutions profiled here, including Emory, Syracuse, Portland State, IUPUI, and Minnesota were *not* faced with an immediate crisis, but chose to act anyway. As noted later, such efforts typically do not involve the same level of resources as those of university "crisis response" strategies, but often, likely due in part to the *lack* of an immediate threat, these partnerships do a better job of taking into account community concerns in the framing and agenda-setting of their initiatives.

As has been true since the Morrill Act, economic and educational motives remain intertwined. In terms of economics, while hardly true of all metropolitan areas, a number of American cities began to rebound after decades of decline. Indeed, efforts such as Yale's in New Haven and Penn's in West Philadelphia are part of a broader trend of urban revival. For example, the nation's capital, Washington, DC, after decades of population decline, saw its population rise by nearly 30,000 to over 600,000 from 2000 to 2010.[11] The fact that urban problems began to seem not quite as "intractable" was buttressed by the increasing realization—borne out both by practical examples such as the early efforts at Penn and Yale, as well as by academic research—that universities, acting in their economic capacity as anchor institutions, could make a powerful, positive contribution to social and economic outcomes.

A number of studies have highlighted this critical university role. In 2002, the Initiative for a Competitive Inner City and CEOs for Cities discussed this untapped potential: "Despite their considerable size, colleges and universities are often an overlooked component of urban economies. Their impact on these economies can be enormous. More than half of all colleges and universities in the nation are located in the urban core: central cities and their immediate surroundings. They have significant purchasing power, attract substantial revenues for their surrounding economies, invest heavily in local real estate and infrastructure, are major employers, and help to train the workforce and nurture new businesses." Nationwide, America's 4,000 colleges and universities spend more than $400 billion annually, own more than $300 billion in endowment investments, and employ roughly three million faculty and staff. As David Perry of the University of Illinois at Chicago and David Cox of the University of Memphis write, "Urban universities are spending up to a quarter of a trillion on salaries, goods and services, which is more than 20 times what the federal government spends in cities on jobs and economic development." David Maurrasse, in a 2007 report for CEOs for Cities, argued that anchor institutions such as universities have "special importance to the re-making of a city and its future."[12]

The term "anchor institution" itself, which once would have surely received blank stares from university leaders, now is regularly a part of university president discourse. In 2007 and 2008, more than three dozen university presidents came together to form the Coalition of Urban Serving Universities, which seeks to promote university engagement in K–12 public schools, community health outreach, and community economic development. In 2009, a number of university presidents—namely, Nancy Cantor of Syracuse University, Gerard Clancy of the University of Oklahoma at Tulsa, Eduardo Padrón of Miami Dade College, Beverly Tatum of Spelman College, and Wim Wiewel of Portland State University—joined with more than a dozen community partnership leaders and researchers to submit a report to HUD secretary Shaun Donovan that, as referenced in the introduction, called on the federal government to help forge a "new compact between government, anchor institutions and their communities" to leverage university resources to meet the needs of urban communities. This group, dubbed the Anchor Institutions Task Force, decided in 2010 to formalize its status as an independent entity of practitioners and leading experts in anchor institution-community partnerships.[13]

University trade associations have also taken note of these developments. For example, in April 2009, the American Association of State Colleges and Universities (AASCU) named Muriel Howard as its president. Howard, who hails from the urban campus of Buffalo State College, where she was president from 1996 to 2009, quickly moved to reestablish the group's urban steering committee. The Association of Public and Land-Grant Universities (APLU) has created a new Office on Urban Initiatives and, in June 2010, appointed its first vice president of urban affairs to direct the new office.[14]

The growth of this anchor institution movement has also gained a great deal of academic support. Leading scholars of the 1990s (including Derek Bok, Ernest Boyer, and John W. Gardner) helped to build the argument that by strategically focusing their many resources—from academic programs and research to business practices—on locally identified problems, universities can improve their core intellectual and academic work, in part by giving students and faculty real-world experience that can inform both research and teaching. Boyer, for instance, offered a new definition of scholarship. His "scholarship of engagement" has four functions: discovery, integration of knowledge, teaching, and application. Boyer's definition has been widely adopted—meaning that many community partnerships (a form of application) are now part of the definition of the university's central educational mission.[15] Gardner, who served as secretary of Health, Education, and Welfare under President Lyndon Johnson, and as president of the Carnegie Corporation, called for government to facilitate new forms of interaction between all sectors of society (public, private and non-profit), including higher education institutions, to strengthen families and communities. Building on both of these ideas, Bok, who served as Harvard's president from 1971 to 1991, sharply criticized universities for not doing enough to help solve America's most urgent social problems. He urged academic leaders, foundations, and government to work together to encourage universities "to respond effectively to the full agenda of national needs."[16]

Today, this growing understanding of enhancing teaching, research, and learning through community engagement—and, further, the related understanding that the campus, as an anchored part of a broader community, cannot thrive if surrounded by a sea of poverty, disinvestment, dilapidated housing, and other signs of a failing social structure—has become an increasingly important element in reducing internal academic resistance to community engagement strategies. Indeed, to some extent, the extension of those strategies has become seen as central to achievement of the university's mission.

But while community engagement has gained prominence at many higher education institutions, the rhetoric far surpasses the number of tangible, mutually beneficial initiatives. John Saltmarsh and his colleagues in a 2009 white paper on democratic engagement further caution, "Engagement defined by activities connected to places outside the campus does not focus attention on the processes involved in the activity—how it is done—or the purpose of connecting with places outside the campus—why it is done."[17] Even when engagement initiatives are carried out, clarity regarding the purpose of university engagement in surrounding neighborhoods is often lacking. For example, "engagement" (meaning greater interaction between the community and the university) may be seen simply as an end unto itself; or engagement may also be seen as a *means* for higher education institutions to act in a way that will lead them to invest in the long-term economic development and improved quality of life of their local communities.

As we head into the second decade of the twenty-first century, the field is asking itself some critical questions about institutionalization, accountability, and the true impacts on those most in need.

David Cox, executive assistant to the president at the University of Memphis and former director of the Office of University Partnerships for the U.S. Department of Housing and Urban Development (1998–99), discusses one of the field's central concerns: "We need agreed upon metrics and accountability. People write up what they are doing and get great [public relations] coverage. But you have to read it with a grain of salt. We need to get beyond that. Right now, when you ask universities, 'Do you really do what you claim you're doing?'—The answer is usually 'Trust me.' We're moving on ideology, and we have to move beyond that to take this work to the next level."[18]

Henry Taylor, professor and director of the Center for Urban Studies at SUNY-Buffalo, speaks from experience about the challenges of effecting real change: "The majority of outreach programs operate under the framework of what I call 'liberal do-goodism.' [The university is] more comfortable with the sound of rhetoric without concrete action—there's a lot more PR than substance. The university wants to 'appear' involved, and it is, but it's not strategically focused. And, as long as it's not strategically focused, then it's not about bringing real change."[19]

Elizabeth Hollander, senior fellow at Tufts University and former executive director of Campus Compact, emphasizes the particular challenge of community wealth development: "In thinking about the university role in improving a community without gentrifying it, it's hard to do, no matter who you are. When university and city government are equally committed, then chances are improved. Most of where this work is right now, is people being proud of doing anything at all—we too easily slide over true wealth development and the true impact on residents."[20]

To begin to answer some of these questions, in this study we examined in depth the community development initiatives at ten universities to see *how* they are partnering with their communities, *why* they have chosen to act in these ways, and *what* are their intended—and realized—impacts. Much of the literature on community-university partnerships focuses on the level of the individual partnership—or what might be called the "micro" level. For example, a 2006 Community Partnership Summit convened by Community-Campus Partnerships for Health and a number of foundations identified key factors behind productive partnerships, including identifying clear roles and expectations, creating policies and work processes that honor each partner, having a liaison who can be a "translator" between university and community partners, appropriately compensating community partners, building community capacity, and institutionalizing support within the university. Writing about partnerships with tribal communities, three University of Colorado–Denver researchers highlight the importance of reciprocity and mutual respect in achieving successful partnerships.[21] We concur wholeheartedly with these assessments and indeed highlight many of these themes in this study ourselves.

At the same time, in doing this research, because of our focus on understanding what it means for a university as a whole to pursue an anchor institution mission, we wanted to apply our analysis also to the *totality* of a university's partnership programs and corporate practices. In particular, we aimed to see whether, from the perspective of the *institution* one could discern different macro-level strategies. We did not enter this research with any preconceived categories or assumptions as to what these macro-level approaches might be. But in our research, we did find three principal patterns that emerged among the institutions' policies and practices—that is, three general strategies in anchor-based community development. In this study, we label these approaches the *facilitator* model, the *leadership* model, and the *convener* model. This taxonomy is discussed in the next chapter.

Three Strategies of Anchor-Based Community Development

A growing number of universities are engaged in anchor institution work, but not all anchor institution strategies seek to meet the same goals. As we noted briefly in the preceding chapter, in our site visits to ten campuses, we found three principal patterns that emerged among the institutions' policies and practices—that is, three distinct approaches to anchor-based community development. Often "community engagement" is treated as a broad, catchall category that fails to consider important differences that may exist among universities. In our research, we have sought to advance the discussion of university-community partnerships to think more clearly about what it means for a university to pursue an *anchor institution mission*. We hope the classification schema we offer here of *facilitator*, *leadership*, and *convener* strategies provides a useful step in that direction.

Taking the various community engagement practices together, as well as the overall institutional approach toward community development, begins to paint a picture of what one can expect to see at each set of schools. Schools adopting a *facilitator* model tend to place special emphasis on educational opportunity, including a focus on access, academic engagement, and public education and health partnerships, as well as providing in-kind resources for local capacity building across a broad geographic region. Schools adopting a *leadership* model also emphasize education and health partnerships, but tend to focus more strongly on pursuing comprehensive community revitalization, using their business practices for community economic development, often with a specific focus on disinvested neighborhoods that are immediately adjacent to the university. Lastly, schools adopting a *convener* model, like the leadership model, place a heavy emphasis on comprehensive community revitalization, but often place greater emphasis on building local capacity and sharing agenda-setting power with other community stakeholders. It is also not uncommon for a university adopting a convener approach to focus its community development work on a neighborhood that is *not* adjacent to the campus.

As with any taxonomy, these lines of demarcation with the above breakdown are imprecise. No school perfectly fits in one category. Nonetheless, we believe this taxonomy does provide a useful analytical tool to analyze the anchor institution activity of colleges and universities *as institutions* and to begin to answer, in a "real world" sense, Barry Checkoway's classic question of "university for what?"[1]

For example, a university adopting a facilitator role is making a choice to operate as a kind of "partnership taker"—that is, it is responsive to community needs, but spreads its resources thinly. This has the substantial political benefit that the university avoids playing favorites and, importantly, maintains a reputation as a fair broker in the community. On the other hand, dispersal of university resources naturally reduces the ability of the university to affect outcomes (whether those outcomes be in the area of community health, public school education, economic development, or some other area of concern) in any particular neighborhood. By contrast, universities adopting a leadership model make a specific choice to be a "partnership maker" and focus time, attention, and resources on specific neighborhoods; in part because such efforts aim to achieve neighborhood-wide effects in an area that is immediately adjacent to campus, leadership strategies tend to be better financed than facilitator model approaches (i.e., a higher budget and more involvement of the corporate side of the university).

Convener strategies fall somewhat between these two modal types—unlike universities operating in a facilitator mode, certain neighborhoods are explicitly favored for the delivery of university academic and corporate resources over others. However, unlike universities operating in a leadership mode, the neighborhoods in question are often *not* adjacent to campus, making the university less of a "central player" than if the neighborhood was next door. And regardless of whether a neighborhood is adjacent or far away, a convener approach places considerable energy into building a strong coalition that links the university to foundations and outside funders, the business community, and community groups to achieve significant neighborhood improvement. The convener approach thus involves less direct university agenda setting and more give-and-take with community partners than a typical leadership approach. A benefit of a leadership approach may be speed and the ability of the anchor institution to both shape and implement a specific transformative vision. A benefit of a convener approach may be the ability to bring more stakeholders into the vision-building process, and, perhaps, achieve broader, long-term community support for the transformation as a result.

Of course, although we have outlined these modes as if it were a pure "choice," in reality, structure plays an important role in influencing which path a university adopting an anchor institution mission is likely to follow. A leadership strategy requires a greater financial resource commitment than a facilitator strategy does, so it is hardly surprising that two of the schools profiled here that have adopted a leadership strategy (Penn and Yale) are Ivy League schools, nor is it surprising that large, resource-poor, state universities like IUPUI and Portland State have adopted more of a facilitator strategy. It is also true that location matters—not all urban universities have adjacent low-income communities. Clearly, the options facing a university with immediate low-income neighbors are different from universities surrounded by a set of middle- or upper-class neighborhoods, such as Minnesota and Emory.

While we fully acknowledge the importance of structural factors, this does not mean that structure is absolutely determinative. LeMoyne-Owen College, for example, is a resource-poor, historically black college based in Memphis. Nonetheless, through a community development corporation that it founded, LeMoyne-Owen has played an important role in revitalizing an adjacent neighborhood that it has helped rename as "Soulsville." In short, resource limitations did not stop LeMoyne-Owen from focusing on its adjacent neighborhood; however, its limited resources may well have been a large part of the reason why in many respects its overall approach more closely reflects the coalition principles that underlie the "convener" model that we outlined above. Also, the same university may adopt different approaches at different times—it is not uncommon for a university that begins with a facilitator approach to move toward a convener approach over time as it builds relationships with community groups in certain areas and makes decisions to focus resources in neighborhoods where it sees itself having the greatest impact. Nor is it uncommon for a university that adopts a leadership approach in response to a "crisis" situation in an adjacent neighborhood to transition, over time, to a more consensus-oriented approach that may focus on a broader set of issues or neighborhoods.

Figure 1 outlines in "ideal type" fashion some of the key differences that we have found these three approaches to involve.

Most universities, naturally, as we noted above, employ a *combination* of approaches, albeit with significantly different emphases, rather than one "pure" modal version. That said, these distinctive patterns are relatively easy to discern. For instance, at universities that most closely follow a *facilitator* approach, one typically finds that administrative leadership supports a civic engagement mission but corporate investments directed at community development (i.e., local purchasing, hiring, investment, and real estate) are limited. IUPUI, Miami Dade College, and Portland State provide examples of this approach.

Figure 1. Three Roles of Universities in Anchor-Based Community Development

Key Issues	University as Facilitator	University as Leader	University as Convener
The Engaged Community	• Dispersed partnerships rather than geographic focus • Respond to partnership opportunities from across broader community	• Focus on adjacent neighborhood • Revitalization often initiated in response to crisis or threatening conditions	• Targeted efforts often focus on non-adjacent neighborhood • Strategic choice to engage (not required by history or immediate threat)
Partnership Programs and Goals	• Focus on academic engagement, public education and health partnerships, and in-kind resources to build local capacity	• Focus on comprehensive neighborhood revitalization—especially education, health, and community development—through academic and non-academic resources	• Focus on capacity building, as part of neighborhood revitalization • Public school and health partnerships often part of broader agenda

Figure 1. *(Continued)*

Key Issues	University as Facilitator	University as Leader	University as Convener
Institutional Support and Leadership	• Strong administrative support for broad civic engagement mission • Designated community partnership center with focus often on academic engagement	• Strong administrative support often directly overseeing revitalization efforts • Additional partnership centers promote university-wide engagement	• Moderate to high administrative support often with designated, high-powered staff to oversee revitalization efforts • Additional partnership centers promote university-wide engagement
Funding and Resources	• Low endowment • Limited budget • Limited corporate investments • Moderate leveraging of external resources	• Moderate to high endowment • High budget • Significant corporate investments • Internal investment leverages considerable external resources	• Moderate to high endowment • Moderate budget • Moderate corporate investments • Significant leveraging of external resources
Principles of Economic Inclusion	• Emphasize access to education • Limited but focused efforts toward support of small and local business owners	• Emphasize innovative corporate practices for community economic development (e.g., local purchasing, real estate development)	• Emphasize capacity building • Developing targeted corporate practices that support diversity, with increasing focus on local community
Nature of Community Relationships	• Good neighbor: responsive to community's or city's agenda • Typically reactive (partnership "taker," not "maker")	• University agenda setting • Strong community dialogue, but plans often presented "to them" rather than developed "with them" • Hire from within rather than from community • Create stand-alone organizations to pursue agenda; heavily brand efforts	• Co-agenda setting among university and community partners • Hire community people to work in partnership centers—translator function • Partner with new or existing community organizations with shared leadership; low-key branding
Impacts on Community	• Large-number of nonprofits benefit from partnerships • Neighborhood-wide impacts difficult to measure due to extensive geography of effort	• Significant university interventions in community development, public health, and K-12 schooling show promising indicators • Major improvements in public safety • Often result in higher real estate values in target areas	• Substantial increase in nonprofit and community capacity • Efforts centered on target neighborhood(s) relatively new, making long-term impact difficult to assess

Educational opportunity is a focal point of these schools' community development efforts; thus, they seek to provide engaging, supportive learning environments for both their students and the broader community. To this end, universities serving as facilitators often emphasize service-learning opportunities as well as public school and health partnerships, with large numbers of students and faculty involved. These efforts reach a significant number of community partners, with the work typically dispersed throughout the greater community rather than focused on a specific neighborhood. In other words, these institutions clearly recognize their roles as anchors but tend to focus this charge on broad rather than deep engagement. For some, this may be part of a deliberate decision to focus their energy and resources on regional development. For others, it may be a conscious or subconscious choice to take on less "risky" forms of engagement, particularly when there is little or no direct threat from the surrounding neighborhoods.

Perhaps due, in part, to the lack of financial strength to contribute to comprehensive neighborhood development, strong relationships are particularly emphasized in the anchor strategies of universities serving as facilitators. They are seen as "good neighbors" who are responsive to agendas set forth by their local community or city. Despite limited resources, these institutions aim to help build the capacity of community organizations, primarily by providing in-kind resources, including facilitation of community forums. While it is clearly expressed that city and community partners benefit from the university's engagement, neighborhood-wide impacts are difficult to measure due to the extensive geographic range of such efforts.

Universities who serve as *leaders* in community development agendas often act in response to crisis, most often urban crime or, at a minimum, the *perception* of crime. Improving conditions in their adjacent neighborhood is necessary for a cleaner, safer environment that will attract top students and faculty and maintain the university's stature. These institutions are older, often private, universities with large endowments and the capacity to make significant investments in their communities. In response to threatening conditions, top administration directly oversees—and commits significant institutional resources toward—these efforts. In turn, this often attracts significant external resources and support. Although the community is frequently consulted, universities as leaders primarily set the community development agenda, with programmatic focus often on the "big three" issues—public health, K-12 education, and community development. As the crisis subsides, these institutions often take steps toward more collaborative initiatives. Examples of this approach can be found at Cincinnati, Penn, and Yale.

Finally, universities serving as *conveners* in anchor-based community development make strategic choices to engage in neighborhood revitalization. Like universities operating in more of a leadership framework, these institutions too are often older, private universities with large endowments and the capacity to make significant investments in their communities. Unlike universities operating in a leadership role, however, these universities most often are surrounded by well-to-do, rather than low-income, neighborhoods.

As a result, convener universities often work in non-adjacent neighborhoods. Community development is not required by history or immediate threat but rather comes to be seen as part of their institutional mission. Indeed, a focused "urban agenda" or "place-based strategy" is often just a portion of these universities' broader engagement agendas. Administrative support is strong but corporate investment in targeted neighborhood projects often limited; thus, significant external resources may need to be leveraged to carry out community development plans.

Universities acting in a convener role are more likely to forge broad coalitions with community stakeholders in a collaborative fashion, where the university may as a result yield significant decision-making power to partner organizations. Examples of this approach are provided at Emory, Minnesota, and Syracuse. We also include LeMoyne-Owen in the category, because its approach follows similar principles of collaboration, even if structurally its situation (small endowment with an adjacent low-income neighborhood) could not be more different than that faced by Minnesota, Emory, or Syracuse.

We examine each of these three overarching strategies in more detail in the remaining chapters. But before proceeding to analyze our ten profiled institutions, we turn to a broader discussion of the areas in which urban universities and colleges have frequently sought to invest their resources.

Higher Education Approaches to Urban Issues

In our site visits to the ten universities featured in this study, we chose to analyze six major areas in which urban colleges and universities have, in recent decades, sought to work in partnership to improve the welfare of their surrounding communities: (1) comprehensive neighborhood revitalization; (2) community economic development through corporate investment; (3) local capacity building; (4) public school and health partnerships; (5) academic engagement; and (6) multi-anchor, city, and regional partnerships.

The higher education institutions chosen for this study demonstrate some of the most innovative and effective approaches to leveraging their resources as anchor institutions. In part, their success is due to the understanding of these approaches as a powerful pedagogical strategy. In other words, these universities realize that by actively engaging in community work, they can make important new contributions to learning, teaching, and research. Moreover, these institutions understand that these areas of engagement are not mutually exclusive, and indeed, have come to develop multifaceted anchor approaches. Demonstrating the patterns among our three clusters of institutions (facilitator, leader, and convener), figure 2 presents the approaches and tools typically implemented by each set of schools—in other words, how these universities generally express their role as anchor institutions.

In particular, the facilitator model places special emphasis on academic engagement, as well as providing in-kind resources for local capacity building and public education and health partnerships and, at times, working with other city and regional partners. The leadership model also emphasizes education and health partnerships but places an equally strong, and sometimes stronger, focus on comprehensive community revitalization, using institutional business practices for community economic development and often collaborating with other anchors or city partners to increase overall impact. Finally, the convener model focuses on local capacity building *as part of* comprehensive community revitalization, as

Figure 2. Expressions of the Anchor Institution Role			
	University as Facilitator	**University as Leader**	**University as Convener**
Comprehensive Neighborhood Revitalization	• Not very common in this model, unless approached as partner for community-led revitalization effort	• Very descriptive of this model; usually university-led	• Typically part of this model; joint university-community planning
Community Economic Development through Corporate Investment	• Not very developed within this model	• Leading examples of business practices such as local purchasing and endowment investment	• New and/or evolving practices that support local investment
Local Capacity Building	• Individuals, local businesses, and organizations supported through educational programs, incubator space, and in-kind resources	• Included among goals, but not always carried out in practice (university maintains heavy influence)	• Key focus, seen through practices such as resident engagement, trainings, and participatory leadership
Public School and Health Partnerships	• Often led by individual faculty or interdisciplinary teams • Typically emphasized over community development	• Large institutional initiatives in these areas often support focused community revitalization agenda • Faculty and students also engage on project-by-project basis	• Institutional initiatives in these areas often support broad community engagement agenda • Faculty and students also engage on project-by-project basis
Academic Engagement	• Strong programs in service-learning, capstones, and community-based research; primary focus on student experience, with little connection to community development efforts	• Strong programs in service-learning and community-based research; may or may not be connected to community development efforts	• Strong programs in service-learning and community-based research; may or may not be connected to community development efforts
Multi-Anchor, City, and Regional Partnerships	• Some collaboration with city and regional partners • Fewer partnerships with other anchors	• Initiate the collaboration with other anchors, city partners, and/or regional consortia	• Some collaboration with other anchors and/or city partners • Occasionally part of regional consortia

well as engages in broader K-12 education and health initiatives and in multi-anchor, city, and regional partnerships.

We now provide a more general overview of the practices and considerations involved in the six areas of partnerships, drawing upon examples from both our ten profiled institutions, as well as a few others. This is intended to provide a more general overview of the potential of various forms of engagement. In the following sections of this book, we further discuss how—and why—the institutions profiled in this study have emphasized certain areas of engagement over others.

Comprehensive Neighborhood Revitalization

A number of universities, including several of those featured in this book, have engaged in comprehensive neighborhood revitalization efforts. Such an approach requires galvanizing and organizing internal and external resources to carry out an extensive development plan. In this manner, these universities attempt to effect broad, systemic change in multiple areas such as safety, housing, economic development, education, and health. Such a multipronged approach almost always requires collaboration with other partners, including other anchor institutions, so that resources can be leveraged collectively.[1] This approach tends to be a particular focus among universities who emphasize what we have classified as a leadership role—Penn, Yale, and Cincinnati. Long-term neighborhood revitalization efforts include community residents and other local stakeholders as partners throughout the planning, implementation, and evaluation phases—but to varying degrees. Universities that have assumed the role of conveners—LeMoyne-Owen, Minnesota, Syracuse, and Emory—tend to give particular focus to this collaborative process when engaged in comprehensive neighborhood revitalization. Collectively identified goals guide the work and provide meaningful measures of impact.

This pattern largely reflects the location of the institutions and whether they choose to adopt a place-based strategy. For instance, universities that employ a leadership role tend to focus intensely on their immediate, challenged neighborhood with a significant investment of resources, while universities serving as conveners often choose to concentrate some level of resources in a poor neighborhood that is slightly removed from campus. Universities serving as facilitators, on the other hand, often do not adopt a place-based strategy, instead dispersing programs and resources throughout the broader community. Occasionally these schools may focus some resources on a specific neighborhood, particularly when approached to serve as a partner in a community-led revitalization effort. This is the case, for example, with IUPUI's dedication of resources to the Near Westside as a partner in the community's quality-of-life plan.

Community Economic Development through Corporate Investment

The mere size of universities means their business and financial practices impact local economic development, whether positively or negatively, intentionally or unintentionally. A growing number of universities have come to embrace their role as purchaser, investor, workforce developer, incubator, and real estate developer. Whether they choose to direct their economic power toward community development is a key question of this study. By strategically leveraging their assets and business practices toward community economic development, universities can play a critical role in community revitalization. They can also attract significant outside investments and stimulate key public-private partnerships. These practices are particularly true of the universities we have identified as using a leadership model—that is, Penn, Cincinnati, and Yale. These sites have demonstrated that more quantifiable impacts result when universities establish specific goals and targets for their financial practices to influence surrounding neighborhoods.

One economic practice that some universities have adopted is redirecting their purchasing dollars to support their local community. This often requires internal changes to the institution's procurement policies, whether that means providing unique opportunities for local, minority, and women vendors to do business with the university (as seen at Syracuse) or providing incentives for purchasing officers to engage in such strategies (as seen at Penn). Additional resources or staffing may also be needed to build up local vendor capacity in order to do business with the university. By investing dollars that they would already be spending on goods and services into their local community, nonetheless, higher education institutions can help create healthy, stable, and viable communities. As Henry Webber of Washington University in St. Louis notes, "All anchors will do some local purchasing, but building or improving a local business community often requires active outreach to local vendors and intensive efforts to improve the capacity of these vendors."[2] A larger number of universities have made special efforts, such as hiring local contractors or mandating minority and local hires among their general contractors. (Of course, minority contracting is often required of public universities, but exceeding these expectations and focusing on local hires is certainly less common.) This may be linked to an apprenticeship program that enables residents to develop specialized skills on the job; Minnesota provides a leading example of this approach.

Another business practice geared toward community economic development is local workforce development and hiring. Some universities have targeted recruitment and training programs that prioritize hiring local residents. Through such programs, training in a core skill set linked with mentorship and real job opportunities can lead to significant economic opportunities for individuals while fulfilling specific workforce needs at the institution. Moreover, when universities expand their employment base from within their local neighborhood(s), it also promotes positive environmental practices by cutting down on commuting. The University of Southern California (USC), for example, has adopted a goal to increase employment from the areas immediately surrounding its campus. This goal has largely been realized through local recruitment and channeling applicants to various job opportunities, resulting in one out of seven applicants from the seven surrounding zip codes being hired at USC (a total of 170 hires out of approximately 1,200 positions, as of 2002).[3] Combining these workforce practices with the local purchasing practices described above, one innovative approach is to match university procurement with new community-based businesses that fulfill the needs of the university while creating opportunities for employment and asset building for local residents. Cleveland's Greater University Circle is leading the way in such an approach and will be discussed further in chapter 10.[4]

Universities can also help shape real estate development for community benefit. Simply where institutions choose to erect new buildings has the potential to substantially impact the local economy. However, most higher education institutions have acted alone in their real estate activities, or, minimally, have maintained the lead role.[5] On the other hand, a number of universities have chosen to work with local partners, such as local community development corporations (in whom the community may have greater trust), in order to circumvent some necessary political and financial risks that come with real estate development—as well as address broader community development goals. Other anchor institutions have partnered with private developers who can attract funding for low-income housing.[6] These options often mean ceding some degree of control of the development process. As Ziona Austrian and Jill Norton of Cleveland State University put it, "The direction that a university takes with respect to real estate acquisition and development ultimately depends on its leadership. The university president and top-level administrators set the agenda for physical development. Their vision for the future of the university and their perception of the role of the university as a civic partner determine what they do and how they do it." The authors claim that anchor institution real estate development can most effectively reach mutually beneficial goals when university leaders choose to (1) align their plans with broader community goals; (2) partner with residents, city officials, and other stakeholders; and (3) ensure opportunities for community participation in the planning and decision-making process.[7] Leadership also influences how development agendas are financed. Some institutions have invested major dollars into real estate development in their surrounding community, such as Cincinnati's dedication of $150 million in endowment funds for redevelopment in Uptown. These dollars can leverage significant private investment.

University activity can also stimulate local commercial investment and the local housing market. For example, attracting and building new businesses in the area can provide jobs for residents in addition to bringing services to students, faculty, staff, and the broader community. Employer-assisted housing programs can also help revitalize the neighborhoods surrounding universities by creating more mixed-income areas. It should be noted that these practices may intentionally or unintentionally displace existing small businesses or property owners. One principle to address such issues, according to the *Anchor Institutions Toolkit* developed at Penn, is to "create retail development in context of the surrounding neighborhood—complementing existing mix versus displacing."[8] In addition, universities may choose to—or be required to, based on their funding source—include affordable rental and low-income housing options for residents as part of their development, such as Portland State's agreement with the Portland Development Commission. Although rare in example, universities may also support community land trusts, nonprofit agencies that use nonprofit landownership to maintain permanently affordable housing even in a "gentrifying" area, as Duke University has done through its support of the Durham Community Land Trust.[9]

Local Capacity Building

Some universities have sought to address community housing, business, and economic development challenges by building resident and neighborhood capacity. Specifically, a number of universities have worked in partnership with existing, or formed new, local community development corporations that draw upon community strengths. This approach is especially common among universities identified as conveners—Emory, Syracuse, Minnesota, and LeMoyne-Owen—who also emphasize resident engagement, trainings, and joint leadership in these efforts. Historically black colleges and universities (HBCUs), in particular, have been engaged in building and supporting community development corporations, an effort that grew largely from HUD dollars distributed to minority-serving institutions in the 1990s (funding that continues to this day), as well as grant programs active during the late 1990s and early 2000s supported by Seedco and the Fannie Mae Foundation.[10]

Many universities have helped build local business capacity as part of a broader community development vision. A select number of institutions have helped establish revolving loan funds to support local entrepreneurs. Indeed, such was a founding purpose of the LeMoyne-Owen College CDC. Another strategy is depositing university money in community development financial institutions and local minority-owned banks, thereby provided a larger pool of funds to lend to area businesses, as both Yale and Duke have done. Some universities operate business incubator facilities, providing a nurturing environment for emerging small businesses to develop and flourish. Other institutions provide workshops and technical assistance for local entrepreneurs. This focus on building local capacity through in-kind resources and educational programs is particularly emphasized by universities serving as facilitators—IUPUI, Portland State, and Miami Dade College. In supporting local business development, Henry Taylor emphasizes, "The level of training should focus not only on providing market access to goods and services for the university, but actually developing groups of business owners that can go back into their community and help it grow."[11]

Some university-community partnerships aim to strengthen existing community institutions. Many of the higher education institutions in this study, for example, have increased the capacity of local nonprofits through the placement of student interns and volunteers, as well as through faculty research. Many of these universities also provide trainings for local nonprofits and small businesses, led by professionals from throughout the institution and the broader community. In some cases, it is necessary for the university to commit to building local capacity in order to have a strong, on-the-ground partner organization for its community development agenda. Some universities have engaged other partners—often community foundations or well-established CDCs—to take on a more focused community capacity building role. As David Maurrasse discusses in *Beyond the Campus,* community-based organizations and residents need a "certain level of technical capacity and political savvy" to benefit most from their partnerships with higher education institutions.[12]

Public School and Health Partnerships

In recent years, the importance of community health and public education in urban revitalization has received mounting national recognition. Urban colleges and universities, in particular, have demonstrated growing interest in developing research and project-based partnerships in these areas. Indeed, public education and health partnerships are a common element among all of the institutions profiled in this study.

As the 2009 HUD Anchor Institutions Task Force report emphasized, "Successful community development and successful schooling are interconnected and interdependent." Moreover, successful public schools are intrinsically linked to the success of higher education institutions. Not only do public schools prepare the next generation of college students, but also universities train the next generation of K-12 teachers and principals. Moreover, universities need strong neighborhoods to succeed, and strong neighborhoods rely on strong public school systems. Furthermore, public schools have a direct economic impact, as completing high school is one of the most important predictors of a young person's lifetime earning potential. According to a 2009 study by the Alliance for Excellent Education, if the number of high school dropouts in the nation's fifty largest cities and their surrounding areas were reduced by half, these 300,000 new graduates would collectively earn in excess of $4.1 billion in additional wages in an average year compared to their expected earnings without a diploma. As a result of higher incomes and increased spending, these graduates would also increase local tax revenue by nearly $536 million during the average year.[13]

One promising model of university engagement in public education is the development and support of community schools, employing a school-centered community development approach. A community school serves as the hub of its neighborhood, drawing in partners and community resources to improve student learning, strengthen families, and promote healthier communities. A growing body of research shows that community schools have a significant impact on increasing attendance, reducing the dropout rate, improving student academic performance and behavior, increasing parent involvement, and strengthening adult education. Moreover, more efficient use of school buildings, increased security, and better rapport between students and residents contribute to more stable neighborhoods.[14] Two of the universities featured in this study—Penn and IUPUI— have served as anchors in community school partnerships in their local neighborhoods. Through this university-assisted community school approach, and others, universities can provide a wealth of resources to local school partners, including the use of undergraduates in tutoring, mentoring, and staffing of after-school programs. Professors and graduate students can also help develop curriculum and provide assistance with professional development for K-12 teachers.

A number of universities have taken a different direction in public school partnerships by adopting local schools or opening new schools (often charters) designed for low-income students. These approaches typically involve significant financial investment and intensive professional development, such as the University of Pennsylvania's support of the Penn Alexander School in West Philadelphia.

Improving community health is not only an intrinsic element of the university-assisted community school approach described above, but is also an increasing focus of health professional schools.[15] IUPUI, with the nation's largest nursing school (in terms of degrees offered) and one of the largest medical schools, exemplifies the mutually beneficial potential of neighborhood clinical outreach as a means of educating health professionals. Public health programs are also growing at universities across the country, with or without academic medical centers, through which faculty and students are engaged in community-based participatory research, health education, and outreach. Community-Campus Partnerships for Health is a growing network of over 1,800 communities and higher educational institutions across North America that demonstrates this trend.[16] Community health partnerships need not have an economic focus in order to have an economic benefit—scientific studies have proven that healthier individuals learn better, work harder, and have greater productivity. Going one step further, Victor Rubin of PolicyLink claims, "Health is such a large industry. If a university puts a new [health] clinic in a low-income neighborhood, it can have its own economic impact by creating jobs and real estate. It becomes sort of a mini-anchor."[17] Miami Dade College's Medical Center Campus and Penn's Netter Center have both helped to open community health centers in their local neighborhoods. These centers are providing much needed services to community residents, as well as invaluable experiences to college students in the allied health fields; they may one day enjoy the spillover economic benefits to which Rubin refers.

Academic Engagement

Academic engagement refers to the variety of ways that universities can leverage their *academic* resources to achieve community development objectives, generally carried out in ways that are mutually beneficial for the university, including enhanced learning, research, and teaching. Academic engagement may include service-learning, yearlong, or semester "capstone" projects, practicums, health clinics, internships, community problem-solving research, and more. In one form or another, scholarly engagement is a common feature among all of the institutions in this study; still, service-learning and community-based research is *most* emphasized by universities identified as facilitators, largely driven by their emphasis on student and faculty engagement while meeting partnership requests. Indeed, IUPUI, Portland State, and Miami Dade College have three of the largest service-learning programs in the nation.

Some universities, including several in this study (Syracuse, Portland State, Minnesota, and IUPUI), have made revisions to their tenure and promotion guidelines to include a broader definition of scholarship. For example, in addition to IUPUI's "Public Scholar" designation for faculty hiring, and faculty awards from the Chancellor's Office, the university also encourages effective faculty engagement by providing fellowship opportunities to work in one of five targeted areas of community revitalization. Such policies and practices can encourage faculty to conduct more, and more ongoing, community-based participatory research. Other institutions have worked to embed service-learning opportunities within their curriculum, helping to create a "culture of service" in a generation of youth. Service-learning, per se, although it is perhaps the most visible result of the growing university engagement movement, is not a major focus of this study, in large measure because the nature of the work (the overwhelming majority of which is tied to the academic calendar of quarter-long or semester-long courses) does not easily lend itself to transformative community change.[18] Still, students in service-learning courses can provide labor for immediate nonprofit and public school needs. They can also be linked to sustained partnerships and programs, providing a consistent source of volunteers and the potential for greater impact.

Some institutions, like Portland State and Emory, provide yearlong capstone courses as a means to engage students in deeper relationships with community partners, as well as connect students' experiences to a broader field of study. These capstone projects involve interdisciplinary teams of students working collaboratively with community partners to identify, and aim to solve, pressing community problems or assist community partners in pursuing important new opportunities for improving the well-being of their residents and neighborhood.

When scholarly efforts are connected to sustained partnerships, such as IUPUI's Faculty Community Fellows working in the Near Westside, Emory's yearlong Community Building and Social Change Fellows program for students, and Penn's faculty and students working in community schools through academically-based community service, the potential for community transformation is greatly enhanced.

Multi-Anchor, City, and Regional Partnerships

Many colleges and universities have looked to expand and deepen their external partnerships—including with other educational institutions, medical institutions, corporations, and city and state government—in order to share resources and services invested in their local community. The common rationale is that urban revitalization efforts may have a greater chance to succeed if there are collective resources, ownership, and accountability among many partners. In some cases, the university may choose to partner with local government for more strategic reasons, such as acquiring funding and land. As Perry and Wiewel observe, "Relations between universities and city governments tend to be project- or task-oriented, episodic, and subject to political and personal vagaries. Given the importance of universities to their cities and the importance of local government to university projects, it would make sense for both to engage in more systematic, continuous, and comprehensive joint planning."[19] Portland State (where Wiewel has served as President since 2008) offers a leading example in which the university and the city have participated in joint planning that has met the needs of the university while contributing to the vitality of the neighborhoods surrounding campus.

Four of the universities in this study—Penn, Syracuse, Cincinnati, and Minnesota—have formed consortiums with higher education or other anchor institutions in their region. In other words, multi-anchor partnerships are most common among universities emphasizing a leadership or convener strategy. Such collaboration provides an opportunity to share and leverage resources as well as learn from each other. Similar to coordinating activities across one campus, bringing together the strengths, assets and programs from multiple institutions has the potential for greater collective impact on the community. Of course, multi-anchor partnerships should also pay attention (and perhaps give even greater attention than individual anchor initiatives) to building on the skills of local residents and the strength of neighborhood associations, in order to promote community development that will be supported and sustained. Cincinnati's experience in this area, which is discussed more in chapter 6, provides an opportunity for others to learn from.

Addressing the Challenges

Colleges and universities that incorporate any, or all, of the forms of engagement just described face numerous challenges and critical decisions along the way. We briefly discuss several of these issues below: creating an engaged community; establishing partnership programs and goals; institutionalizing an anchor vision; securing funding and leveraging resources; building a culture of economic inclusion; sustaining participatory planning and robust community relationships; and, where the rubber hits the road, actually meeting at least some of the key needs of the low-income residents and neighborhoods who are partners in these efforts. These same issues will be explored further in each of the comparative segments of chapters 5, 6, and 7. It is also worth noting that institutional type, scale, funding, resources, demographics, and culture are all important characteristics that play a role in shaping campus-community partnerships. This idea is woven throughout the rest of the book as we discuss individual strengths and approaches among our cross section of cases.

Creating an Engaged Community

Individuals, groups, and entities across the world define community in many different ways, and higher education institutions are no exception to this rule. Some universities view their community as the scholars who work and study within the boundaries of their campus. Others see themselves *within* a broader community—for many urban institutions, a community of poverty and blight—one with which they may or may not choose to engage. A growing number of universities have begun to see themselves as *part of* their surrounding community, their futures intertwined with the success of their neighbors. As Michael Morand of Yale puts it, "The inextricable bond [of a university as a community institution] is expressed by the fact that our marvelously urbanized campus is continuously intersected by public streets and sidewalks, that the art museums are free and open to the public as are over a thousand lectures, concerts, and events each year. That engagement and rootedness is what fundamentally sets places like ours apart from hospitals, foundations, banks, corporations, and others that support community development."[1]

For universities that have taken the view that they are *within* and *part of* their surrounding community, definitions and tactics still vary. The historical relationship between the institution and the community plays a key role in the approach to engagement. Several universities have engaged in community development in response to crisis, such as violent crimes in the neighborhood surrounding campus. Some universities strategically focus on neighborhood-level impacts, while others look to impact regional development. Some do both. Syracuse University, for example, has taken on the entire city of Syracuse as its engaged community while still focusing on revitalization of two specific neighborhoods. Not all urban universities are immediately surrounded by poverty. In such cases, they may choose to focus their partnership efforts on relations with their immediate neighbors and/or government agencies, such as Emory's early partnership programs in the Clifton Corridor and surrounding neighborhood area. Or they may choose to invest at least some level of focused resources in a targeted neighborhood that is not directly adjacent to campus but is most in need of the resources and relationships that a university can provide, such as the University of Minnesota's efforts in North Minneapolis or Emory's more recent work through the Office of University Community Partnerships in low-income metropolitan Atlanta neighborhoods.

Regardless of their definition, the universities in this study have all demonstrated meaningful impacts on their surrounding communities. We argue, however, that those who adopt a place-based strategy, focusing resources on specific geographic area(s), have greater *potential* to directly influence community economic development. This is discussed further in the final chapters of the book.

Establishing Partnership Programs and Goals

The specific programs and activities enlisted by campus-community partners vary greatly, although they generally align with the partners' chosen methods of engagement, such as the six areas outlined in the previous chapter. They also depend upon the identified assets and needs of all local partners. A community needs assessment may be conducted to assess these prioritized areas, while asset mapping may be conducted to identify the capacities and strengths of local individuals, organizations, and institutions. The selected programs and goals will also depend upon existing relationships, financial capacity, and leadership. As Henry Webber and Penn's *Anchor Institutions Toolkit* both suggest, anchors may want to conduct a risks-and-benefits analysis when evaluating potential strategies and projects.[2] In the most collaborative approaches, community residents and other key stakeholders are involved in these assessments and at all stages of the planning process to collectively identify goals and activities that will mutually benefit both the community and the institution.

Another distinction among higher education institutions engaged in their communities is whether the university takes a reactive or proactive approach to community development. As previously described, a growing number of universities have taken a lead role in community revitalization efforts. Some universities are reacting in response to a crisis within or on the edge of campus, as mentioned above, while others take a more proactive approach to turn around a nearby blighted community. Other universities do not have the capacity to lead a community revitalization effort, but have served in a convener role, pulling resources and stakeholders together. Still other universities have served as key partners in a collaborative effort for community revitalization but have not taken the lead role, instead allowing community leaders, or other anchors, to guide the initiative.

Institutionalizing an Anchor Vision

As defined by the Carnegie Foundation for the Advancement of Teaching, "institutionalized practices of community engagement" among universities and colleges demonstrate "alignment among mission, culture, leadership, resources, and practices."[3] For universities and colleges implementing anchor institution strategies, there are no substitutes for high-level administrative support. University presidents and chancellors, in particular, set the institution's vision and priorities, as well as its budget. When these leaders support community engagement efforts—beyond rhetoric—partnerships work more effectively, more efficiently, and achieve greater impact. As a 2002 Urban Institute report stated, "The president or chancellor plays a major role in setting the institution's priorities and establishing it budget. Leadership at this level is the only efficient way to mobilize resources and support for community outreach and partnerships from across all the major divisions of the academic institution." For instance, during Judith Rodin's tenure at Penn, responsibility for the West Philadelphia Initiatives resided directly in her office and with several of her vice presidents. As Richard Meister, former executive vice president of academic affairs at DePaul University, notes, leadership is needed because true engagement demands a change in thinking: "Engagement requires an institution to recognize that it is a corporate citizen or entity that has to model certain behaviors. It is quite a contrast from the traditional version of the ivory tower—removed and afloat, critiquing from above."[4]

Still, sustainable community partnerships must go beyond the commitment of a few dedicated individuals or presidential leadership. Otherwise, few efforts will persist beyond a single administration. Depending on the university's anchor approach, this may mean developing such measures as increasing the number of faculty as leaders in community-based research and curriculum or changing the culture among purchasing officers to focus on local procurement. To be certain, engaging faculty members—who do the vast majority of teaching and research at the university *and* who are often the longest standing members of the institution—plays a critical role in institutionalizing an anchor vision.

Further, community development efforts have greater potential impact when the administrative and business sides of the university work together with the academic side.[5] One promising approach to internal coordination and collaboration—and sustainability—is the presence of a centralized unit that promotes and manages outreach activities. Some of these units are focused almost exclusively on service-learning, while others have broader community partnership agendas. At the same time, major community development efforts led by university administration are often managed—and funded—separately from their community partnership centers. The degree to which these approaches, and their resources, are strategically aligned has much to do with the institutional leadership and the specific programs and goals being implemented, and largely affects how the *university* is impacted by engagement with its community.[6] At many of the universities featured in this study, for example, high-powered faculty or staff person(s) often lead a centralized partnership center whose efforts are supported by, and closely aligned with, the central administration. For instance, the University of Minnesota has a dean of extension and two associate vice presidents in positions that are responsible for community engagement: Beverly Durgan, Andrew Furco, and Geoff Maruyuma, respectively. All of these leaders report to senior vice president Robert Jones, whose commitment to advancing both the community engagement agenda and the urban agenda has helped bring together university-wide efforts. This leadership and alignment often promotes more effective—and efficient—use of internal resources by focusing them on specific, strategic objectives.

Securing Funding and Leveraging Resources

While federal, foundation, and donor dollars have supported many universities' engagement efforts, internal funds are essential for sustained community-campus partnerships. Endowment and operating fund allocations are two ways to leverage university assets for community development. Targeted alumni-giving campaigns have also raised dollars for partnership efforts. Although state institutions often have more restricted funding, those in this study have been able to draw from their central budget to support community partnership activities. University leaders often feel greater justification in the use of core funding and endowment dollars toward community engagement when the activities also help realize the core missions of their institution; this investment typically involves annual expenditures to campus partnership centers and programs that are also helping to advance research, teaching, and learning. In several cases, it involves substantial capital expenditure.

Higher education institutions can also leverage their resources in ways that require less direct expenditures—and which often serve to effect a greater institutional cultural transformation—such as through adopting economic inclusion practices in their employment, purchasing, hiring, investment, and contracting, as noted above. Efficient use of internal resources also requires the reallocation of existing funds to community partnership activities, such as faculty time, whose research or students are focused on community problem-solving.

External funding, even when it is limited, can often have a catalytic impact. Many of the universities in this study have been supported through federal dollars, such as Office of University Partnership (OUP) grants administered through the U.S. Department of Housing and Urban Development (HUD)—typically in the range of $400,000–$700,000 over three years. Reaching more than 300 universities in its first decade, OUP has had significant influence on the evolution of university-community partnerships, although funding for the program has always been limited.[7] The universities in this study have also received significant grants from local and national foundations. Too many campus-community partnerships, however, rely on grant funding, which are often limited in dollar amount and in time. External grants often do not allow for the necessary time to build relationships and have an inclusive planning process, which is essential for any ongoing efforts for community revitalization.

Many universities and colleges have looked to diversify and expand their funding base for community partnership efforts. Universities focused on real estate development, in particular, have been able to leverage funding through tax increment financing, new markets tax credits, revenue bonds, standard commercial loans, and other sources. Some universities have helped form nonprofit organizations that operate as independent entities but remain closely associated with the institution. This allows not only for the organization to attract funding using the university name but also to avoid bureaucratic and other restrictions on university funds. The LeMoyne-Owen College Community Development Corporation is one example of this type of approach. Here the college, even with limited funds of its own, has been able to participate in community development activities through association with and support of this separate 501(c)3 entity, because the CDC's leadership has had the vision (and with the college's backing, the stature) to attract external community development grant and loan support.

LeMoyne-Owen is not unique in creating a separate entity to support its community development work. This approach has also been used by Ohio State University, for example, which formed Campus Partners for Community Urban Redevelopment as an independent entity to lead the development of the multiuse (retail, commercial, residential) South Gateway project. Urban planning and mixed-used real estate specialists David Dixon and Peter Roche explain Ohio State's rationale:

- The revitalization should be led by an entity with a clearly defined mission and full-time staff dedicated to this task. Flexibility and effectiveness in conducting planning and real estate development activities would also be key, and the university itself could not provide that expertise.
- Clear authority for making decisions, independent of the very collegial decision making process of the university, would be critical.
- Distance from the university structure would be important, both to shield OSU from potential controversy and to inspire community acceptance.
- Campus Partners would need to live up to private-sector expectations by playing the dual role of the redevelopment authority (assembling land and handling relocation, demolition, and environmental cleanup) and the source of "patient capital" (taking early risks related to planning and market studies, land purchases, etc.).[8]

Campus Partners also demonstrates that a strategy that benefits both the university and the community can often attract considerable external support. In particular, Campus Partners, with the backing of a $28 million endowment investment from Ohio State University, was able to raise $35 million from new markets tax credits and over $100 million in external funds from other sources.[9]

As Campus Partners illustrates, however, the commitment of internal funds remains critical. Some of the schools discussed in this report, particularly those following what we have labeled a leadership strategy, have made direct investments in the hundreds of millions of dollars. Still, as a number of the other cases in this book illustrate, smaller scale efforts can also result in significant community benefit. As we will discuss later, most commonly it is the integration of internal and external resources that fosters the most sustainable and successful anchor partnerships.

Building a Culture of Economic Inclusion

While many university-community partnerships have led to reductions in the rate of neighborhood crime, few have resulted in significant reductions in poverty rates. Similarly, while considerable success has occurred in a number of partnership programs, these efforts have rarely been sufficient to eliminate the health disparities and educational achievement gap that poverty most often brings. In an essay entitled "Can Universities Contribute to Sustainable Development," Stephen Viederman claims, "Most efforts at social change are, in effect, ameliorative: they seek to remedy immediate problems, but do not deal with root causes."[10] At the same time, a range of strategies has emerged in the last fifteen years to begin to directly and systemically address such issues and create greater economic opportunity for local residents. Some universities have dedicated intellectual and human resources to solving these real-world problems through service-learning, community-based participatory research, internships, and fellowships. More tangible economic benefit—though more limited in example—comes through the dedication of purchasing and contracting dollars, employment practices, training and technical assistance, investment, and real estate development toward community economic development. These innovative practices are largely being demonstrated by universities serving in leadership roles.

Several other institutions in this study have been encouraged by state or city policies to offer assistance to minority and disadvantaged business owners. Many of the studied universities have also supported local entrepreneurs and small businesses through training, technical assistance, and seed funding. Universities emphasizing a convener strategy typically embrace this capacity-building focus as a means to economic inclusion.

The University of Pennsylvania's West Philadelphia Initiatives is one of the most highly recognized commitments to economic inclusion, which involved a combined effort including the business practices and academic programs described above.[11] This approach, however, can be challenging, as there is often a tension between the economic development mind-set and the partnership mind-set of a university. As Maurrasse phrases it, "As much as higher education appears to be moving toward involvement in local communities, the institutions also are becoming increasingly corporate in nature. The core academic mission holds one set of priorities; economic aspects of the mission drive another set of priorities. The two are intertwined but not always in sync."[12]

For some institutions, providing access to higher education is their primary vision—and perhaps greatest potential—for providing economic opportunity. This is particularly true of universities serving as facilitators. Miami Dade College's open-door policy and Portland State's open transfer agreement with local community colleges both speak to this objective. Miami Dade also offers a number of credit and noncredit courses at no charge to community residents (a practice most commonly seen at community colleges). Clearly, just as they have different interpretations of community, universities view their role in promoting economic inclusion in various ways.

Sustaining Participatory Planning and Robust Community Relationships

Building relationships and trust among campus and community partners takes time. And as Maurrasse wryly comments, "If the historical relationship has been contentious, it takes even more time."[13] Sustainable campus-community partnerships involve inclusive planning processes that allow for an inventory of strengths of the various partners involved, prioritization of the most pressing needs, and agreement upon mutually beneficial practices. Transparency is a necessary element of trust between campus and community. As Rachel Weber, Nik Theodore, and Charles Hoch of the University of Illinois at Chicago write, "Transparency requires that informational channels allow partners to comprehend the interest, intentions, and capabilities of each partner. It does not mean that all information is disclosed indiscriminately (which, in fact, may constitute a dereliction of fiduciary duty), but rather that information be relevant, actionable, and delivered on a timely basis."[14]

Community buy-in is essential prior to—and during—implementation. "For community buy-in, people from the university have to be seen as trustworthy, of their word, and bringing a tangible benefit for the community. One way to be trustworthy is to not be a direct representative of the institution (faculty or student groups, for example); or, be a representative of the institution and admit your past wrongdoings," says Rubin. Being able to cede real power and control in decision-making is also critical in developing truly participatory planning. In 1969, urban planner Sherry Arnstein wrote perhaps the classic journal article, published in the *Journal of the American Planning Association*, on what constitutes effective, as opposed to token, participation in decision-making. In Arnstein's eight-step ladder, the level of community participation in decision-making can range, theoretically, from "manipulation" at the lowest rung of the ladder to full citizen control at the top of the ladder. Later scholars have modified the rungs of the ladder, but the basic concept that partnership depends not just on the number of meetings, but also on how decisions are made in those meetings, remains. Most interesting for our purposes are steps 4, 5, and 6 of the Arnstein ladder; these correspond, to "consultation," "placation" (i.e., consultation with some adjustment based on community views), and "partnership," respectively. It is not always best to maximize community control—particularly if the university's comfort level requires maintaining significant control to be willing to invest its resources—but it is necessary for the university to be up front in its expectations. As Rubin says, "You need to be able to describe what it is the university wants to do, and be clear that you are willing to share the planning and decision making with community groups."[15]

Ongoing communication is also indispensable for sustained partnerships. Forums, town halls, and other gatherings can provide opportunities for community and university stakeholders to exchange ideas and discuss strategies for partnership and redevelopment. In Penn's case, monthly meetings called First Thursdays are held in a public library "to which all community stakeholders and university administrators are invited and regularly attend to nourish the process of transparency."[16] Yale holds a similar monthly forum. Universities may also provide opportunities for residents and other stakeholders to counsel and monitor their partnerships through a community advisory board.

As noted above, power dynamics play an important role in campus-community partner-ships. Austrian and Norton's analysis of university real estate development holds true for many university engagement initiatives: "The extent to which community groups can affect the development process is partly a function of their sophistication. Well-organized groups with highly skilled leaders are better able to exert pressure and more equipped to negotiate with the university."[17] Some institutions have signed community benefit agreements with their neighborhood, in order to negotiate results and expectations. "There's a principle behind this: it's not a benefit if the community doesn't want it," says Rosalind Greenstein, an urban policy analyst. She continues: "[A community benefit agreement] is the second best thing, though. The best thing is a really good community planning process."[18] This process is most successful when there is "consistent, committed leadership on both sides of the partnership—the university and the community," adds Elizabeth Hollander. She also emphasizes the need for "very skilled bridge people who know how to work between the two entities."[19]

Maurrasse goes a step further to discuss the importance of empowering the community. "It is important to ensure that knowledge is being transferred from higher education into local communities, promoting self-sufficiency rather than fostering dependency among local con-stituents. Capacity building would suggest the transference of power from one party to the other. Furthermore, when both parties are treated as if each has something to offer, the opin-ion of the transitional 'recipient' influences the nature of the relationship. Ultimately, the 'recipient' is more likely to buy into the partnership when engaged as a contributor through the process." Such practices reflect an asset-based community development approach.[20]

According to Harry Boyte, founder and codirector of the Center for Democracy and Cit-izenship (now at Augsburg College), the "main obstacle to genuine and productive partner-ships" between higher education institutions and their communities is a "'knowledge war,' full of invisible hierarchies and exclusions" that dramatically limits their capacity to solve neighborhood (and greater societal) problems.[21] Fortunately, through such practices as described above, a small but growing number of university administrators and faculty are recognizing and respecting the value of resident and community knowledge, which helps to break down some of these power structures.

Meeting the Needs of Low-Income Residents and Neighborhoods

For this study, we sought to move beyond public relations and anecdotes to assess the uni-versities' overall approach to community development, how these efforts affect those most in need, and how such strategies can be focused for the greatest positive outcome. As antic-ipated, few universities have engaged in comprehensive, longitudinal evaluation of com-munity outcomes (or university outcomes, for that matter). Much of the assessment to date has been measured against specific goals and targets for individual programs or initiatives, or for reporting to specific funding streams. For example, the University of Minnesota exceeded a 30 percent women- and minority-owned business target for the $2.1 million renovation of their new Urban Research and Outreach-Engagement Center, and Portland State's Business Outreach Program has assisted more than 400 small and emerging busi-nesses to develop, as well as create 150 new jobs, in the last three years alone.

A few institutions are beginning to look at neighborhood-level impacts, including educational achievement, employment levels, and per capita income. IUPUI's partnership with George Washington Community School, for example, helped its 2009 high school graduates enjoy a 100 percent acceptance rate into college. In 2009, Miami Dade College awarded nearly 8,000 associate degrees and 200 bachelor's degrees, as well as helped 600 residents earn their GEDs. Remarkably, LeMoyne-Owen College saw its surrounding neighborhood's per capita income increase from $8,000 to $13,500 from 1999 to 2009, while the percentage of residents earning less than $10,000 per year fell 21 percentage points, from 68 percent to 47.3 percent.

Some impacts of university engagement strategies—particularly those with large development agendas—have also been mixed. The University of Pennsylvania's creation and support of the Penn Alexander School, for example, achieved its desired result of high achievement for local students and attraction of Penn-affiliated families to live in the local community; real estate values have skyrocketed, however, which has displaced some of the families that once lived in the area. Cincinnati has also displaced residents and small business owners through its commercial and real estate development; to combat such consequences, they have helped acquire façade improvement grants for existing businesses as well as provided subsidized rental space.

Some university initiatives have more indirect community economic development benefits. Yale's homebuyer program, for example, has provided $22.5 million in subsidies to support more than 925 university-affiliated individuals or families to buy homes in New Haven. Emory's Office of University Community Partnerships has focused on building capacity among existing community development corporations.

Other university initiatives, while deeply focused on community economic development, are too young to see the desired results. Syracuse's Near West Side Initiative, for instance, has made great strides in its efforts to acquire and renovate land as well as rehabilitate old homes with sustainable green technology. Realization of the initiative's goal to improve the overall quality of life in the Near West Side (through such measures as increased employment and homeownership), on the other hand, can only be seen in time. It is also worth recognizing the deep and terrible impact that the subprime mortgage and foreclosure crisis has had on low-income neighborhoods throughout the United States, including many of the communities that universities have been helping to develop. As Victor Rubin puts it, "I fear a lot of the gains that came about in university-related neighborhood revitalization may be swept away. It is certainly a very critical issue and will shape all these endeavors for years to come."[22] Promisingly, while conducting this study, we saw few signs of campuses pulling back from their community investment.

Summing Up

The last four chapters provided an overview of how universities are taking on the role of anchor institutions, including a history of how they got here, current practices being implemented, and the challenges still faced. In part 2, we explore these ideas further and back up our observations by looking at what is happening on the ground at ten diverse sites.

Case Studies

The convergence of thinking and acting boldly with people requires that our communities' and our institutions' assets be used to create possibilities as well as discover them. We've learned that addressing some of the most difficult societal problems affecting individuals and communities requires a multidimensional view—seeing not only what others see but also the new relationships and new dimensions of complex problems and potential solutions

—Lou Anna Kimsey Simon, president, Michigan State University, in *Engaged Scholarship: Contemporary Landscapes, Future Directions*, volume 1, edited by Hiram E. Fitzgerald, Cathy Burack, and Sarena D. Seifer

As we discussed in the previous chapter, anchor strategies require the multidimensional view to which President Simon refers, because the issues facing our urban communities—such as poverty, crime, substandard housing, and inadequate K-12 education—themselves are multidimensional. Moreover, such efforts require creatively and strategically tapping the assets of the institutions and the communities of which they are a part, and then focusing these resources on specific objectives.

To explore what this work looks like in practice, in this portion of the book, we dive into the particular anchor strategies of our ten profiled colleges and universities, organized into three chapters according to the typology we have laid out.

First, we look at a group of three schools—IUPUI, Miami Dade College, and Portland State University—which have acted as *facilitators* in broad efforts for local and regional development. Next, we look at a second set of three schools—Penn, Cincinnati, and Yale—which have acted as *leaders* in community development efforts, focusing on revitalization of a particular community or neighborhood adjacent to campus. Lastly, we look at a third set of four schools—Syracuse, Minnesota, LeMoyne-Owen, and Emory—which have acted as *conveners*, working to forge coalitions with community stakeholders in a collaborative fashion. We begin each chapter by looking at the general characteristics defining each cluster of schools and then provide brief case studies on those individual institutions. Each chapter concludes with a comparative analysis that discusses some key challenges universities face in community development (as presented in chapter 4), providing further details on how these institutions work to navigate through such issues.

University as Facilitator: IUPUI, Portland State, and Miami Dade College

The three universities reviewed in this chapter—Indiana University–Purdue University Indianapolis, Portland State University, and Miami Dade College—are all young, large, public institutions whose civic engagement missions emphasize educational opportunity. To this end, they seek to provide engaging, supportive learning environments for their students as well as the broader community. Service-learning, community-based research, and public school and health partnerships involve large numbers of faculty and students at all three institutions. Where, or with whom, these university members engage is not constricted by a strategic institutional agenda. Instead, they are seen as "good neighbors," responding to a wide variety of community groups or agencies that wish to partner. Support from top administration helps leverage funding and recognition for engagement activities; however, the commitment of institution-wide resources, particularly corporate investment, toward community development remains limited.

Ziona Austrian and Jill Norton reflect on the limited funding available at many young, public institutions, particularly in regards to real estate development potential: "Portland State University, for example, has not yet been able to rely on its foundation because the university is relatively young, it does not have a large, well-established alumni base, and the foundation's assets are fairly limited."[1] Indeed, the endowments and budgets are limited at all three of these schools. In part *because* of limited funds, these universities focus on building capacity for community organizations and residents through in-kind resources. Miami Dade College, for example, houses and provides fiscal management for several programs targeted at job training and K-12 education for low-income residents. Its downtown campus also facilitates monthly forums for the underserved neighborhood of Overtown. Moreover, by partnering with city departments and established community organizations, these schools are able to facilitate broad, collaborative efforts for community development. Portland State, for instance, works with its city agencies in support of regional growth and development, with particular leadership in transit development and sustainability. At IUPUI, the university has worked in collaboration with its city on several initiatives; however, it is the strong community leadership in the Near Westside that has fostered an opportunity for the university to partner in comprehensive neighborhood revitalization. Indeed, IUPUI's focused academic resources in the Near Westside are a notable exception to the other two schools in this cluster, which do not have a place-based strategy. To date, however, corporate investment in this neighborhood has been lacking, limiting the potential gains that anchor-supported development can foster.

Indiana University–Purdue University Indianapolis

The Center for Service and Learning has been that bridge to pull resources out of the University, but there are no conversations at the upper level about what surrounds us and how they could have direct investment.

—Richard Bray, assistant director of IUPUI's Office of Multicultural Outreach
and former GINI coordinator for the Near Westside, interview by
Rita Axelroth Hodges, Indianapolis, August 3, 2009

Indiana University–Purdue University Indianapolis (IUPUI) was founded in 1969, as a partnership between Indiana and Purdue universities, to serve as Indiana's urban research and academic health sciences campus. Civic engagement is part of the institution's founding mission and seen as a central component not only for student learning but also for impacting its local community. IUPUI has come a long way in mending relationships with the community it displaced in the 1960s for campus development, primarily through the efforts of the Office of Neighborhood Partnerships (ONP). Begun as a special project in the Chancellor's Office in 1997, ONP has found a more focused niche within the Center for Service and Learning. Although ONP's efforts are aligned with the Near Westside's collectively identified areas of need and the Center's resources (particularly faculty and students) have been strategically leveraged to work within these focus areas, the potential for increased university-wide collaboration remains great.

The Center for Service and Learning (CSL) serves as one of several centralized units on campus. According to director Bob Bringle, the Center was built around incorporating service into the three things seen as most important to university students: courses, work experience, and volunteer opportunities. Formally established in 2001 through the merger of the Office of Service Learning, the Office of Community Service, and the Office of Neighborhood Partnerships, the Center's mission focuses on engaging students, faculty, and staff in service activities that mutually benefit the university and the community. As noted above, this amalgamation of offices has led to a more intentional focus of academic and human resources to, and long-term partnerships with, the Near Westside, an area representing five neighborhoods near campus.[2]

Much of the university's efforts in the Near Westside today are directed through the Great Indy Neighborhoods Initiative (GINI) project. GINI is a citywide collaboration for holistic neighborhood revitalization that is being implemented in six Indianapolis communities,

---

Figure 3. IUPUI Anchor Approach

Comprehensive Neighborhood Revitalization
- Partner in the Great Indy Neighborhoods Initiative (GINI) for Near Westside

Community Economic Development through Corporate Investment
- Participation in minority vendor fairs / trade shows
- Some support to local businesses but limited reach (6% annual spend to minority- and women-owned businesses)

Local Capacity Building
- Five faculty community fellows work to build capacity with Near Westside organizations
- Solution Center's Community Venture Fund provides matching grants (average $5,000) to support student internships and short-term business assistance, as well as runs Nonprofit Solutions Initiative (over 100 participants/year)

Public Education and Health Partnerships
- Student service scholars, work-study students, faculty, and staff participate in community school partnerships (integrated focus on academics, health and social services, and civic engagement)

- Professional schools (medicine, nursing, dentistry, allied health) provide clinical outreach, as well as develop spin-off businesses
- Community Learning Network: continuing education opportunities in local community centers

Academic Engagement
- 4,000 students participate in service-learning each year with 250 community organizations
- Several faculty development and grant programs support service-learning and civic engagement
- Chancellor's RISE to the Challenge Initiative (Research, International study, Service learning, and workplace and community Experiential learning) set goal of every IUPUI undergraduate participating in at least two RISE experiences by graduation

Multi-Anchor, City, and Regional Partnerships
- Leader in the Talent Alliance (regional alliance of schools, colleges and universities, and services to support young people from cradle to career)
- Leader in Central Indiana Community Schools Network and regional Center for University-Assisted Community Schools

---

which were competitively selected. "There are lots of resources in our community but we never had a great vision. One of the greatest things we did with GINI is created that vision, and identified partners who could best move us forward," says Diane Arnold, executive director of the Hawthorne Community Center. By being a partner in the GINI project for the Near Westside, IUPUI has been able to participate in focused and strategic initiatives as identified through the community's Quality of Life Plan: housing, public safety, beautification, business and economic development, education, health, and civic engagement.[3]

The Center for Service and Learning's five faculty community fellows each work in one of the focus areas of the GINI Quality of Life Plan. The three-year grants for fellows help "promote interdisciplinary collaboration and accountability for community outcomes in ways that wouldn't otherwise exist," says Professor Darrell Nickolson. As a faculty fellow, Nickolson partners with the local community development corporation and other community organizations on plans to stimulate economic and business development. For example, Nickolson and his students are designing the expansion and new building for the Hawthorne Community Center, which hopes to serve as an anchor project to drive future development in this area. "This is not the first attempt to revitalize this area," comments Nickolson, "but IUPUI's involvement is an opportunity to really push this forward." Faculty fellow Paula Differding-Burton helped brand a new identity for the Near Westside as well as for its new business association. This process helped "bring together five different neighborhoods and five neighborhood associations, which was no small feat," comments Patrice Duckett, GINI coordinator for the Near Westside. Although there is interest in revitalizing the central business district in the Near Westside, many recognize that attracting more students and faculty to live in the area—who would patronize new businesses—is a necessary step. However, crime in the area has been a deterrent for these efforts. Some faculty note that this may be a perfect opportunity for the university administration to step forward with its corporate resources, particularly real estate development, rather than looking to campus expansion in the north.[4]

IUPUI has thus participated in comprehensive neighborhood revitalization, but has done so without taking the driver's seat. This is made possible, in part, due to strong community leadership and the Center for Service and Learning staff's strong history of community work. Hawthorne Community Center serves as the lead partner for the GINI project in the Near Westside. Hawthorne director Diane Arnold also serves on Indianapolis's public school board and is a prominent community leader. Other key partners include the Indianapolis Neighborhood Resource Center, which provides neighborhood development specialists to work on capacity building, and Local Initiatives Support Corporation (LISC) of Indianapolis. Although IUPUI has been a key player since the beginning, community-based organizations have maintained the lead role. "Near Westside's history of getting stuff done was the clincher [in being selected as a GINI site]; this included a strong partnership with the university to get those things done. But IUPUI backed away from the actual presentation of the Quality of Life Plan—they really let the community own it," comments Anne-Marie Predovich Taylor, executive director of the Indianapolis Neighborhood Resource Center. Arnold expands upon the idea of IUPUI as a partner: "IUPUI really collaborates. They don't come in and say, 'We're going to fix you.' Instead, they come and listen. They see what resources they have and can bring to the table. We know it has to be fruitful for them too."[5]

One of IUPUI's most successful areas of engagement, and their area of leadership within the GINI plan, is K-12 education. These partnerships have largely focused on supporting community schools—neighborhood schools that integrate academics, health and social services, youth and community development, and civic engagement to improve student learning and to develop stronger families and healthier communities.[6] IUPUI has provided substantial resources to meet the needs of community schools developing in the Near Westside and is also leading a regional community school effort. Notably, IUPUI proved its allegiance when it stood with community residents to have the local failing high school reopened as a community school. Since reopening in 2000, George Washington Community School has significantly raised both attendance and graduation rates, and 100 percent of 2009 graduates were accepted into a postsecondary institution. Providing adult education in the Near Westside has also been a priority of the community school approach; for instance, IUPUI economics faculty have led financial literacy workshops for nearly 200 residents over the last several years. In addition, IUPUI's Community Learning Network is strategically working with local community centers to offer continuing education through the centers' workforce development programming. Finally, IUPUI's School of Education is preparing the next generation of teachers to work in urban settings through applied research and pre-service training. The School houses several centers focused on issues such as multiculturalism and math and science education, which interact with local public schools and community groups.[7]

A second focus of engagement at IUPUI is in public health. The university boasts the second largest medical school and largest multidisciplinary nursing school in the nation. Medical, nursing, and dental students provide in-kind services to children and families throughout the community as part of their clinical training. IUPUI physiology students staff and manage a Fit for Life program at George Washington Community School's Fitness Center. The Medical and Life Sciences departments, in particular, receive strong attention from the university administration, which hopes to see spin-off businesses developed here; thus, these partnerships have taken on a more corporate approach than the community relationship building approach of the Office of Neighborhood Partnerships.

Opportunities for students to be engaged with the community are abundant. Through the Center for Service and Learning, 4,000 students participate in service-learning each year, contributing labor to over 250 community partner organizations. Institutional research data shows that work experience is particularly important to students at IUPUI, so the Center has built many opportunities for work-study positions and scholarships. Roughly one-third of federal work-study students are community work-study, and more than $300,000 annually is directed to community service scholarships.[8] The Sam Jones Community Service Scholarship Program, for instance, provides opportunities for students with a background in service to sustain their community involvement and leadership at IUPUI. With nearly 180 scholars in 2007–2008, this is one of the largest service scholars programs in the country. The Fugate Scholars Program engages undergraduates with community school programs, such as implementing a college preparatory curriculum at George Washington. A select number of Sam Jones and Fugate scholars go on to serve as community partner scholars, acting as campus liaisons with community-based organizations and facilitating the engagement of additional student workers and volunteers.

Despite its many activities, Bringle explains, the Center for Service and Learning represents "only a small mosaic of what IUPUI does" to embrace its civic engagement mission. The Solution Center, for example, was founded in 2004 to serve as "a front door" to facilitate interactions between the university's community of scholars and researchers, and business, government, and nonprofit organizations. The Solution Center is supported largely through the Lilly Endowment. One of the Center's key activities includes a Community Venture Fund, which matches funds from mid- and small-sized businesses in order to support student internships, research projects, and short-term business assistance. (Grants are typically less than $5,000.) "Some organizations we work with have very limited resources. We try to help them assess their situation and solve their problems creatively," says Krista Hoffman-Longtin, associate director for Internships and Experiential Learning at the Solution Center. "For example, instead of hiring a marketing director on a very limited budget, we may suggest that they hire a consultant and an intern to do the work." The Center also runs the Nonprofit Solutions Initiative, which manages a database of nonprofit consultants, as well as facilitates free networking and workshops for more than 100 participants each year, including an annual conference focused on building nonprofit capacity.[9]

Demonstrating yet another engagement arm, IUPUI's Center for Urban Policy and the Environment conducts applied research in partnership with local and state government as well as social service agencies. For example, professor and policy analyst Laura Littlepage and her students have partnered with the Coalition of Homeless Serving Agencies for the last four years. Their research has resulted in issue briefs for policymakers that focus on homelessness prevention. Littlepage has also launched a study on the impacts of students and service-learning on the nonprofits with whom they work. "We're not assuming it's all win-win," says Littlepage. This Center is largely supported through the Lilly Endowment, as well as university and grant funding.[10]

In all, more than a dozen centers across campus have civic engagement as a defining quality of their work, emphasizing IUPUI's commitment to, and decentralized infrastructure for, realizing its anchor institution mission.

Portland State University

To a certain extent, for PSU to really care about the metro area goes back to our very founding. We were founded to serve returning veterans, and the other Oregon University system members didn't want us to survive after we served the first wave of vets. The only way we survived was getting local unions and politicians to support us—so from the beginning, the University had to make clear how we were serving local business and local government. It was necessary for political survival in a state system that didn't necessarily support our existence.

—Wim Wiewel, president, Portland State University, telephone interview by Rita Axelroth
Hodges, August 13, 2009

For nearly twenty years, Portland State's motto "Let Knowledge Serve the City" has symbolized the university's history of—and ongoing commitment to—engaged teaching and learning. As the only four-year public university in its metropolitan region, Portland State has a special opportunity to serve as a model of an engaged, urban research university. Institutional transformation took place in the early 1990s when President Judith Ramaley made a formal, articulated commitment to engagement that was manifested throughout the undergraduate curriculum. "This work, in large part, grew out of a focus on student learning," comments Kevin Kecskes, associate vice provost for engagement and director of community-university partnerships. "It was not a direct interest in addressing issues of poverty, housing, etc."[11]

Although the university has remained committed to community engagement, its mission has shifted in recent years. Not only are faculty and administration beginning to think of Portland State as more of a research institution, but they have also expanded their definition of community. As President Wim Wiewel explains, "As we've become more of a research university, we have also included engagement of businesses and the government as a legitimate form of community engagement, not just nonprofits. The fact that we're the only game in town means it's easier for us to extend our partnership to all sectors of the metro area." Indeed, Portland State's new economic development strategy is about harmonizing its education and research agenda with the regional economic development clusters defined

---

Figure 4. Portland State University Anchor Approach

Comprehensive Neighborhood Revitalization
- Partnerships largely dispersed throughout greater community
- Some concentrated efforts in University District area in 1990s

Community Economic Development through Corporate Investment
- Support of mixed-use development (40% facilities/real estate not owned by university)
- Focus on sustainability for local supply chain
- Some outreach to emerging small businesses (award extra points on evaluation)

Local Capacity Building
- Business Outreach Program has supported over 420 small businesses
- School of Social Work's Regional Research Institute for Human Services (RRI) provides leadership training and incubator space

Public Education and Health Partnerships
- Many individual faculty involved in community-based participatory research
- Formalized tutoring partnership with 60 Portland Public Schools

- Articulated agreement with all community colleges within 60-mile radius

Academic Engagement
- Revision to tenure and promotion in 1990s to advance scholarship of engagement
- Over 8,000 students, faculty, and staff engage in community-based learning courses each year
- Senior Capstone Program involves more than 230 community-based research projects each year
- Masters of urban and regional planning program and undergraduate degree in community development
- $50M program for sustainability research and teaching

Multi-Anchor, City, and Regional Partnerships
- Strong collaboration with City Bureau of Planning and Portland Development Commission, focused on real estate development and supporting growth in regional economic development clusters (e.g., Portland State Business Accelerator)
- Investment in transit development ($9.5M towards streetcar)

---

by the city.[1] Revisions to the promotion and tenure guidelines in the 1990s also helped advance the scholarship of engagement at Portland State. However, "There were no mandates on *what* or *where* faculty needed to be partnering; rather, that scholarly expressions of their community-engaged work (either community-based learning or community-based research) could count as part of a faculty member's overall tenure review portfolio," says Kecskes. Indeed, across the campus, there is common reverberation of "grassroots" and "diffuse" partnerships that fit with the "ethos" of Portland. Kecskes' office, the Center for Academic Excellence (CAE), oversees one of the largest service-learning programs in the country. In 2007–2008, 7,800 students were engaged in more than 400 community-based learning classes, providing more than 1.44 million hours of service. The Senior Capstone Program alone involves more than 230 courses that feature community-based research projects each year. "The capstone program directs armies of volunteers to do work all over the city. It is a great benefit to our community, and to the students," comments Lynn Knox, program manager for the City of Portland's Economic Opportunity Initiative. Still, "Projects are largely based on personal interests of the faculty, students, and community partners, so their placement is fairly random."[13]

Issues of poverty are addressed more directly through the work of individual faculty and students, particularly from the schools of Social Work, Education, Community Health,

Urban and Public Affairs, and Business Administration. Portland State also is one of only a few universities nationally to offer an undergraduate degree in community development.[14] Students enrolled in this program, as well as graduate students receiving their masters of urban and regional planning (MURP), often form deep relationships with community partners working on issues of community development. MURP students sign memoranda of understanding with their community partners and commit to 400 hours of community-based work as part of their program. Professors like Dr. Stephanie Farquhar in Community Health co-write grants with community and government partners, such as the county health department, to work on issues of health, environmental quality, and social capital among vulnerable populations.[15] Some nonprofits have enjoyed ongoing partnerships with the university, particularly through student intern placements. Each year, for example, one or two masters of social work students intern with Sisters of the Road Café, a local nonprofit working to effect systemic change on issues of homelessness. Sisters of the Road's leaders are also invited to make presentations on community organizing to students in the classroom, as well as inform the curriculum. "The experience working with PSU has been challenging in both ways. That's good for a partnership—to learn from each other and build relationships," says cofounder Genny Nelson.[16]

The School of Social Work's Regional Research Institute for Human Services (RRI), on the other hand, primarily provides research, data, grant writing, and evaluation support for local CDCs, service providers, and government entities. RRI also provides training in leadership development and strategic planning. "Within our evaluation strategies, we focus quite a bit on building community capacity around evaluation. We help them think through logic models and develop tools to measure their impact," says director Laurie Powers. "I think of a successful project being where, when we're done, not only does the partner have some data to answer their questions around effectiveness and processes ('what's working'), but also, where we walk away with a mutual agreement that they have more capacity to do evaluation themselves in the future."

RRI has also provided incubator space for several organizations, helping them write grants and obtain 501(c)3 status, and even acting as a fiscal agent until they become more established. Indirect costs can sometimes be inhibiting: most contracts require a 26 percent overhead cut to the university. However, large federal grants, and a dean who supports equity, can enable community groups to overcome these obstacles by offering them lower rates. "As we grow as a research university, this will probably get harder," says Powers. "But at this point, we have a lot of support from our dean and the Research Office."[17]

Another effort focused on issues of poverty is Portland State's Business Outreach Program (BOP), which began in 1994 through a Community Outreach Partnership Centers (COPC) grant from HUD. The purpose of the program is to provide technical assistance to low-income communities—primarily women- and minority-owned businesses within these communities—as well as provide a community-based learning opportunity for undergraduate business students. Student interns, as well as student teams working on their capstone courses in the business school, augment the program's small staff and help build long-term relationships with clients. Since 1994, BOP has supported over 420 small businesses, and from 2006 through 2009 alone, 146 new jobs were created at these firms. BOP was located in North Portland but moved back to campus a few years ago. Although less focused on a particular impoverished area, the program now receives more in-kind support. The program recently completed a contract with TriMet, Portland's transit agency, to support small business owners who were impacted by their light rail construction. With TriMet funding, BOP provided technical assistance, as well as oversaw low-interest loans, to thirty-three local businesses.[18]

Sustainability is emerging as a theme of engagement across campus, and indeed across the city of Portland. However, sustainability efforts have been aimed more toward improving environmental quality than community development. "Arguments for equity are just not as successful or high-profile or championed by civic leaders," says Knox. A university food contract, for example, was put into place several years ago with specific indicators not only about using local food, but also about a certain percentage of waste that has to be recycled and composted. A sustainability coordinator oversees these efforts. Kesckes reflects, "This is partly because of Portland's reputation, but we're also being opportunistic about it. When the normal university food contract came up for renewal, many students and faculty chose to strategically push to incorporate these changes into the next contract." Sustainability standards are built into purchasing and facilities contracts as well, with a focus on local supply chains and environmental quality. Sustainability has even become a theme for academic engagement. In 2008, Portland State was awarded a $25 million challenge grant from the Miller Foundation, to be matched by an additional $25 million from other donors, to focus on sustainability-related projects. Wiewel argues that academic sustainability efforts have broad implications: "We're very explicit about the triple bottom line, including equity and social sustainability," says President Wiewel. "A lot of projects through the Miller gift focus on issues of inclusion, educational improvement, health care, and access to healthy food."[19]

The university's finance and administration office has particularly robust partnerships with city departments, such as the Bureau of Planning and the Portland Development Commission. "We have a formal planning process with the city. We also see the city as a vehicle to communicate with the neighborhood," says Mark Gregory, associate vice president of finance and administration.[20] The city provides significant funding for the university's real estate projects but also enforces some regulations. For example, Portland State's plans to redevelop an old hotel into condominiums must include at least 150 units of affordable housing. More generally, the university strongly supports mixed-use buildings and has maintained its goal that 40 percent of area facilities and real estate not be owned by the university. This helps keep a percentage of the campus on tax rolls, as well as open to the community. Portland State has also been an anchor of transit use and development, connecting itself to other institutions and to the larger community. However, community economic development is not among the administration's highest priorities. "We educate people first," says Lindsay Desrochers, former vice president for finance and administration. "Economic development can be a by-product of what we do, [simply] because we are a big purchaser, real estate developer, and employer."[21]

"The Portland ethic is collaboration, and Portland State is at the table every time," says Lew Bowers, Central City Division manager for the Portland Development Commission.

Nonetheless, despite acting in this role in some specific projects, Portland State, as an institution, has yet to take on a coordinated, strategic approach to community development. The leadership of Wim Wiewel, president since 2008, may help carry Portland State into a new era as a model engaged, urban research university. In his first year, for example, Wiewel created a presidential taskforce partnership with Portland Public Schools. While institution-wide resources may become more thematically focused, however, they are unlikely to be concentrated in specific geographic areas. "We're trying to figure out how to identify the most important problems and how we can concentrate our resources there without losing our grassroots, diffuse principles," says provost Roy Koch.[22]

Miami Dade College

> Miami Dade College's mission mandates our collaboration with our community. Those are my marching orders and they are closely in tune with what I believe. My central belief is that a community college, particularly one like MDC that embraces a community mission, is as important as any institution in the community.
>
> —Eduardo J. Padrón, president, Miami Dade College, e-mail interview by
> Rita Axelroth Hodges, June 5, 2009

In 1960, Miami Dade Community College was born out of the needs of the community. It became the first public higher education option in south Florida and focused on workforce skills. In 2003, its name changed to reflect the addition of four-year degrees, but its commitment to the community has remained steadfast. Today, with an open-door policy and eight campuses that enroll approximately 96,000 credit students and 71,000 noncredit students annually, Miami Dade College awards more associate degrees than any other college in the country. Among its enrolled students, Miami Dade College serves a unique population that reflects the demographics of the county as a whole (and, indeed, 96 percent of credit students are Miami-Dade County residents): 68 percent of students are Hispanic; 19 percent are black non-Hispanic; 34 percent are non-U.S. citizens; 52 percent are first-generation college students; 72 percent work while attending college; 39 percent come from families below the federal poverty level, and 61 percent are low-income. "Miami Dade College has a unique vantage point," comments Daniella Levine, executive director of the Human Services Coalition of Dade County. "They [provide] an opportunity pipeline."[23]

The college employs a workforce that also mirrors the community: across the eight campuses, ethnic minorities account for 74 percent of full-time employees, while 59 percent of full-time faculty are ethnic minorities and 53 percent are female. "Everyone got their start at MDC—they trust us, they respect us, and they send their kids here," says Ted Levitt, director of Miami Dade College's Division of College Communications.[24]

The Carrie P. Meek Entrepreneurial Education Center is among the College's most focused initiatives to effect community change and wealth building. The Meek Center opened in 1989 as college and community leaders recognized the need to expand access and opportunity to education, job training, and entrepreneurial development for local residents. The Center started with a single mission: to build entrepreneurship with small, local

---

Figure 5. Miami Dade College Anchor Approach

Comprehensive Neighborhood Revitalization
- Many efforts dispersed, but several focused initiatives in Overtown, including Hospitality Institute and monthly forum
- Meek Entrepreneurial Center focused on small business development in black business corridor of Liberty City

Community Economic Development through Corporate Investment
- Inclusive hiring practices: 74% of full-time staff are people of color; 59% of full-time faculty are people of color and 53% are female
- 20%–27% of purchasing dollars to minority businesses (primarily Hispanic)
- Minority and small business coordinator enhancing policies and procedures for economic inclusion
- Reverse trade shows (procurement officers set up displays and targeted vendors are invited to attend)

Local Capacity Building
- Cultural and arts programming for broader community (e.g., Miami Book Fair International)
- Meek Center provides entrepreneurial and educational support to micro-enterprises, nonprofits, and individuals

- In-kind resources, including housing of K-12 education and adult workforce programs

Public Education and Health Partnerships
- Open-door policy and student support services help provide 7,800 associate's degrees and 200 bachelor's degrees each year to 61% low-income and 87% minority students
- School of Community Education provides adult education, leading to 600 GEDs earned each year
- Creation and leader of the South Florida America Reads Coalition
- Strong tutoring partnerships with Community in Schools of Miami
- Medical Center Campus outreach and collaboration with Miami Rescue Mission Health Clinic

Academic Engagement
- 5,900 students in service-learning courses taught by 285 professors; spread across 220 community partner sites
- Civic engagement part of core learning theme for all students

Multi-Anchor, City, and Regional Partnerships
- Partner in Miami Children's Initiative for educational pipeline in Liberty City

---

businesses in the black business corridor of Miami. The Center now provides credit and noncredit courses as well as dual enrollment options for high school students, with a particular focus on entrepreneurship. For example, the Center's FastTrac New Venture and FastTrac Planning Programs, initially offered through the Kauffman Foundation, provide educational support to emerging micro-entrepreneurs. For nearly five years, through a partnership between the Meek Center and Neighbors and Neighbors Association (NANA), the City of Miami has provided micro-enterprise grants of $10,000 to $20,000 to fifty small businesses. Utilizing grant proceeds, the business owners enroll in the Center's FastTrac program to obtain up-to-date skills and information on operating their businesses more effectively and efficiently. "This program focuses on increasing the business owners' capacity in order to make them more competitive in the marketplace," says Meek Center executive director H. Leigh Toney. "Therefore, in our entrepreneurship courses, the emphasis is always on application and real-time strategies and tools for entrepreneurs to apply in their businesses right away. We also seek to gauge and address any fundamental educational needs that may arise by making basic literacy and remediation courses available to the students when needed." Nonprofit organizations have also sought support in strengthening their services to the community, and the College's credit or noncredit programs (some grant-supported) aim to help meet those needs as well.[25]

Community engagement also plays out in Miami Dade College's curriculum, with more than 5,900 service-learning students working with 220 community partners in 2008–2009. "The community has become their learning environment in a real way. Entire departments have also begun to work together to develop cohesive departmental approaches to community engagement," says Padrón. All nursing and dental students, for example, are required to participate in service-learning. Service-learning courses, America Reads, and other community-campus partnerships are coordinated through the Center for Community Involvement, which has offices at all eight of the college's campuses. As director Josh Young puts it, the Center "is the highly visible point of entry for community groups that wish to partner with the college in civic activities."[26]

Miami Dade College's School of Community Education also aims to meet the educational needs of the community not served by traditional college programs. The program is self-supported through revenue from its 2,000 courses. However, the School receives college and federal funds to provide adult education and GED courses for free at six of the college's campuses; these efforts reach 10,000–30,000 students a year. The School strives to provide relevant and comprehensive programs that are linked to growing industries; for example, director Geoffrey Gathercole is looking to establish a Green Technology Training Institute for entry-level "green collar" jobs.[27]

Overtown, a community marred by high-profile riots that occurred in response to police brutality in the early 1980s, has been the site of several programs, and the college's downtown campus president hosts monthly meetings for Overtown stakeholders.[28] In 2009, the School of Business launched the Hospitality Institute in Overtown (funded through South Florida Workforce) to provide customer service and job-readiness training to longtime unemployed and homeless individuals who are committed to reentering the workforce. The program connects residents to job opportunities in the local hospitality industry. In its first year, 350 individuals went through the Institute. The School of Community Education has also worked with the Collins Center for Public Policy to conduct community health worker trainings on campus for residents from Overtown. The Collins Center is working with other agencies to improve the civic infrastructure and help revitalize the Overtown neighborhood. "There are great opportunities for Miami Dade College to be an even stronger partner in the new and emerging Overtown," says Phil Bacon, vice president for Neighborhood and Regional Initiatives at the Collins Center.[29]

The College's Medical Center Campus has a strong partnership with the Miami Rescue Mission in Overtown. For several years, volunteer nursing students and faculty have run health and screening centers for the Mission's homeless clients, many of whom have enrolled and earned degrees from the college. The Miami Rescue Mission Health Clinic opened in May 2009 as part of a long-term collaborative effort with the college's School of Nursing.[30] The Medical Center Campus is providing a medical director for the Clinic, and all thirteen disciplines on campus are involved. Much of this work started through the dedication of nursing professor Annette Gibson, who coordinates education and outreach service-learning programs involving nursing and health sciences students and faculty.

"Professor Gibson's vision is to see this done by community colleges across the country by having them partner with nonprofits and community-based organizations already working with community residents," says Marilyn Brumitt, director of community development for Miami Rescue Mission.[31]

The Human Services Coalition of Dade County is another strong partner of the college, which has been addressing critical issues surrounding poverty and social capital in the area for over fifteen years. Service-learning and volunteer partnerships deepened this relationship over time. Challenges in funding and power structures (experienced citywide), however, have inhibited some of the partnership potential. "In 2006, there was a critical moment to establish clear, mutual expectations, but the money from outside investors wasn't there, and that put undue pressure on the college for support. We needed a broader communication strategy to engage more partners," says Daniella Levine.[32] Indeed, Miami's city and county governments have not sufficiently invested in community-based organizations, which has weakened their ability to affect community economic development, attract private investment, and partner with large anchors, like Miami Dade College.

Another key element of the college's engagement efforts is providing cultural opportunities. Vivian Rodriguez reflects the common thread of success stories at Miami Dade College: the daughter of Cuban exiles and a college alumna, she now serves as vice provost for cultural affairs and resource development. Rodriguez's office oversees the college's arts and cultural partnerships, including the Miami Book Fair and the Miami International Film Festival, which have contributed to what the college's administration calls a "downtown renaissance." The film festival, for example, brings filmmakers from around the world to Miami, which has a positive impact on local artists, the local art scene, and the local economy. The college's Cultural Affairs Department also operates a residency program through its citywide performance series, which works to develop future local artists and audiences through educational outreach and professional development opportunities. "We have two distinct constituencies in everything that we do," says Rodriguez. "First are our 170,000 students. Second is the community. We want to make a difference in every household. As Dr. Padrón says, 'We're Democracy's College,' and we have a commitment to making a difference."[33]

Although it has had a diversity policy designed to support equitable opportunities for minority- and women-owned businesses since 1994, the college appointed its first full-time coordinator in 2008 to enhance policies and procedures for economic inclusion of small and local businesses. At this time, the Minority and Small Business Enterprise (MSBE) Office relocated from the Purchasing Department and incorporated with the Human Resources Department under the direction of the Office of Equal Opportunity Programs, which has given the MSBE Office more autonomy. "We're taking a proactive approach to be visible to the community and show them that we want to use small, local, and minority businesses and vendors, but they have to come being ready, willing, and able," says coordinator Sheldon Edwards. "It's a priority for the college—this comes from the top. They brought me in because I have over eighteen years in the field." Among other things, Edwards is enhancing the college's current database to track and verify certification and expenditures to minority, local, and small vendors.[34]

As a community college, Miami Dade College provides significant in-kind resources to community organizations, including the housing of several programs. For example, Take Stock in Children, which works with first-generation students from low-income families, has had an ongoing relationship with the college and has enjoyed fiscal management by the college since 1997. The program provides a unique set of resources for at-risk middle school students, including mentors, advocacy, and guaranteed scholarships. "The college provides us not only with our office space and general office services (utilities, telephone, Internet) but also classrooms, college facilities, and the use of college professional staff for our program delivery," says former director Alex Alvarez. "It is a win-win for our organizations and the community." Of the program's graduates, 70 percent attend Miami Dade College and then transfer to another four-year college. The Miami Dade College Foundation enjoys two matching donor programs, most of which the college has allowed to be directed to Take Stock's scholarship funds.[35]

Finally, Miami Dade College also houses a local branch of Working Solutions, a state-funded workforce program for displaced homemakers. The program provides free, specialized training (in financial management, computer skills, and so forth) to roughly 300 new clients each year and refers them to social services. Over one-third of their clients have found full- or part-time work. Program manager Dr. Linda Scharf also hopes to help clients matriculate into degree programs. "We're an institution of true believers," sums up Levitt. "Our mission is to turn lives around—to shift the tenor of the community by giving chances to get a degree and a job in a competitive workforce."[36]

Looking across the Cases

Creating an Engaged Community

Although commitment of in-kind resources is significant, institutional investment in community development remains scarce for higher education institutions, such as those described in this chapter, that lack major endowments. Instead, available resources tend to be dispersed throughout an extensive geographical area.

IUPUI demonstrates one of the more neighborhood-focused efforts among this set of schools. More than 1,000 homes and hundreds of families were displaced from the historically black neighborhood that now houses IUPUI. Nearly three decades later, the Office of Neighborhood Partnerships was founded to build relationships with the university's displaced neighbors now living in the Near Westside. Efforts have continued through the university's involvement in the GINI plan. "We've had limited resources lately, so the focus [remains] on the Near Westside, even though I've been asked to work in other neighborhoods," says ONP coordinator Starla Officer. "We have thought about providing technical assistance to other local colleges who could partner with these neighborhoods."[37]

Several mixed-income neighborhoods and the downtown business district surround Portland State's campus. These areas are vibrant today, in part because of the university's development.[38] In the 1990s, Portland State worked with city and business officials to revitalize the area around the university (known as the University District). The university is now entering into a second phase of redevelopment in this area, which is to be named an Urban Renewal Area by the city. Academic partnerships, however, have remained "grassroots" and dispersed throughout the metro region. "We debated last year whether we should focus on one neighborhood," says President Wiewel of his first year on campus. "We deliberately and consciously decided no. It would be too arbitrary."[39]

Similar to Portland State, Miami Dade College's decision to develop a new campus downtown in 1970 helped revitalize the downtown area. Some level of resources and focus has been given to the Overtown community, which neighbors the college's downtown campus, as well as to Liberty City, the black business corridor of Miami. However, the majority of engagement initiatives are scattered throughout the larger community. Having enrolled more than 1.7 million students in a community that now registers a population of 2.4 million, and hosting events such as the Miami Book Fair International that draws more than 300,000 visitors annually, there is the sense—across campus and community—that Miami Dade College has touched nearly every household in the county.

Establishing Partnership Programs and Goals

These three universities are largely nonresidential; for many of their students, the courses in which they enroll—and the scholarly experiences they have—often take on an even deeper significance. Addressing this need and their civic missions, IUPUI, Portland State, and Miami Dade College have all institutionalized service-learning in their curriculum. IUPUI's Center for Service and Learning strives to provide a continuum of engagement opportunities for its students and faculty that crosses the university's core mission of teaching, learning, and research. Many of these research and curricular activities have been focused toward the Near Westside. The curricular activities of Portland State and Miami Dade College, on the other hand, have not focused deliberately on neighborhood-level impacts. "It's not really about changing the community or a neighborhood overall," says Miami Dade College's Young. "It's more about what individual partners' needs are and putting that out to students and faculty and making those matches."[40]

These three institutions are also focused on K-12 educational partnerships, in part because they enroll a large number of local students. In Indiana, IUPUI is not only leading the regional community school effort, but is also a key player in the Central Indiana Talent Alliance, which aims to build an educational pipeline from cradle to career. Miami Dade College is also strengthening the educational pipeline for local students. The Miami Children's Initiative (formerly the Magic City Children's Zone)—modeled after the renowned Harlem Children's Zone program in New York City—was conceived at the college's Meek Center, and director Toney formerly served as the chairman of the initiative's board of directors. The goal of the initiative is to create an integrated system of services to support positive youth development and increase high school graduation and college-going rates by strengthening the capacity of youth-serving organizations and expanding the quality and availability of out-of-school time programs for the black and Hispanic community of Liberty City in Miami. The state of Florida has allocated $3.6 million to the ten-year pilot project.

The college also has a strong partnership with Miami-Dade County public schools, providing professional development, student teachers, tutoring and mentoring, and scholarships to many low-income children and classrooms in the county.[41] The college created and leads the South Florida America Reads Coalition, which provides tutoring to more than 1,000 of Miami's most at-risk children annually. Similarly, Portland State's Graduate School of Education has a formalized tutoring partnership with Portland Public Schools that has benefited over 18,000 migrant and high poverty K-12 students across sixty schools.[42]

Community health partnerships also play a key role in these institutions' engagement agendas. Medical, nursing, and dental students at IUPUI all engage in outreach activities, such as screenings, physical exams, and health education. At Portland State, the School of Community Health leads community outreach and community-based research, in which faculty, staff, and students all participate. Miami Dade College's Medical Center Campus provides health services to impoverished communities across south Florida; most notable is the campus's collaboration with the Miami Rescue Mission to open and staff a community health clinic.

All three of these universities provide direct assistance to local nonprofits and entrepreneurs, through programs and centers such as the Meek Center at Miami Dade College, the Solution Center at IUPUI, and the Business Outreach Program at Portland State. Portland State also hosts the Institute for Non-Profit Management, housed in the College of Urban and Public Affairs. In addition to its teaching mission to produce well-prepared leaders for the nonprofit community, the programmatic and research functions of the Institute for Non-Profit Management are focused on building capacity in community-based organizations, locally and statewide. However, at both IUPUI and Portland State, the administration tends to focus more on technology transfer and incubation of spin-off businesses, rather than small and emerging business owners.

Institutionalizing an Anchor Vision

These three institutions have strong civic engagement missions as well as the commitment of their top administration, both in rhetoric and through selective resources. Chancellor Bantz of IUPUI and President Wiewel of Portland State both serve on the board of directors for the Coalition of Urban Serving Universities, which advocates for public urban research universities to fuel the development of the nation's cities and metropolitan regions. President Padrón currently serves as the chair of the American Council on Education and is the immediate past chair of the Association of American Colleges and Universities. He also sits on the board of Florida Campus Compact and was a long-serving member of Campus Compact's national board. All three of these presidents are also members of the Anchor Institutions Task Force.

IUPUI's Center for Service and Learning receives $1.5 million in core funding annually from the university. Unlike many partnership centers at American universities, external grants have become a smaller percentage of their pie, and the Center's twelve full-time employees are all supported through core funds. As mentioned previously, the Office of Neighborhood Partnerships began as a special project directly under the Chancellor, who was deeply interested in mending relationships with displaced neighbors. The scholarly work and leadership of William Plater, executive vice chancellor and dean of the faculties at IUPUI from 1987 to 2006, also significantly deepened the institutional support for service-learning and civic engagement on campus.[43] Indeed, Dean Plater personally attended many of the community meetings throughout the 1990s. Today there is some disconnect between IUPUI's corporate goals and those of its partnership center. "For the past ten years, Westside neighbors have wanted to see the university grow west. That's evidence of the positive relations we've built," says Bringle. Nickolson has worked with developers on potential plans for new student housing and mixed-use buildings in the Near Westside; however, the university is currently planning to expand north of campus instead of west. Indeed, the university has yet to invest capital, real estate, or commercial assets in the Near Westside, which could help stimulate development in the area.[44]

In a similar manner, the Collins Center, which is leading much of the revitalization efforts in Overtown, would like to see Miami Dade College work with a development company to build affordable student housing in this neighborhood. "Simply having a physical presence could bring a big boon to the area," says Bacon.[45] Classroom facilities have necessarily been the college's priority given its enrollment growth, but President Padrón is undoubtedly committed to a major community presence: "Engagement with the community [is] in Miami Dade College's strategic plan, and that plan is systematically addressed at all levels of the institution. We do try to make it a genuine tool in our prioritizing and decision-making. Truth be told, community engagement existed long before we had a coherent strategic plan. It's in the DNA of the institution, deeper than culture." Gathercole comments, "The best support you can have is from the top administration, and we have that. Dr. Padrón takes a leadership role in this area and is a big proponent of [the School of] Community Education. We receive $1.5 million dollars annually in College money [to support free adult education programs], even though we're self-supporting [through tuition programs]."[46]

At Portland State, President Wiewel has created a new position of vice president for research and strategic partnerships (with the first appointment made in July 2010). "This will be a senior-level person who will be focused on both research development and serve as the highest person of coordination of all [partnership] efforts, which includes a lot of grassroots, dispersed projects. Having this as one position makes it very clear that we see our engagement activities as contributing to our research mission: we will build our research university status on our engagement strategy," says Wiewel.[47] However, faculty members have expressed some tension between the institution's commitment to community engagement, including access to education, and its desire to be a leading research university. This new structure of leadership may provide the opportunity to reconcile these ideas and create a more unified vision.

Securing Funding and Leveraging Resources

Decreases in state funding in both Oregon and Florida have hindered some of the engagement activities of Portland State and Miami Dade College, respectively. With a commitment to educational access, institutional funds are being reserved for financial aid and remedial education. "As President Padrón would say, 'We're beyond the point of our elasticity at this point,'" says Levitt. "Every penny has to go to the classroom. We provide a door into the economic mainstream through education. Money must be spent on student support services first." Still, the college dedicates more than $1.6 million internal dollars annually to support institutional engagement, such as the Center for Community Involvement's service-learning activities and the Miami Book Fair International. In 2007–2008, these dollars leveraged nearly ten times their value in external funding for engagement activities at the college. The Florida Department of Children and Families, for example, provides $8.6 million for the college to deliver a refugee vocational education program. In just three years, approximately $3.7 million in scholarship funds were raised through the annual Alumni Hall of Fame event.[48]

Portland State's development efforts are largely focused on land use, real estate, and transit. For such projects, the university receives significant funding from its city partners, including the Portland Development Commission and the Bureau of Planning. The university has also put millions of its own dollars toward transportation projects, including participating in a local improvement district that contributed $9.5 million toward the construction of the Portland Streetcar. Community Outreach Partnership Centers (COPC) funds from the U.S. Department of Housing and Urban Development (HUD) helped launch the small business incubator at Portland State in 1994, now known as the Business Outreach Program. The program has subsisted through funding from service contracts, grants, and in-kind donations; the university covers another 20–25 percent of the program's budget. Since 1996, this program has received funding through the HUD-sponsored Economic Opportunity Initiative.[49]

COPC funds in 1997 and 2003 also helped to expand IUPUI's Office of Neighborhood Partnerships, particularly its work with the Near Westside. More recently, the Center for Service and Learning has directed some of its institutional dollars to this community: Faculty Community Fellowships were specifically designed to reallocate funding for faculty engagement to the Near Westside. The Solution Center also receives university funding as well as significant grants from the Lilly Endowment and several other foundations. Through its Community Venture Fund, the Solution Center provides matching grants to community partners that may not be able to fully support a project or internship on their own. From 2004 to 2006, $1.4 million in Venture Fund grants leveraged $1.2 million in match funding from local organizations, which helped the Center secure additional grants. In the end, the majority of IUPUI's engagement dollars remain dispersed throughout the campus and its many schools and programs. "I haven't seen that big of an institutional commitment yet. There is 'no big check campaign' here," says Bray.[50]

Most of the funding for Near Westside revitalization goes straight to community partners, although IUPUI's partnership has certainly helped leverage grants. The GINI grants provided $2 million over three years for their demonstration projects ($1 million from the Lilly Endowment, and $1 from LISC and other small funders). Near Westside partners also secured a $1 million Neighborhood Stabilization Program grant to return blighted property to productive use. Going forward, LISC will continue to concentrate resources within many of the GINI neighborhoods. "A lot of funders are beginning to recognize the significance of the Quality of Life plans [for the GINI neighborhoods] and place-based funding," comments Anne-Marie Predovich Taylor, executive director of the Indianapolis Neighborhood Resource Center. "Together, we're trying to work for systems change, so that institutions are working *with* neighborhoods, instead of neighborhoods reacting to the institutions' plans."[51]

Building a Culture of Economic Inclusion

When speaking of economic inclusion, all three of these universities give particular focus to educational access for underserved populations. As Ethan Seltzer, professor and former director of Portland State's School of Urban Studies and Planning, puts it, "When you're talking about long-term prospects for wealth building, it's about access to education, access to opportunity! It's far more important for Portland State to have a seamless pathway with community colleges and reduce barriers to higher education, rather than community development strategies, which are somewhat marginal projects here." To this end, the university has a formal, articulated agreement with all the community colleges within a sixty-mile radius to have students' credits transfer over to a four-year program at Portland State. Seltzer goes on, "We're also discussing ways to have community development folks, from partner organizations, finish their education here."[52]

In Padrón's view, "Community colleges are often the only option for the great majority of young students and non-traditional students seeking a fresh beginning in the workforce. Eighty percent of new jobs require some form of post-secondary education. Miami Dade College enrolls 61 percent of graduates of the local public school system (the fourth largest in the United States) who attend college in Florida. Seventy-five percent of these students are under-prepared for college. Miami Dade College is their only option." College access and success for low-income populations remains the core element of the college's community development agenda, notes Levitt: "Our primary focus is on the educational development of each individual, and in turn the social and economic well-being of the community. And we believe that engagement with the challenges faced by the community is critical to student learning."[53]

The Meek Center's Institute for Youth Entrepreneurship builds on this philosophy by not only introducing local high school students to the basics of a business plan but also giving them exposure to the college environment. "It increases their self-confidence that they are college material, thereby making the transition from high school to Miami Dade College fairly seamless," says Toney. Regarding many of the adult programs the Meek Center offers, Toney adds, "Once they are enrolled, they get to take advantage of all of our free resources and programs available to Miami Dade College students, from the library and computer courtyard to free lectures and seminars, designed to support the college's learning outcomes and prepare our students for the workforce." The college also offers a special program for Cuban refugees. "We have a lot of immigrants with medical degrees who can't practice here. REVEST (a refugee vocational training program) helps them gain employment in an allied health field and work on English language skills," says Dr. Norma Goonen, former provost for academic and student affairs and current president of the College's Hialeah Campus. Overall, says Toney, "It's about meeting people where they are and giving them an opportunity to pursue higher education. The goal is for a more educated community."[54]

At IUPUI, a new Office of Multicultural Outreach reaches out to Latino and African American students, and their families, from local neighborhoods to let them know that IUPUI is an option for them. This office also works with the local community college in order to send students, who are not academically prepared for IUPUI, there first. "As long as the university maintains and increases its commitment, we'll see more local students coming to this institution," says Richard Bray, assistant director of IUPUI's Office of Multicultural Outreach.[55]

Sheldon Edwards, minority and small enterprise coordinator at Miami Dade College, seems to speak for all three of these institutions when he says, "As far as economic inclusion, we do a great job of educating the students in our local community; on the business side, we're getting there."

Miami Dade College's charter sets clear targets for contracting with minority- and women-owned businesses, and executive leadership has committed resources toward enhancing its Minority and Small Business Enterprise program. Of the college's annual dollars spent in purchasing, says Edwards, over 20 percent goes to minority, predominantly Hispanic, businesses throughout Miami-Dade County. Miami Dade College also provides "reverse trade shows"—where suppliers and contractors have the opportunity to be attendees, networking with procurement officers and other university officials—and Edwards is looking to specifically invite minority vendors to these events. He is also developing a workshop that will provide guidance to minority firms on how to better compete in bidding opportunities. "We're trying to change business practices and create awareness of what we're trying to get done," says Edwards. "For example, if we're bundling contracts, I'm now looking at whether we should break them out so minority [firms] can handle it, such as lawn cutting—each campus should have their own contracts, so we can work with multiple, smaller contractors."[56]

IUPUI has been a member of Indiana's Regional Minority Supplier Development Council since 1977, providing broad-based exposure both for the suppliers and university staff. Efforts have been in place since this time to increase the participation of minority-, women-, and disabled-person-owned businesses in IUPUI's vast and diverse procurement activities. IUPUI's purchasing director, Rob Halter, provides an analogy of getting up to bat: the more opportunities they can give to disadvantaged business owners, the more chances they have of success. For example, Halter established a relationship with a local, minority, family-owned moving company in the early 1990s, and helped "develop them into the company our department needed them to be." Known as Stewarts' Movers, this company now has a $250,000 annual contract to handle all internal moves on campus, as well as contracts with many other big institutions in the city. The Purchasing Department also partnered with the university's School of Business to bring a local chapter of Main Street USA to campus, which provides training to small businesses and entrepreneurs; by working with Indiana Workforce Development, Purchasing arranged to have 90 percent of course costs covered for individuals in the program. "These small business owners may not ever be able to do business with us, but we helped them start to sell to someone," says Halter. Despite these efforts, IUPUI's annual spending on women and minority business owners remains modest: 2 percent goes to minority-owned and roughly 4 percent goes to women-owned businesses.[57]

Portland State's contracting and purchasing offices have established programs to reach out to minority contractors, although there is no preference as to a specific neighborhood, and annual spending has also remained limited. "[Legally] we can't identify by race or gender, but most minority vendors are small businesses, so we can target that way," says Karen Preston, manager of purchasing and contract services. If a company provides an emerging small business certification from the state of Oregon, the purchasing department will give them ten extra points on their evaluation. However, this does not include any self-reported small business owners or local small businesses across the Washington state line. The focus again turns to sustainability: "We're really looking at supply chain and working on incorporating conditions in our contracts that address sustainability," says Preston. For example, all new buildings have to achieve, at a minimum, LEED Silver certification, a policy that will be mandated throughout the Oregon University System.[58]

Sustaining Participatory Planning and Robust Community Relationships

These three young, public institutions have not faced the traditional town-gown relationships seen at the other universities in this study and many campuses nationwide. Portland State and Miami Dade College, in particular, have made their borders very permeable to the community. "We were never going to be an enclosed campus. We'll always have other commercial business and private citizens in the area. We want that—it adds vim and vigor to our community," says Lindsay Desrochers of Portland State.[59]

Community colleges have always been adept at rethinking the campus/noncampus divide. "We're a community college in the essence of the word," says Levitt of Miami Dade. "We extend beyond the four walls of the classroom—invite people in through our Community Education program and serve as a center where people can find things to improve their quality of life."[60]

When IUPUI's Office of Neighborhood Partnerships was formed, "The agenda was forged very much with the community. Education, economic development, and neighborhood capacity were clearly identified as priority areas," says Bringle. The office received a grant from Campus Compact to host two community dialogues, an opportunity for university staff to genuinely listen to issues concerning the university's role and involvement in the Near Westside. Today's agenda for the Near Westside is shaped by the GINI Quality of Life Plan. The office already had strong relationships with community leaders, which facilitated their role in the plan. Further, office coordinator Starla Officer has a long history with nonprofits in the area. "IUPUI was at the table the whole time," says Diane Arnold, speaking of the GINI process. "Basically, we have these ideas we want to work on, and then IUPUI helps us develop them and go even deeper," comments GINI coordinator Patrice Duckett. The Center for Service and Learning also recently formed an advisory board with representatives from each of its main constituencies (students, faculty, alumni, and community).[61]

Kevin Kecskes views community partnerships analytically in terms of three competing frames—egalitarian, hierarchical, and individualist. "It's pretty clear that, as university leaders, we use egalitarian language. The practice is mixed, but there's much more hierarchical ('we can fix you') and individualist ('we're buying up and taking over because we can') tendencies. We need to better align rhetoric with practice," says Kecskes.[62] Portland State learned some lessons, too, when the university looked at possible expansion along the waterfront in 2004. Despite pulling together a coalition of local stakeholders, communication was not filtering down to residents. The neighborhood organized against the development, and the university decided to back off from its plans. One way that Portland State is resolving such issues today is by aligning its economic development and master campus plans with the citywide economic development plan. "The City gets to broker those deals with the neighborhoods [for the University]. It's part of a bigger conversation—we're taking a 20-year look at development," says Lisa Abuaf, senior project coordinator for the Portland Development Commission.[63] Portland State is viewed positively compared to other institutions in the area, such as the University of Oregon's extension campus in Portland, which has encroached on neighborhoods and even displaced feeding areas for the city's homeless.[64] Many Portland State professors, as well as their partners, argue that their strongest relationships are built on an individual, informal basis. Although these relationships often foster reciprocal collaboration, they have also meant that some engagement initiatives have ebbed and flowed under different leadership.[65]

At Miami Dade College, community stakeholders were deeply involved in the college's overall strategic plan. Each of the college's twelve professional schools also has a community advisory board. Elizabeth Mejia, executive director of Communities in Schools (CIS) of Miami, says of her partnership with the college: "When they say they want to work with the community, they really mean it. They never asked us for money and never said, 'What are *we* going to get out of this?' which is the second question out of many other universities' mouths." Miami Dade College has been heavily involved in CIS's tutoring and mentoring program for low-income, at-risk students. "Miami Dade College is the place to go for our students; most go on to higher ed here. It is their beacon of hope," says Mejia.[66]

While many community partners enjoy the participation of service-learning students coordinated through Miami Dade College's Center for Community Involvement, some mention that they have lacked institutional bridges from the college to explore and develop longer-term collaborations.[67] Likewise, the Center for Service and Learning at IUPUI and the Center for Academic Excellence at Portland State are focused most intently on academic engagement. This method results in many valuable projects, but as Paul Leistner of the City of Portland's Office of Neighborhood Involvement observes, it also often means that there is "not really a coordinated strategy from the university; they don't all talk to each other."[68] A university-wide partnership center that extends beyond service-learning and academic engagement to strategically engage and make accessible the institution's economic and other non-academic resources might help boost these efforts.

Meeting the Needs of Low-Income Residents and Neighborhoods

Impacts can be difficult to measure when programs and resources are dispersed across the campus and community. Still, IUPUI has taken several steps to foster community wealth building in the Near Westside: the Financial Literacy Workshop Series led by economics faculty has engaged more than 200 residents; faculty community fellows helped form a new business association, created youth entrepreneurship programs, and are planning for redevelopment in vacant areas; and the university's partnership with George Washington Community High School has placed hundreds of students on pathways to postsecondary success. Still, the university could make deeper impacts on the Near Westside if it chose to strategically invest institution-wide resources (i.e., academic *and* non-academic) in this area. "We have a community that's articulated its Quality of Life Plan. This is an opportunity for the [whole] university to look at it and see how they could apply problem-solving and resources to what

the neighborhood is trying to do," says Aaron Laramore, program officer for LISC Indianapolis.[69]

Miami Dade College, on the other hand, supports several community development
objectives but continues to focus primary resources on its student population. Levitt comments, "I don't know how much we can/will grow in the next few years. We want to keep
our doors open, and we need enough remedial support for our students, which is expensive.
We have to surround them with support. If President Obama's goal of doubling bachelor's
degrees is to be achieved, community colleges will play a huge role." Indeed, with 61 percent
low-income and 87 percent minority students, Miami Dade College provides a door into the
economic mainstream through education for thousands of young people. Besides the 7,800
associate degrees and 200 bachelor's degrees awarded in 2009, 600 local residents earned
their GED through Miami Dade College's School of Community Education. In Overtown, the
college has also trained two cohorts of forty people each as community health workers, and
more than 600 residents have received certification from the Hospitality Institute, with a 35
percent job placement rate. The College's K-12 partnership programs are also showing
promising results, such as I Have a Dream Overtown, which guarantees college scholarships
for participants who stay in school, remain drug-free, and complete the program. This is a
mutually beneficial outcome, since 61 percent of graduates from the local public school
system who attend college in Florida choose Miami Dade. With even more concentration
on impoverished communities like Overtown, the college may begin to see greater neighborhood-level impacts.[70]

At Portland State, the Business Outreach Program has produced the most tangible
impacts for community development. As mentioned previously, the program has assisted
more than 400 small and emerging businesses and created more than 150 new jobs in North
and Northeast Portland. As at IUPUI and Miami Dade College, community engagement is
also driven into Portland State's curriculum. Most notably, the Senior Capstone Program
engages nearly 250 groups of students every year to work on problem solving with community organizations. Much of the engaged curricular and research projects across the campus,
however, remain dispersed throughout the greater community. Greater collaboration and
coordination, perhaps, could lead to a more sustained impact. According to President
Wiewel, the new vice president for research and strategic partnerships will be in a position
not only to demonstrate "that we see our engagement activities as contributing to our
research mission," but also "see *whether* we can achieve more by greater collaboration and
coordination. At times, this may include geographic concentration. But I think there are
strengths in addressing things in a more cross-cutting way."[71]

University as Leader: Penn, Cincinnati, and Yale

The community partnership efforts of the three universities reviewed in this chapter—the University of Pennsylvania (Penn), the University of Cincinnati, and Yale University—are marked by four key factors: (1) each has enjoyed strong institutional leadership that has made community engagement a continued top priority; (2) each of the campuses is adjacent to at least one low-income neighborhood with a high percentage of African American residents; (3) each of their efforts evolved in large measure in response to threatening conditions in the areas surrounding campus—in Cincinnati, general neighborhood deterioration and crime helped move the university toward greater engagement, while at both Penn and Yale the schools' administrative-led efforts were spurred by murders of community members (a faculty member at Penn and a student at Yale); and (4) in response, each of these universities made long-term investments totaling over $100 million.

Implicit in the four factors named above is a fifth—all three schools have the scale, endowments, and hence the *capacity* to finance their initiatives. The University of Cincinnati has the smallest endowment of the three, ranking seventy-third in the nation in June 2009, but with a still significant total, even after the 2008 financial crash, of nearly $833 million. (It should also be noted that Cincinnati's endowment ranks twenty-fourth for public institutions.) Yale and Penn, both Ivy League colleges, not surprisingly rate much higher nationally, with Yale ranking second and Penn tenth. Yale's endowment, before the recent economic crisis, topped $22.8 billion, while Penn's exceeded $6.2 billion. After the crash, as of June 2009, Yale's endowment had fallen to $16.33 billion, while Penn's endowment had fallen to $5.17 billion.[1] In terms of annual budget, Penn's annual turnover is $5.67 billion (although this figure falls to roughly $2.5 billion if Penn Health System is excluded), Yale's annual turnover is $2.31 billion, and the University of Cincinnati's is $1.02 billion.[2]

Given the role crime played in spurring community work, it should be no surprise that all three schools share a focus on improving conditions in adjacent neighborhoods.

They also share some other traits marked by this focus. Because at Penn and Yale, at least in the immediate crisis aftermath, community work was seen not as a "plus," but as an *imperative*, efforts have involved major resource commitments, not only in terms of budget, but also in leadership energy and administrative support. To be sure, it is not true that the *only* reason for these two schools' community partnership work is as a response to tragedy. Indeed, both schools had engaged in some partnerships beforehand. Nonetheless, tragedy has shaped both the size and direction of these universities' engagement efforts. In Cincinnati, deteriorating business districts and neighborhoods on the borders of campus led to similar commitments of resources and leadership. The power of these institutional initiatives should not be underestimated. At the same time, it poses a major challenge to "partnership" principles, for in these efforts, the university acts much less as a facilitator of community groups and much more in a direct leadership role. To be sure, consultation is important, and indeed obtaining community support is a necessary element of this approach, but there is no question of who is "first among equals." At the same time, as crisis has subsided and threatening conditions have gradually improved, more collaborative approaches are beginning to emerge at all three schools.

University of Pennsylvania

> The parents did not want to hear us talk about what we planned to do. They wanted to see immediate results, or else they would pull their children out of Penn. And to make sure we got the point they . . . booed us off the stage. The time for further study was over. Penn's future was at stake. We needed to act.
>
> —Judith Rodin, president, University of Pennsylvania (1994–2004), quoted in John Kromer and Lucy Kerman, *West Philadelphia Initiatives: A Case Study in Urban Revitalization*, Philadelphia: University of Pennsylvania, 2004, 8

Penn is often viewed as the national leader of community partnership work—and not without reason. The extent of Penn's effort is unusual in both its scope and its duration, spanning several university presidencies and more than two decades. In examining Penn, therefore, some historical context is helpful. Penn's partnership efforts began *before* the crisis brought about by the murder of a Penn faculty member in 1996, to which Rodin refers above, but pre-crisis support from the university trustees and administration was limited. As a result, the early years of Penn's partnership efforts, beginning in the mid-1980s under the leadership of President Sheldon Hackney and university professor Ira Harkavy, displayed a much more "grassroots" partnership feel.[3] According to Tom Burns, a Philadelphia community development consultant who taught for a number of years in the late 1980s and early 1990s at Penn's Wharton Business School, the period of Hackney leadership was a "great period of opening up doors and building relationships." Among other things, this period was when Penn began its efforts to improve local public schools in West Philadelphia. Initiated by Harkavy and a few other faculty members in 1985, by 1992 the effort had grown to sufficient scale that Penn established the Center for Community Partnerships (which would later be endowed by Barbara and Edward Netter) to

Figure 6. Penn Anchor Approach

Comprehensive Neighborhood Revitalization
- West Philadelphia Initiatives: public safety, housing, retail development, business development, and public school partnership efforts begun in 1990s
- Netter Center coordinates academic, institutional, public and private resources with a focus on public education, urban nutrition, and community development in West Philadelphia

Community Economic Development through Corporate Investment
- Local Purchasing Program spent $100.5 million locally and purchased $100.3 million from minority-owned suppliers in FY10; sourcing managers rewarded for economic inclusion
- 35% of all Penn construction jobs to minority and women workers, and 26% of all contracts to minority- and women-owned businesses
- Employer-assisted housing in West Philadelphia
- Health care career ladders and construction apprenticeship programs evolving

Local Capacity Building
- Nonprofit Institute trainings for members of local organizations
- Small Business Development Center at Wharton School of Business
- Strengthening CDC partnerships through LISC's Sustainable Communities Initiative–West Philadelphia

Public Education and Health Partnerships
- University-assisted community schools: local public schools serve as hubs for community transformation for more than 5,000 children and their families
- Created Penn Alexander K-8 School and provides $750,000 annual subsidy
- School of Education: district contracts to manage two public schools
- Public health focus with school partnerships and through Schools of Nursing and Medicine and Center for Public Health Initiatives

Academic Engagement
- Academically based community service courses engage more than 50 faculty and 1,500 undergraduate and graduate students each year to solve real-world problems in West Philadelphia

Multi-Anchor, City, and Regional Partnerships
- Lead funder of University City District, a multipurpose business improvement district, with other community institutions
- Hosts Philadelphia Higher Education Network for Neighborhood Development, a consortium of 36 colleges in greater Philadelphia area
- Local and national replication of university-assisted community school model

institutionalize community partnership work. Penn also began its initial efforts to promote local purchasing.[4]

Rodin brought a shift to the more comprehensive effort that Penn is known for today, with greater attention placed on the use of *institutional* resources. As Burns explains, "In the Rodin administration, it was a new model. She understood rightly that it was absolutely in the university's self-interest to reshape the quality of life in the community. From a management point of view, it was an effective style. [But it was a] style of initiating things in a somewhat unilateral way—an 'enlightened self-interest' frame, which was very different than the impulse that the Hackney administration followed." According to executive director of public affairs Tony Sorrentino, since the beginning of the Rodin effort, Penn has spent over $500 million on a combination of physical redevelopment expenditures (especially build-out costs for new retail and commercial facilities) and ongoing support to other programs, notably annual funding of the University City District business improvement district, the Penn Alexander K-8 School, and the Netter Center for Community Partnerships.[5]

Under Rodin, Penn's efforts were focused in five areas: public safety, housing, retail development, business development (through procurement from local businesses), and public school partnerships. The school partnership work built on existing Netter Center for Community Partnerships initiatives, while also expanding the effort in other ways, most notably by creating a brand new public K-8 neighborhood school (Penn Alexander) near campus. The other areas involved a broader effort to leverage institutional resources for community development. Between 1996 and 2003, Penn financed the acquisition and reha-bilitation of over 200 rental buildings (most of which are inhabited by community members not affiliated with Penn), developed 300,000 square feet of retail space, boosted its local purchasing (from $20.1 million in fiscal year 1996 to $61.6 million in fiscal year 2003), and employed local residents in construction projects, with over 22 percent of contracts let out to women- and minority-owned firms. The university was also successful in attracting out-side investment. Penn estimates that its $150 million in investments in retail development leveraged an additional $370 million in private investment. An evaluation of the first seven years of the stepped-up Rodin effort found considerable success. Among the key findings: housing values in the neighborhood had more than doubled, while reported crime fell 40 percent.[6]

Amy Gutmann, who became Penn's president in 2004, has taken what might best be described as a middle road between the Hackney and Rodin approaches; the institutional work has continued, but is less heavily emphasized as a neighborhood revitalization effort, while more energy has been focused on relationship-building, academic engagement work, and eastward expansion. Some outside observers believe this has resulted in reduced atten-tion to West Philadelphia. D. L. Wormley, formerly of the community group Neighborhood-sNow, puts the matter this way, "[With Penn expanding eastward toward Center City] will Amy [Gutmann] make sure that West Philadelphia gets its due in terms of retail, employees, and services? Maybe. With Judy [Rodin] there was no question. With Amy there is a question: 'What does she do, and does she know that we exist?'" Richard Redding, director of com-munity planning for the City of Philadelphia, concurs that direct institutional involvement in West Philadelphia real estate has declined under Gutmann. "Rodin was bigger on physi-cal development," Redding notes.[7]

By contrast, with public school partnerships and academic engagement, there is no question as to Gutmann's strong backing. Redding emphasizes that under Gutmann there has been "a lot of support" for academically based community service. Netter Center for Community Partnerships director Ira Harkavy agrees, pointing out that "Amy [Gutmann] got us an endowment. The [educational partnership] programs at local schools have grown. Our efforts, as a national model, have blossomed under this president." Budget numbers confirm Harkavy's assessment. Since Gutmann's presidency began, direct university sup-port to the Center has increased by more than 50 percent, from roughly $600,000 to over $1 million annually, while the Center's overall budget has more than doubled from $2.1 million in 2004–2005 to over $5.3 million in 2008–2009.[8]

One place where Penn's community development effort has been particularly strong is in its use of institutional purchasing. The numbers are impressive. Ralph Maier, former director of purchasing at Penn, noted, "When we launched 'Buy West Philadelphia' in the

1980s we were doing about $800,000. Today [2009], twenty-three years later, we are on pace to procure locally in West and Southwest Philadelphia [about] $95 million. This year, our total spend year-to-date is down 8 percent, but we've increased the percentage of purchasing from local businesses from 11 to 13 percent, and diversity spend [minority business purchasing] has gone from 9 to 11 percent of total spend."[9]

Penn has also extended its economic influence in many other ways, notes Sorrentino. This includes ensuring that at least 20 percent of the $200 million or so in "large" construction contracts (valued at $5 million or higher) are let out to minority- and women-owned firms. Glenn Bryan, assistant vice president in Penn's Office of Community Relations, concurs: "There is a lot of responsibility at Penn to train local residents to be in the trades. We do very well in construction—the numbers for minority, women, and local contracting are high." An estimated 35 percent of all Penn construction jobs have gone to minority and women workers. As well, Penn exercises considerable influence through the retail buildings it owns. Sorrentino estimates that Penn owns and operates 450,000 square feet of retail (roughly twice the square footage of a typical Walmart store), which houses 111 businesses that have combined annual sales of $200 million.[10]

Two other pieces of Penn's economic development efforts are its housing program and its sponsorship of the University City District (UCD). The housing program was a centerpiece of Rodin's efforts. During her tenure, 386 "Penn affiliates" purchased homes with Penn assistance, making effective use of a mortgage guarantee program that had long been available to assist Penn faculty and was expanded to include all university staff in the mid-1980s during the Sheldon Hackney administration. In the past few years, the program has continued with a somewhat slower pace; Sorrentino estimates that at least 200 more have used the program since 2004.[11] UCD is a multipurpose business improvement district organization. Initially Penn provided a dominant share of UCD funding. As recently as fiscal year 2003, UCD board members, led by Penn, provided 70 percent of its then-$5.2 million budget (or $3.6 million). By 2009, UCD's annual budget had grown to nearly $9.6 million, but board member contributions had fallen to 40.6 percent of total revenues. Penn remains UCD's largest funder, contributing well over $2 million, but as a whole Penn is now responsible for less than 30 percent of the organization's revenues. Known best for its "safety ambassador" program of quasi-police security guards, UCD has also through its Neighborhood Initiatives program developed streetscape improvements that have helped support local retail development. Since 2008, UCD has been an enthusiastic participant with other community-based organizations in developing a broad array of economic and workforce related programs, such as the LISC-supported Sustainable Communities Initiative–West Philadelphia (SCI-West). To date, the initiative has attracted millions of dollars of support from the William Penn Foundation, as well as other foundations outside the Philadelphia area.[12]

While less directly related to specific community development objectives, it bears mention that Penn has also put a lot of emphasis on building a culture of engagement on campus. Coordinated by Civic House, founded due to a student campaign in 1998, today more than 1,500 students engage in what Civic House director David Grossman categorizes as "active volunteering," while more than 4,000 students annually participate in at least one of Civic House's events. Penn is also a leading supporter of an independent consortium of thirty-six colleges and universities known as PHENND (Philadelphia Higher Education Network) that currently connects over 200 undergraduate students from eight area colleges with over 400 high school students. Academically, the Netter Center also works to engage the curricular end of the spectrum. When the Center began, there were only four academically based community service courses at Penn, which involved a total of three faculty and 100 students. In 2009–2010, there were more than sixty courses involving fifty faculty members and over 1,500 students in West Philadelphia.[13]

Partnerships with Philadelphia public schools are one last but central area of emphasis for Penn's community work. Penn runs programs in twenty-three schools and provides training for teachers at even more schools, but most activities are concentrated in nine schools in West Philadelphia. The best known of Penn's efforts is the Penn Alexander School, a K-8 school with an estimated enrollment of 531 students, which Penn helped create and continues to provide $750,000 a year on top of normal public school funding. As James Lytle, professor in Penn's Graduate School of Education, notes, that kind of money "allows you to do a lot. It's a really nice public school. You could walk in there and you would think you were in the suburbs. . . . It still has a group of African American families, although that group has diminished. Penn Alexander gets regular visitors from across the country. It also gets high involvement from parents—it is the equivalent of a private school education." Demographic data largely confirm Lytle's assessment. In 2004–2005, the first year of full enrollment at Penn Alexander, the student body was 58.4 percent African American, 22.5 percent white, 13.2 percent Asian, and 5.8 percent Latino; by contrast, five years later, in 2009–2010, the student body was 39 percent African American, 32 percent white, 14 percent Asian, 6 percent Latino, and 10 percent "other" (or declined to state).[14]

At several other public schools, Penn, through the Netter Center for Community Partnerships, operates in a community school framework. This approach focuses on utilizing the school as a community center that can provide a wide range of support services, such as classroom assistance, after-school programming, tutoring, literacy training, and nutritional education. The Center's "university-assisted community school" approach is concentrated on a set of schools within three high school catchment areas in West Philadelphia. Sayre High School enjoys one of the most developed efforts. In part due to these supports, Sayre met all thirteen targets for "Adequate Yearly Progress" in 2006–2007, one of only five neighborhood high schools in the district (out of over thirty) to achieve this goal. The school-based Sayre Health Center (opened in 2007 and staffed by Penn doctors and third-year medical students) now serves over 300 patients per month. At two community schools (Henry C. Lea, a K-8 school, and Alexander Wilson, a K-6 school), Penn also operates as an EMO (educational management organization), which involves an explicit contract with the Philadelphia public school system to provide services that will assist in "turning around" the schools. At these two schools, Penn's Graduate School of Education receives a management fee from the public school district for its services, which works out to about $500 per student (or $350,000 a year) and pays for the schools' classroom and professional development support, focused on training teachers and principals. Penn's performance as an EMO has been lauded; of the six groups in Philadelphia with EMO contracts, Penn is the only organization to be rewarded by the school district with a multi-year contract.[15]

While Penn's achievements have been impressive, the Netter Center's staff is continually looking at ways to better link the various outreach efforts to achieve greater overall impact. Netter Center associate director Cory Bowman notes, "We get the evaluation numbers as required either at a site or thematic, but the most important change is to integrate our work . . . that is the least talked about form of evaluation, but also the most important one." Center director Harkavy makes a similar observation. "Penn has made tremendous progress. But fundamentally the problems of West Philadelphia have not been effectively solved. The potential," Harkavy adds, "for full throttle engagement is great. We need to have a more conscious conversation. The necessary steps haven't been taken. To be fair, it's very hard to do."[16]

University of Cincinnati

Universities, by design, are in it for the long haul, and they have to take a long-term view of all their investments. This is particularly true at an urban institution.

—Monica Rimai, former senior vice president for administration and finance and interim president, University of Cincinnati (2006–2009), telephone interview by Rita Axelroth Hodges, October 5, 2009

Figure 7. Cincinnati Anchor Approach

Comprehensive Neighborhood Revitalization
- Uptown Consortium led to investment of $400 million in community; broad socioeconomic goals set, but activity focused on real estate development to date

Community Economic Development through Corporate Investment
- Use of $150 million out of endowment as "patient capital"
- Participate in two small statewide programs that direct purchasing dollars to minority businesses (average 6%–8% annually) and goods and services from socially and economically disadvantaged businesses (average 4% annually)
- Open bidding process through Office of Contract Compliance

Local Capacity Building
- Formation of seven community urban redevelopment corporations in Uptown neighborhoods, each with majority community representation

Public Education and Health Partnerships
- Strive, a public-private partnership to support young people from cradle to career, with particular focus on college access

- Cincinnati Pride Grant, a "last dollar scholarship" for Pell-eligible students from the local school district
- $20 million to GEAR UP for services to over 4,700 public school students
- Development of STEM schools in community

Academic Engagement
- Service-learning part of general curriculum but unquantifiable to date

Multi-Anchor, City, and Regional Partnerships
- Uptown Consortium: shared resources and goals of major employers in the area
- Agenda 360: collaboration with regional partners to transform southwest Ohio's economy
- Center for the City: web portal to connect campus to the broader community
- Strong collaboration with multiple City of Cincinnati offices, including Community Development, Economic Development, and Transportation

On the hilltops above Cincinnati's Central Business District, in an area known as Uptown, crime and blight on campus edges created a sense of urgency for the University of Cincinnati and spurred their active involvement in creating a safe, clean, and vibrant community. "We were trying to deal with a situation that threatened our existence," comments Gerry Siegert, associate vice president for community development at the University of Cincinnati. These circumstances, combined with visionary leadership, took the university's service mission to a whole new level. Over the last decade, the University of Cincinnati has invested significant resources, mainly human and monetary, to develop its surrounding neighborhoods.[17]

Particularly notable about Cincinnati's effort is the decision to forgo the standard university practice of maximizing returns on its endowment and instead leverage that endowment to support the university's social and community goals. Mary Stagaman, former associate vice president for external relations and presidential deputy for community engagement, explains the university's view of its investment "as patient capital" that can be made available "very long term, at very low interest rates." This creative use of its endowment allows the university to make a unique investment in the community that it would otherwise be unable to finance. Specifically, over the last ten years, the university has dedicated nearly $150 million from its endowment pool—or approximately 13.6 percent of the school's entire endowment (before the financial crash)—to finance low-interest loans, as well as an additional $8 million dollars in operating grants for community redevelopment efforts. Siegert states that they have experienced a nearly three-to-one leveraging of their endowment money through tax-exempt debt, loans from banks, and other sources: "In total, our loans represent [an estimated] 20–40 percent of the entire redevelopment effort."[18]

Also notable about Cincinnati's effort is the strong level of collaboration with other area anchor institutions. In 2003, the University of Cincinnati, an urban public university, joined with four other large local nonprofit employers (three health care organizations and the local zoo) to form the Uptown Consortium. Holding several summits involving hundreds of community residents, the Consortium developed a plan to invest $500 million to improve the quality of life in Cincinnati's challenged Uptown neighborhoods. Most of the funding provided to date—totaling nearly $400 million, including outside investments—has been directed to real estate development.[19]

Not all community partnership efforts at the University of Cincinnati, of course, date from the creation of the Uptown Consortium. Starting in the late 1980s, under President Joseph Steger, the university undertook a new master plan to redevelop its campus from within. This physical transformation set the stage for change in many ways: new student housing transformed the student experience; campus borders became more permeable; and dialogue increased between those internal and external to the university. Faculty, staff, and students became increasingly involved in problem-solving curriculum and community partnership efforts; still, the university had yet to affirmatively claim its position as an urban institution and engage in university-wide partnerships.[20]

When Nancy Zimpher arrived as president in 2003, she led a strategic planning process—involving a wide range of university stakeholders—to draft the university's vision for its future. The plan, *UC|21: Defining the New Urban Research University,* helped to reposition Cincinnati as a leading research *and* a leading urban university. "This notion of bringing university resources to address great urban community challenges is in Nancy [Zimpher's] DNA. It has been part of her agenda for a long time," says Monica Rimai. Through Zimpher's leadership, the institution began to understand not only that leveraging resources to address urban community challenges was the right thing to do, but also that the university's core mission of research, teaching, and service could greatly benefit. This vision was not without some internal dissent, although the tides have been slowing turning. "The mission of UC|21 is great, but now we have to hold people accountable to it," comment Michael Sharp and Kathy Dick, who direct the university's service-learning and student volunteer offices.[21]

Zimpher continued the efforts of her predecessor, Steger, for physical redevelopment, and set out to transform the neighborhoods surrounding Cincinnati's campus through extensive community development. In many ways, the work off-campus became an extension of the transformation of the campus itself. The university's trustees were on board to make a significant financial investment to these efforts. Of course, it was the full backing of the most senior financial officers of the institution, including the senior vice president for administration and finance and the chief investment officer, that made it "more palatable for institutional budget managers to accept, and support, the initiative," notes Siegert. It was expected that the short-term return on investment would be safer and cleaner neighborhoods that would attract more students to the university and improve town-gown relationships, which would ultimately benefit the bottom line. Indeed, the university has begun to enjoy initial returns such as dramatically increased enrollment rates in the last handful of years.[22]

As noted above, Cincinnati encouraged a partnership among the area's largest institutions—the university, Children's Hospital Medical Center, TriHealth Inc., the Health Alliance (now known as UC Health), and the Cincinnati Zoo—to create the Uptown Consortium. Formally established in 2003, the Consortium marked a key milestone in Uptown to have five chief executives come together and share ideas and resources.[23] Additionally, the university established seven community urban redevelopment corporations (CURCs) in the neighborhoods of Uptown. Each has a five-member board consisting of four representatives from the local business and neighborhood associations and one university representative.[24]

The Uptown Consortium, in particular, began with a very broad mission to improve economic opportunity and quality of life in the area. According to Stagaman, this reflects the idealism and optimism of the executive leaders.[25] However, both the Consortium and the CURCs have remained largely focused on real estate development to date. Other neighborhood goals set out by the Consortium revolve around homeownership, business retention, employment, safety, and transportation. According to a market study, between 2004 and 2008, Uptown experienced an 8.2 percent decrease in the total number of Part 1 crimes (the City of Cincinnati overall saw a 10.3 percent decrease during the same period) and a 9.5 percent decrease in neighborhood crimes. A total of seventy-eight permits, representing 199 housing units, were issued in Uptown between 2002 and 2008, mostly dedicated to student housing.[26] The potential of several other programs has yet to be realized. For instance, the Uptown Mortgage Program, modeled after Cincinnati's Walk to Work program, aimed to attract employees to live in the area and, therefore, increase purchasing power; limited finances, however, have led to little traction with either housing program.[27]

The University of Cincinnati has also shown leadership through its educational partnerships, with particular focus on college access. Strive, a public-private partnership aimed to support young people from cradle to career, began when Zimpher convened university presidents in the area to discuss the challenges of college access. She then partnered with the KnowledgeWorks Foundation, which volunteered staff members to begin research on existing data and programs. When Strive was formally established in 2006, the model was based on a "Roadmap to Success," key transition points from pre-K through college, which were identified by university faculty and graduate students. Cincinnati's dean of the College of Education, Criminal Justice and Human Services, Larry Johnson, continues to be a major organizational leader for Strive, and the university's new president, Gregory Williams, now sits on the executive committee.[28]

The university also began the Cincinnati Pride Grant as a "last dollar scholarship" for Pell-eligible students who graduate from Cincinnati public schools to be able to attend the university free of charge. Students who receive this grant are required to participate in the Cincinnati Pride Program, through which they are encouraged to utilize various academic support services available, such as academic coaching, counseling centers, and foreign language labs. Strive partners are looking to the Kalamazoo Promise in Michigan as a model for possibly expanding Pride Grant eligibility to any graduate from the Cincinnati school district, as well as to other universities.[29] Though the current economy has curtailed fundraising, the university continues to make these scholarships part of its $1 billion capital campaign.[30]

The College of Education, Criminal Justice and Human Services has also directed $20 million to GEAR UP, a federal college awareness and readiness program for low-income youth. The college serves as the program's lead agency and provides administrative and fiscal leadership for the services delivered to over 4,700 public school students. "We hope to leverage our funds to help bring more resources [to disadvantaged students]," says Dean Johnson. "Helping kids graduate from high school is the biggest economic driver we can have."[31]

The University of Cincinnati's leadership, particularly in helping to form the Uptown Consortium, has established a strong foundation for anchor-based community development, as well as brought significant leveraging power. The Consortium now represents "a collective voice," says assistant city manager for the City of Cincinnati, Scott Stiles. The university's Community Development office—which oversees the community redevelopment corporations—has a very close working relationship with the city's Department of Community Development.[32] Additionally, the university is a partner in Agenda 360, a regional action plan for building talent, jobs, and economic opportunity. Agenda 360 has engaged leadership from many public and private partners all over the region, including several other anchor institutions, providing a variety of expertise and resources.[33]

Looking toward the future, the university's community development efforts are going through a period of transition. A new president, Gregory Williams, who had previously been president of City University of New York, was installed at the university in November 2009. In early 2010, there were other adjustments as well. The Uptown Consortium director left his position after five years, and the Health Alliance had been dissolved (replaced later in the year by a new nonprofit institution, UC Health). Moreover, the redevelopment efforts in Uptown have a long way to go to realize the broad community goals laid out more than five years ago. With all of these changes, many who remained were concerned about whether the work of the Consortium and the University of Cincinnati would be sustained. Fortunately, such fears appear to have been largely unfounded.[34] Indeed, with the addition in 2010 of community leaders on the Consortium's Management Operations Committee, and reaffirmation, by the board of directors, of its broader social mission, there lies great opportunity to *begin* to address these greater socioeconomic issues.

Yale University

> There were [thirty-four] homicides in New Haven in 1991. But the murder that captured Yale's attention—and sparked a fundamental change in the way the university thought about its hometown—was the February 17 killing of sophomore Christian Prince '93.
>
> —Mark Alden Branch '86, "Then . . . and Now: How a City Came Back from the Brink,"
> *Yale Alumni Magazine,* May–June 2009, 43.

As noted above, although antecedents of Yale working in New Haven can be identified going back to the 1950s, at Yale it was tragedy—specifically the murder on campus of Yale student Christian Prince in 1991—that mobilized the Yale community to greatly expand its

---

Figure 8. Yale Anchor Approach

Comprehensive Neighborhood Revitalization
- Support for housing, public schools, libraries, and youth programs in Dixwell, Dwight, and Hill neighborhoods

Community Economic Development through Corporate Investment
- Contract goals of 25% minority, 20% local, 6.9% women, and 14% first-year apprentice hires
- Real estate development: owns 350,000 square feet of retail that is leased to 100 stores
- Yale Homebuyer Program: $22.5 million in subsidy dollars facilitated over 925 home purchases

Local Capacity Building
- 550,000-square-foot incubator in downtown New Haven; helped start 40 companies, which have raised $450 million in venture capital
- $2 million grant to support community development financial institution, First Community Bank

- Helped secure initial funding for Greater Dwight Development Corporation

Public School and Health Partnerships
- Support to 20 public schools, and particularly strong relationships with two magnet schools
- Focus on literacy, arts, and science education with 10,000 public school children participating in university programs annually
- Public health outreach by professional schools

Academic Engagement
- Limited service-learning

Multi-Anchor, City, and Regional Partnerships
- Joint planning with the city
- Lead funder of Town Green business improvement district and Market New Haven
- Strong collaboration through long tenures of university president, city mayor, and school district superintendent

community partnership efforts.[35] Sheila Masterson, a cofounder of the Greater Dwight Development Corporation, a local community development corporation, explains, "True successes are not based on altruism; they are based on need. What happened here in New Haven was that a student was murdered. There were people at Yale who got up and said, 'Holy cow! Our pool of applicants has dropped 10 percent and we've got to do something.'" The Greater Dwight Development Corporation's other cofounder and executive director, Linda Townsend Maier, says an added factor was that the overall high level of crime created "pressure for the community and Yale to say, 'What you're experiencing we are experiencing, so we have to come together.'"[36]

In its work, Yale has made a number of important investments in community partnerships and related community economic development. In particular, Yale has been a national leader in leveraging real estate development for community benefit.

As noted above, the murder of a student on campus was a major factor in spurring Yale to increase its community partnership efforts. These efforts did not truly accelerate, however, until current president Richard Levin was inaugurated in 1993. In Levin's first two years, Yale successfully applied for a community outreach partnership center (COPC) grant in the Dwight neighborhood, established a director of university real estate to better manage nonacademic real estate property holdings, and began to invest in retail and streetscape revitalization. Additionally, Yale launched its housing program in 1994 (subsidizing New Haven home purchases for 200 affiliates in its first two years), created the Office of New Haven and State Affairs in 1995, and made the office director a vice president position in 1997.[37]

Nonetheless, even as Yale under Levin picked up the pace of its community partnership work, it still moved more deliberately to work with existing organizations, rather than create *de novo* organizations. Part of what allowed for this was scale. The entire population of the city of New Haven (125,000) is only three-fifths that of the West Philadelphia section of Philadelphia, for example. Sheila Shanklin, director of cooperative management at Housing Operations Management Enterprise (HOME), explained the "small town" nature of New Haven this way: "The language of the university and city officials can be different," Shanklin notes, "but I have a good relationship with them all because I have worked in the neighborhood a long time. I knew the mayor before he was mayor. His kids went to school with my grandkids. My husband was his soccer coach. I could talk with him differently. If you have relationships with people, what may be difficult for others is easier."[38]

Yale's effort has focused on four areas. President Richard Levin, speaking in 2003, described these components as follows: (1) economic development, with a focus on promoting biotech start-ups; (2) strengthening neighborhoods, with a focus on housing and school partnerships; (3) promoting improved safety, appearance, and vitality in downtown; and (4) marketing the city, an effort in which Yale's retail arm, University Properties, has played a key role.[39]

Notably, while "strengthening neighborhoods" makes the list, reducing neighborhood poverty per se is *not* an explicit goal of Yale's efforts. Jon Soderstrom, director of the Office of Cooperative Research, who heads Yale's biotech business development support effort, is very direct on this point: "Yale didn't decide, 'Let's alleviate poverty in New Haven.' What

Yale decided is—where we could have a positive economic impact, we would try to do so . . . our goal is to remain one of the great universities in the next century. Our goal is not to transform society—in a macro sense, through knowledge, yes—but in a micro sense, no." The scale of Yale's efforts in economic development, particularly in the area of business development, has been significant. In the past decade, Soderstrom points out, his office has developed a 550,000-square-foot incubator in downtown New Haven that has enabled forty new companies to be created. Combined, these businesses have raised about $450 million in venture capital and leveraged $3 billion in total equity, including five companies that have "gone public." Soderstrom also notes that the office helped create an incubator to support the start-up efforts by students. One student business—Higher One, Inc.—has been hugely successful, raising $10 million and employing 300. There have been a total of thirty-five start-up student businesses to date, of which seventeen have full-time employees.[40]

Yale's contributions to economic development in lower-income neighborhoods have been more episodic, but not unimportant. Overall, Yale's Office of New Haven and State Affairs estimates that graduate and professional schools have spent $14.39 million on outreach over the past two decades, including $1.27 million in fiscal year 2009, as well as provided significant in-kind resources. For example, Yale Law School faculty did pro bono work "which was worth a fortune" to enable the Greater Dwight Development Corporation to attract a Shaw's Supermarket to the Dwight neighborhood in the 1990s. The CDC has also benefited from pro bono public planning assistance from Yale's Urban Design Workshop.[41]

In terms of its direct neighborhood work, Yale's signature effort has been its homebuyer program, an employer-assisted housing initiative that aims to create more "mixed income" neighborhoods in New Haven by encouraging Yale faculty and staff to become New Haven homeowners. Efforts focus on helping renters become homeowners and encouraging new staff and faculty to buy homes in New Haven. In its fifteen years of existence, the Yale Homebuyer Program has provided $22.5 million in subsidy dollars that have facilitated over 925 home purchases (with an estimated combined value of over $150 million or an average home price of about $162,000) in New Haven by Yale faculty, staff, and affiliates. To date, about 45 percent of participants have been unionized staff, 80 percent have been first-time homebuyers, and about 50 percent of participants are people of color. According to Michael Morand, associate vice president of the Office of New Haven and State Affairs, there have been only two foreclosures in the history of the program. The subsidy amount per household is presently set at $30,000—$7,500 at closing, and $2,500 a year for nine years for each year of continued residency—with an additional $5,000 for people who buy in the Dixwell neighborhood, a low-income neighborhood near campus, which is a focus area of Yale's current efforts.[42]

In addition to its homeownership program, the other major arm of Yale's neighborhood building efforts has concerned its efforts to improve New Haven public schools. Yale's investment in this area is significant. In fiscal year 2009, Yale calculates that its investment in school partnerships was $3.9 million; in the past two decades, Yale estimates it spent $53 million on school partnership programs, or, more than twice the level of expenditure for its homebuyers' program.[43] Claudia Merson, director of public school partnerships at Yale's Office of New Haven and State Affairs, notes that while Yale partners with twenty of New

Haven's public schools, it works particularly closely with two magnet schools: Co-op High School and Hill Regional. Co-op High School has 600 students, with a focus in five areas of the arts and humanities. According to Suzannah Holsenbeck, Yale's support work, which includes the establishment of her staff position as an on-site partnership coordinator, as well as access to in-kind resources (including a range of activities from Yale tutors assisting with fundamentals to workshops with graduate students in Yale's drama program) have helped Co-op High achieve "safe harbor" status in math, while reading scores climbed twenty percentage points from 2008 to 2009.[44]

Another long-standing partnership is the Urban Resources Initiative, a community forestry partnership program supported by Yale since the mid-1990s. According to Colleen Murphy Dunning, director of the initiative, the group works annually with "fifty to sixty organizations on some kind of community forestry." The group aims to plant 10,000 trees in New Haven between 2010 and 2015.[45]

In terms of public safety, one important aspect has been for Yale to make voluntary payments in lieu of the property tax revenues that it would be providing the city were it not a nonprofit institution. In fiscal year 2009, Yale's contribution to the City of New Haven was $5.1 million, which has helped the city finance public services. Over the past two decades, Yale's voluntary payments to the city have exceeded $44.7 million.[46]

Another important aspect of Yale's strategy has been its management of its retail portfolio. While Yale's direct contribution to neighborhood and downtown real estate totaled only $100,000 in fiscal year 2009, this figure is deceptively low. Over the past two decades, Yale invested a total of $57.5 million in downtown and neighborhood real estate.[47] The benefit of this investment is substantial. As Abigail Rider, associate vice president and director for university properties, explains, Yale's property ownership enables it to leverage its real estate assets to achieve ancillary public safety and marketing goals. "We treat our portfolio as if it were a mall. So we secure it. We maintain it. We run events. We support our tenants. We have massive and continuous marketing," notes Rider. All told, Yale owns 310,000 square feet of retail, with leases to 110 stores, a residential portfolio of 500 units, and a small amount of upstairs (above retail) office space.[48]

According to Rider, Yale's ownership enables it to actively shape city development. "We pay for ourselves, but we are not under pressure to get a 25 percent internal rate of return," Rider explains. "The important thing is to get a decent return, since part of the return of this activity is a social return . . . [so] if there's a small business that we think is unique, we can afford to take a slow approach to rent." Rider adds: "Our ideal is not Rodeo Drive. We want . . . all of the [services] the community needs—hair salons, spas, dry cleaners, laundry, hardware store—these are things that are hard to do. It is harder than clothing or apparel. The flight to suburbia drew these uses out. What we need is a walkable city: where residents can get what they need here."[49]

Overall, Yale's efforts remain focused on the four areas outlined by President Levin in 2003: that is, economic development, strengthening neighborhoods through housing and public school partnerships, public safety, and downtown retail development. Yale also continues to expand its efforts in these areas. Most notably, in November 2010, Levin joined with New Haven mayor John DeStefano Jr., superintendent of schools Reginald Mayo, and

Community Foundation president William Ginsberg to launch a new effort to support the New Haven public schools called "New Haven Promise." Yale has committed to be the primary donor to the program, which will be administered by the Community Foundation. Patterned after similar programs in Pittsburgh and Kalamazoo, Michigan, the new program will cover full tuition to attend in-state public colleges and up to $2,500 per year for independent, nonprofit colleges for qualifying New Haven public high school graduates with a 3.0 GPA or better. The program will be phased in over four years, with the full benefit available to the graduating high school class of 2014, and represents a significant expansion of Yale's community partnership activity.[50]

Looking across the Cases

Creating an Engaged Community

Penn, Yale, and Cincinnati are all immediately adjacent to low-income neighborhoods. Penn, for example, is bordered on its east by the Schuylkill River and on its west by the West Philadelphia section of Philadelphia. According to the 2000 census, roughly 220,000 people live in West Philadelphia (a collection of twenty-two neighborhoods), of whom 71.8 percent are African American and 23.4 percent are white. The poverty rate as of 2000 was 24.4 percent, while unemployment was 11.2 percent, and the median household income under $21,000. City planning director Rick Redding estimates that as of 2009 the population of the area has fallen to 209,000.[51]

The University of Cincinnati is located in an area known as Uptown, comprised of several neighborhoods diverse in their socioeconomic and racial makeup. In 2008, an estimated 50,820 people lived in Uptown. African Americans, Asians, and other minorities comprise around 58 percent of Uptown's population (compared to 50 percent citywide). The poverty rate in 2008 for Uptown families was 23 percent. With five of the tri-state's top ten employers, however, Uptown employs around 40,000 individuals, rivaling the Central Business District of Cincinnati (just 1.5 miles from the south end of the University of Cincinnati's campus). Homeowners made up just 23 percent of Uptown residents in 2008, compared to 61 percent citywide.[52]

New Haven is a diverse city with a number of middle-class and even wealthy neighborhoods, but Yale University is close to many low-income neighborhoods, especially on its west side. Indeed, in 1999, New Haven was one of fifteen cities selected nationally for a ten-year "Empowerment Zone" designation (which requires a poverty rate of 25 percent or higher within the designated census tracts), with a focus on the six low-income neighborhoods of Hill, West Rock, Newhallville, Dwight, Dixwell, and Fair Haven. These six neighborhoods combined have an estimated population of nearly 42,000, a poverty rate above 31.5 percent, and an unemployment rate estimated to exceed 17.9 percent.[53]

Each of these institutions hence faces similar challenges, yet each has sought to connect to surrounding low-income neighborhoods in different ways. As detailed in our discussion of relationship building and participatory planning below, these universities have used a variety of mechanisms to reach out to and engage the community. This has included everything from holding monthly community meetings to developing *de novo* organizations to working to build local capacity and partnerships with pre-existing community-based organizations.

Establishing Partnership Programs and Goals

Penn, Cincinnati, and Yale all seek to promote neighborhood revitalization. But all do so with a mixture of motives. On the one hand, there is a genuine desire to be a "good neighbor" and to provide substantially enhanced services to low-income residents who were previously neglected (and sometimes directly exploited) by these institutions. At the same time, all three universities clearly identify their efforts as a response to safety concerns over what happens in adjacent neighborhoods, where many of their students and some faculty live. In some cases, a key (often unstated) goal of "revitalization" is to move the invisible "boundary line" between the resource-rich "gown" and the much poorer sections of "town" just a little further away from campus—or, at the least, to create a safe corridor along these shared edges. In a sense, the development of retail districts along Broadway and Chapel in New Haven; of Calhoun Street in the Clifton Heights district and Short Vine in the Corryville district of Cincinnati; and of Fortieth Street in West Philadelphia all serve this purpose. Such mixed-use developments help create new urban zones that provide amenities for both town and gown, but with the important ancillary benefit for the university of increasing the safety of the campus community by literally moving the poorer areas of the surrounding city at least a few blocks further from campus. The Penn Alexander School in West Philadelphia, which Philadelphia housing expert Kevin Gillen estimates to have increased the average real estate value of homes within its "catchment" area by "about $100,000," is another example of this effect at work, albeit with a focus on creating a residential, not commercial, buffer zone neighborhood.[54] This is no accident. Again, ensuring public safety for the campus community in these cases was *primary* to the entire effort.

At the same time, all three universities aim to go beyond creating safe spaces for students and faculty. As Morand of Yale puts it, "There are extraordinarily deep, broad, thick, marvelous and inextricable bonds of a community institution called Yale. . . . Continuous engagement is the reality here. . . . We are not mere 'partners'—we are 'part of,' fellow stakeholders, fellow citizens, neighbors."[55] While these institutions certainly view themselves as "part of" their community, there is no question that resource and power imbalances exist. In places like Yale or Penn, but also (albeit to a lesser degree) Cincinnati, once the period of high crime and "crisis" has subsided, an opportunity to deepen and broaden efforts to be more inclusive of community goals clearly exists. One might even say that the initial crisis response often generates a "need" for a broader response. For example, a 2006 internal report at Penn warned that "Penn must work to avoid the creation of two West Philadelphias"—one that is close to campus and favored (the urban buffer zone) and the larger region, which risks suffering from continued neglect. In response, the authors made a number of recommendations including strengthening direct hiring and workforce development of West Philadelphia residents, a greater focus on housing for lower income residents, a strengthening of the local network of community development corporations (CDCs), expanded community health work, and support for local business development through such means as a business incubator and a community development credit union.[56]

Informed by this vision, efforts are under way in at least two of these areas at Penn: local hiring and CDC partnership development. Regarding the former, Netter's Cory Bowman notes that the key question is, "What can you do to connect West Philadelphians to West Philadelphia jobs? The issue is not that jobs don't exist, but connecting them. . . . Every kid should be able to get an entry-level job. We want to identify five or six kids at every high school, 800 kids citywide, help them graduate, and then get entry-level jobs or go on to college," Bowman explains. "We're still at square 0.5, but we're making progress." Bowman adds that the Netter Center is now working with large health care employers in Philadelphia to develop effective health care career ladders for area residents and youth through the Skills Development Center. In 2007–2008, the Skills Development Center trained 700 incumbent workers at the Penn Health System and the Children's Hospital of Philadelphia.[57]

Randy Belin, senior program officer at the Philadelphia office of the Local Initiatives Support Corporation, describes LISC's Sustainable Communities Initiative–West Philadelphia (SCI-West), a program supported by the William Penn Foundation that aims to coordinate the activities of the University City District and three local community development corporations. Belin notes, "Penn did a needs assessment in 2004. It lines up well with SCI-West. The main issues are similar: affordable housing, workforce development, public safety, and health." Penn's Glenn Bryan serves on Philadelphia LISC's advisory board, and his participation is a sign of the university's commitment to this process. "There is only opportunity and potential," Belin says.[58]

At Cincinnati, the university leadership is beginning to think more strategically about how it can leverage all of its resources to align with the comprehensive needs of the community. However, some disconnect still exists between administrative-led initiatives and the faculty and staff whose partnership efforts have been built on more grassroots efforts. Michael Sharp speaks frankly about this challenge: "Similar to other large institutions, the left hand of the university and the right hand of the university don't know what each other is doing. But, over the last several years, we've been making strides in the right direction."[59] Communication from the top to the bottom and across schools and centers at such a large institution is often challenging. Yet both the leadership of the university and those running the partnership centers do agree that increased collaboration and communication—both externally and internally—are essential. In the meantime, the university has created a more visible portal for the greater community called Center for the City. The virtual portal is partly intended to make the divisions among engaged centers and faculty invisible to the community. It will connect the university and its resources to local nonprofits, government, and the corporate community. Through efforts like this, and the university's role in Agenda 360 (more below), Cincinnati appears to have turned *some* of its community engagement focus toward citywide partnerships.[60]

At Yale, perhaps because of the continuity of presidential leadership, there has not been as thorough an evaluation of its community partnership work as Penn experienced after Rodin's departure; nonetheless, the effort at Yale has evolved in recent years. Traditionally, notes Reggie Solomon, program director for the Office of New Haven and State Affairs, Yale had not invested "in the area between nine o'clock and noon" (northwest quadrant) that extends into the impoverished Dixwell neighborhood. One notable effort to invest in Dixwell has been the Rose Center project, where Yale, with the participation of local community members, has built a new police substation and 3,000-square-foot community center, which includes a sixteen-person computer lab and a fifteen-person meeting room. Yale has also invested $500,000 in a local park (Scantlebury Park).[61]

More recently, Yale's professional schools have also deepened their efforts. For example, Yale has supported the development of a new community development financial institution, First Community Bank, both with a $2 million capital grant from the Office of New Haven and State Affairs, as well as in-kind assistance from Yale Law School and Yale School of Management. Yale's Medical School has also increased its public health outreach work, with Yale being one of thirty Clinical Translational Science Award grant recipients nationally. The Community Alliance for Research Education, with an annual budget of $300,000–400,000, is targeting six neighborhoods in New Haven with the worst health status and aims to reach 2,500 people.[62]

Institutionalizing an Anchor Vision

To a large extent, all three schools aligned their institutional priorities for engagement in the immediate post-crisis period. However, the schools have maintained their focus differently over time. Penn has perhaps the most developed structure to support community engagement. Under President Rodin, for instance, the board of trustees set up a Committee on Neighborhood Initiatives that would be on par with Finance and other committees of the board and oversee the effort at the trustee level; this committee has continued its work under current President Gutmann. A big part of the strength of Penn's efforts has indeed been consistent presidential support, as well as the prominence of the Netter Center. The importance of the Netter Center is signaled by the fact that its director, Ira Harkavy, also has the rank of associate vice president. The Netter Center reports directly to the vice president of government and community affairs and the dean of the School of Arts and Sciences, but with a strong link to the university president.[63]

At Cincinnati, from 2003 to 2009, Nancy Zimpher provided tremendous leadership for the university's repositioning as an urban, engaged university. As president of the Greater Cincinnati Foundation Kathy Merchant, puts it, "Nancy Zimpher brought a gale force wind and enthusiasm for the role that the university can and should play for community economic vitality and quality of life." Not only did Zimpher understand and support the development efforts, but also there was active participation. As Siegert notes, "Despite the huge demands on the President's daily schedule, time was dedicated to serve on the Board of Trustees of the Uptown Consortium and often communicate directly with neighborhood community leaders who sought counsel with her and/or members of her administrative cabinet." However, many university faculty and staff know that institutional change is not often an easy course. "Nancy tried to set the table on what an engaged university is, but the institution is a big machine and is slower to change. I'm optimistic that we'll get there . . . eventually," says Michael Sharp. Moreover, Cincinnati recognizes that a more conscious linking of the corporate and academic sides of the university could bring about more systemic change, in part by leveraging each other's resources. Professor Michael Romanos remarks, "The School of Planning is supposed to be knowledgeable about urban development in the city . . . we don't even know what the [Uptown] Consortium is doing. We're informed through newspapers of the redevelopment. There is disconnect between the Consortium and university academic resources."[64]

When Cincinnati began its presidential search after Zimpher's departure in June 2009, there was a public board resolution to retain the institution's commitment to the community. Zimpher also elevated the status of her associate vice president for external relations, Mary Stagaman, to presidential deputy for community engagement. Stagaman helped orchestrate relations between the university and the broader community, as well as to organize efforts internally. Monica Rimai, who served as senior vice president of finance and administration and helped to execute Zimpher's vision of community engagement, served as the interim president. The new president, Gregory Williams, installed in November 2009, hails from City College of New York (where he was president from 2001 to 2009) and thus has a strong urban background, which augurs well for continued commitment to Cincinnati's anchor institution strategy. Still, to ensure sustainability, efforts going forward will likely need to engage a broader range of university leaders.[65]

Yale has relied largely on the leadership of President Richard Levin. His nineteen-plus year term has allowed for the institutionalization of a broad effort coordinated by the Office of New Haven and State Affairs and the Office of University Properties. Since 1990, when Bruce Alexander, a Yale alumnus who formerly worked for the Rouse Corporation, a leading real estate firm, was hired, the director of the Office of New Haven and State Affairs has had the status of vice president (with the formal title of Vice President of New Haven and State Affairs and Campus Development), giving the office "cabinet rank." Jon Soderstrom confirms the centrality of presidential support to the whole effort.[66]

Michael Morand describes the work as follows: "Our office is about doing, not telling. Incorporating facilities work with community engagement has a major impact: our guys in facilities get it. They implement local and minority construction programs—no arm-twisting required. First-floor retail—it works more seamlessly here. You have senior officers of the university focused on New Haven. Local impacts are at the table when corporate decisions are made. And the president of the university supports this, so you have the bully pulpit effect."[67]

Securing Funding and Leveraging Resources

Each of the three institutions has contributed considerable financial resources to community engagement that total in the hundreds of millions of dollars. For the University of Pennsylvania, this investment has involved both annual expenditures as well as more substantial one-time capital expenditures. Regarding the former, the contributions remain relatively modest: direct Penn contributions to the Netter Center, Penn Alexander School, University City District, and employer-assisted housing program total roughly $5 million to $6 million a year—and perhaps with other partnership programs might reach $10 million a year. Of course, these programs also leverage much greater external support, with UCD raising more than $5 million for landscaping and transportation from 1997 to 2003, and Netter raising more than $4.5 million in 2008 alone. Regarding the latter, capital expenditures during the Rodin period are estimated to total $510 million; in essence, this was done by leveraging existing real estate and construction budgets to serve both real estate development as well as broader community development goals.[68]

The University of Cincinnati has committed $148.6 million, over a ten-year period, out of its endowment to real estate development in Uptown. According to Siegert, a good portion of the nearly $150 million invested has been recovered as projects matured or as alterative funding sources were identified and implemented; however some loans remain outstanding. "Although the outstanding balance of original endowment loans has ranged between $80 and $90 million, the diversity of the projects funded with these loans has attracted over $250 million in other financing resources," notes Siegert. Reserves have been provided to recognize the fact that not all investments may be recovered. These reserves include approximately 20 percent of principal and a portion of accrued interest. In addition to endowment loans, the seven community redevelopment corporations have collectively received an average of one million dollars in operating funds each year, over the last eight to nine years, from the university's general funds. The university's chief investment officer, Tom Croft, takes a long view on how these investments fit into the university's endowment portfolio: "While these loans aren't publicly traded, investment-grade bonds, we are comfortable that we will get our money back over time and ultimately see a return on our investment. Moreover, these investments, which are appreciably improving surrounding neighborhoods for both our students and the community, have strategic value that goes far beyond their direct rate of return."[69]

The Greater Cincinnati Foundation has also invested in the university's community development efforts, in addition to funding health and education initiatives. Most recently, the foundation has provided program specific funding through low-interest rate loans, similar to the university's investments. Program investments are going directly into real estate deals with expectation of repayment long term.[70]

Yale has also made a sustained investment in community development in New Haven. According to an estimate compiled by the Office of New Haven and State Affairs, Yale spent over $7.7 million on outreach and community development programs in 2008–2009 and a total of $164 million since 1990. Included in this amount is $54.5 million in supporting the development of New Haven's retail district and $22.5 million to support employer-assisted housing. These investments have leveraged significant additional investment. For example, the $22.5 million in employer-assisted housing dollars helped leverage home purchases in excess of $150 million. If one includes Yale's voluntary payments to the City of New Haven— which are on top of state-mandated PILOTs (payments in lieu of (property) taxes)—then the total Yale expenditure for 2008–2009 increases to $12.8 million and the total direct expenditure since 1990 rises to $209 million.[71]

Building a Culture of Economic Inclusion

Penn has taken very deliberate efforts toward economic inclusion, and is using its economic and purchasing power to create opportunities for local, minority, and women business owners. Penn's local purchasing effort began in the 1980s, as discussed above, and has continued to grow in breadth and depth over the last couple of decades. One recent change made by Penn has been to strengthen its community outreach by partnering more with nonprofit groups with similar aims, such as the Pennsylvania Minority Business Development Council and Minority Business Enterprise Center. Additionally, economic inclusion has become more embedded into the institutional culture at Penn: "We used to have a director of minority business development. But by having that position, we had created silos. We constantly ran into battles between that position and sourcing managers. Our decision when the minority business development director left was to not replace that position and instead make economic inclusion a core duty of each sourcing manager . . . A single structure creates no excuses for incompetence," says Maier. University City District, in partnership with the Netter Center, has also recently embarked upon more focused workforce development efforts, including running an apprenticeship program with the University of Pennsylvania Health System for eighteen- to twenty-four-year-old high school graduates from West Philadelphia, as well as developing a database that defines pathways into entry level and career ladder jobs across West Philadelphia's institutional employers.[72]

At Cincinnati, the university's Office of Contract Compliance works closely with the Central Purchasing Department to offer assistance to minority and disadvantaged suppliers, although their reach has been limited to date. The office administers two statewide programs: (1) the set-aside program, which sets goals for state entities to have 15 percent of purchasing dollars go to state-certified minority business enterprises (MBEs) participating in the program; the university averages 6 to 8 percent each year; and (2) the EDGE program (Encouraging Diversity, Growth, and Equity), which sets a 5 percent goal for goods and services from socially and economically disadvantaged businesses; the university averages 4 percent each year in this area. By state law, the university is allowed to give a 10 percent economic advantage to certified MBEs for goods and services only. The Purchasing Department keeps a very open bidding process, inviting minority and disadvantaged businesses to visit the office and review old bids, both successful and unsuccessful.[73] Several other Uptown Consortium partners have been closely attuned to workforce development and minority inclusion. For example, University Hospital has been working with the city to form a health care workforce development track for underemployed workers within the hospital. The city's Workforce Development Board has adopted this model for tracks in construction.[74]

Yale has done relatively little in the areas of workforce development and purchasing, but has a very strong program in contracting. Michael Morand notes that Yale requires "our contractors to meet the same goals as the City in terms of local, minority, women, and first-year apprentice hires. These goals are 25 percent for people of color, 20 percent local, the federally determined 6.9 percent for women, and 15 percent for first-year apprentice hires. Yale does $100 million in construction this year [2009]. We probably did $200 million last year. Trades jobs pay twenty-five dollars an hour and include benefits."[75]

Sustaining Participatory Planning and Robust Relationships

All three institutions have spent time developing relationships with their local neighborhoods as well as involved residents and other stakeholders in the planning of their community development initiatives. But, in general, the universities have taken more of a direct leadership—rather than "partnership"—role. Perhaps nowhere is this more obvious than in the decisions by Penn and Cincinnati to form new community organizations to be their primary "community" partners, rather than choosing to partner with existing community organizations and work to build community capacity. At Penn, the most important of these partners has been the University City District. At Cincinnati, of course, the most important partner has been the Uptown Consortium, along with seven community redevelopment corporations that Cincinnati also set up from scratch. Given the high level of university funding of these groups, it is obvious that, at least initially, these partner organizations served more as outreach conduits than truly independent interlocutors. One explanation for this lack of independence at Penn, of course, is the "emergency" conditions that led to the efforts in the first place. Lucy Kerman, who worked in the Office of the President under Rodin, and co-author John Kromer note that one reason Penn rejected "a CDC-driven structure was the time required to organize and implement the Initiatives through a separate entity with its own mission, board leadership, and staffing. University leadership was convinced that immediate action was required and that taking the time to establish a nonprofit/CDC leadership and administrative role was not an option."[76]

Michael Romanos suggests that it was declining enrollment linked to poor quality student housing that led the University of Cincinnati to take action in the late 1990s. "The only way UC could solve this problem was to work with the community; thus, the first community development corporations in the Uptown were formed," writes Romanos. It should be noted that university officials intentionally allotted themselves non-majority seats on the redevelopment corporation boards in an effort to empower the community, although university leadership and resources in establishing these new organizations (as well as continued financial support) have certainly maintained a certain level of influence and occasionally created tension from differing expectations.[77]

Meanwhile, the Uptown Consortium leaders made explicit goals to include the community in the planning and design process. Three Uptown summits were held between 2004 and 2005 for the Consortium to interact with community residents, with each Summit growing in attendance. This was one of the opportunities for Consortium leaders to hear about community-identified problems and for partners to collectively identify solutions. Key changes were made in the Consortium's plans based on residents' feedback at the summits. Several town-hall meetings, workshops, and public forums were also held to include residents in the planning.[78] However, these events slowly petered off, and communication between the Consortium and the community diminished. The first big development was completed, which was a parking garage for Cincinnati Children's Hospital. As Matt Bourgeois, director of one of the redevelopment corporations puts it, while parking was a necessity, this fed the community's fears: instead of the community benefits that they were promised, the community saw the institutions' neighborhood revitalization plans as "a conduit for institutional goals." The Uptown Consortium continued to set the agenda and consult with the community only moments before implementation. Over the next couple of years, tension grew between some of the neighborhood organizations and the Consortium.[79]

Yale, too, has relied largely on its own organizations, notably University Properties and the Office of New Haven and State Affairs. However, unlike Penn or Cincinnati, Yale has a long-standing partnership with an independent CDC, Greater Dwight Development Corporation. Yale helped the CDC secure its initial funding through a grant from the Community Outreach

Partnership Centers (COPC) program at the U.S. Department of Housing and Urban Development (HUD). The CDC has gone on to develop a supermarket in the Dwight neighborhood to the west of Yale's main campus. It has also been an important partner in Yale's efforts to reduce crime through community policing, led the effort to develop a neighborhood master plan, and has taken a leadership role in developing neighborhood childcare. To be sure, the partnership has not proceeded smoothly at all times. Greater Dwight cofounder and executive director Linda Townsend-Maier notes that there have been times where some individuals at Yale tried "to control us. They helped create our CDC, but we were not a Yale CDC." Sheila Masterson, a fellow Greater Dwight cofounder, agrees: "I remember rumblings that we were Yale's CDC. Maybe that was everybody's version on the Yale side, but we were strong. It's been a learning process from both sides." Nonetheless, the partnership has survived and grown through the conflicts. Greater Dwight staff and community members concur that the partnership has helped achieve broader community goals.[80]

More recently, both Penn and Cincinnati have sought to strengthen their collaborative efforts. Penn, while operating largely outside the framework of existing community development corporations, has long endeavored to include community members in other ways. Particularly important has been its monthly "First Thursday" program, at which community members are invited to share breakfast, listen to a speaker from Penn, and provide critical feedback with Penn administration leaders in the room. D. L. Wormley, formerly of Philadelphia's neighborhood-focused intermediary organization NeighborhoodsNow, notes, "One of the best things that Penn has done is First Thursday. People are beginning to try to resolve issues."[81]

The Netter Center also has a specific community outreach component, which includes a Center-wide community advisory board, as well as program-specific community advisory groups. The Center's strategic plan, published in February 2008, however, identified the lack of integration of the community advisory board with Center governance as an institutional weakness and called for changes in structure to address that. Center director Ira Harkavy indicated that in the time since the strategic plan came out, "The community board has been getting more aggressive and stronger" and has played a key role in setting the Center's partnership agenda.[82]

More broadly, Tom Burns of Urban Venture Group, who has worked as a consultant with LISC on the Sustainable Communities Initiative–West Philadelphia (SCI-West) program, says that he senses a shift in Penn. There may be, Burns suggests, "an opening to move away from the 'do it our own way' approach to an approach that seeks out opportunity for sensible collaboration that is well aligned with the institution's goals. Potentially it is a much more mature framework in place for sustaining some of this work." Burns suggests the goal of community partnership should be what he labels *shared development.* "It has a planning frame," Burns notes. "Underlying the idea is the principle of shared development that locks anchors and CDCs in a development agenda of mutual interest. I don't think we have that in West Philly at this point," Burns cautions, but he is hopeful that the SCI-West effort could develop in that direction.[83]

In Cincinnati, community groups have responded to past shortfalls by approaching Consortium leaders, particularly University administrators, about the need for stronger community representation. This led to a year of dialogue. Much like the Consortium itself, the ability of five community councils to come together with a collective voice not only was a significant milestone but also has given community leaders greater leverage. In 2009, the Uptown Consortium partners, in collaboration with the five community councils, re-examined the Consortium's mission. As part of that process, the Consortium committed to increasing community participation in decision-making and to working more collaboratively. One example is that two community council representatives have been invited onto the Consortium Management Operations Committee (one rung below the board, but where key decisions get made). Leadership recognizes that they must still build a way for these representatives to take the messages back to the neighborhood, so everyone is engaged and aware of the process.[84] Going forward, it will also be essential that the university—as a key leader of the Consortium and other community development efforts—set appropriate expectations to both the internal and external community. "When we first began, we became the solver of all problems regarding economic development, and the community and city began to expect that," reflects Rimai. "We [eventually] came to recognize our own limitations, be transparent about why and how we were doing what we were doing, and communicate that to people in a way that they understood. We've come a long way; we are much more open and much more honest about each other's needs, wants, and abilities. Our partnership has never been stronger."[85]

Yale has modified practices over the years as well. Like Penn, Yale has a "First Thursday" breakfast event to provide a regular monthly site for interaction between community members and Yale administration staff. Unlike Penn, Yale's Office of New Haven and State Affairs lacks the formal community advisory board structures that Penn's Netter Center has. Another key component of Yale's community outreach worth emphasizing has been close collaboration with city leaders. Here Yale has had a unique advantage that neither Penn nor Cincinnati has enjoyed. As Claudia Merson points out, since the mid-1990s in New Haven, "We've had the same mayor, the same high school district superintendent, and the same university president. That's not to say there haven't been changes under them, but we have these partnerships and these partnerships are stable."

Broadly speaking, Yale's approach has been more initiative-by-initiative, rather than the formal comprehensive efforts launched at Penn and Cincinnati. Michael Morand characterizes Yale's approach as follows: "You can try the grand-slam approach to urban revitalization—a mega-mall or a stadium—but if you can hit enough singles and a couple of doubles, you'll get more runs on the board." Yale's community collaboration efforts likewise largely follow this model.[86]

Meeting the Needs of Low-Income Residents and Neighborhoods

Because of the intense revitalization efforts focused on low-income neighborhoods immediately adjacent to resource-rich universities, all three efforts bear a gentrification—or, to use a less loaded term, displacement—risk. On one hand, all three schools have clear, physical impacts on their communities through real estate investment. All three schools have also made significant investments in community institutions, especially through partnerships with local public schools. On the other hand, the impact on quality of life for residents has been more mixed. Certainly, the neighborhoods are more pleasant, with greater retail availability, improved façades and streetscapes, and improved neighborhood safety. At the same time, there are obvious shortfalls. Except for the construction industry, none are all that strong on hiring locally or providing workforce development. Purchasing, even at Penn, has holes in terms of its effectiveness. More broadly, the poverty rates of the surrounding communities remain high. The cover article in the May–June 2009 issue of *Yale Alumni Magazine* touts the undeniable reality of a "New Haven Renaissance," and yet the same article cites data showing that New Haven's poverty rate has climbed slightly since the mid-1990s and stood as of 2007 at 20 percent. One is reminded of the comment of Paul Grogan and Tony Proscio in their analysis of the role of community development corporations in reviving the South Bronx: "What changed the South Bronx from Fort Apache to a functioning community was not a sudden influx of wealth, but a careful restoration of order." In short, the challenges faced by universities that undertake comprehensive community engagement efforts are not altogether different from the challenges faced by community developers in the United States more generally.[87]

Penn, Cincinnati, and Yale have dealt with these challenges in different ways. At Penn, to prevent a bifurcation of West Philadelphia into "two west Philadelphias," the goal has been to broaden the "catchment" area. To some, this has meant a reduced focus, but to others it represents an opportunity to rebalance and refocus efforts. In the words of a January 2006 internal Penn memo, "The goal of 'engaging locally' includes strategies for both the so-called 'inner' ring (campus to 52nd St, Haverford Ave to the River) and the 'outer' ring (52nd to 63rd, north to Parkside, and inclusive of Southwest Philadelphia), as well as the eastern campus development. Fundamental to Penn's efforts is a commitment to ensuring that longtime residents throughout West and Southwest Philadelphia benefit from developments around campus, and an appreciation of the need to work collaboratively with the community to address their needs and interests." Various policy changes have been made at Penn to implement this vision, including a shift in the employer-assisted housing program to cover a larger geographical area. Tom Burns of Urban Ventures views this new direction positively. "I am kind of a hopeful guy," Burns says, "This could be a period when a more mature relationship emerges with the leadership of the community, who are in some ways less angry and possibly more strategic in thinking about how to work that relationship in ways that deliver benefits to the community.[88]

Cincinnati is at an earlier stage in its efforts, but is building on its experiences, both positive and negative, regarding community development. For instance, some of the redevelopment has had unintended consequences: as retail prices increased dramatically, some smaller businesses have been forced to leave, and a number of low-income individuals have also been displaced by new market-rate apartment buildings around campus. To address these issues, the Uptown Consortium has made several more focused efforts to help existing residents and businesses benefit from revitalization.

For example, with around 16,000 residents and 32 percent of families below the poverty line, Avondale is the second largest, and poorest, neighborhood within Uptown. It is comprised of roughly 90 percent African Americans; unemployment stood at 14 percent in the 2000 census, and the business climate has been fairly stagnant.[89] Today's revitalization in

Avondale's Burnet Avenue business district is the result of an $85 million joint project of Cincinnati Children's Hospital Medical Center, the Avondale Community Council and the Uptown Consortium. This mixed-use development will have retail on the first floor and house the *Cincinnati Herald* (the city's only African American newspaper) on the second floor. The architect for this project is an African American who partnered with a local construction company to create opportunities for minority involvement in the construction. According to former Consortium director Tony Brown, "We plan to subsidize about 7,500 square feet of retail to attract small businesses to come back into the neighborhood." Drugs and crime have been a significant problem in Avondale. According to Brown, the Consortium first weeded out businesses that served as storefronts and then "contracted with the Greater Cincinnati Micro Enterprise, a community development financial institution, to help existing, legitimate businesses with a business plan, while UC's Community Design Center is helping them work on design plans." The Consortium has also partnered with a residential development firm, The Model Group, that attracted $13 million in low-income tax credits to build approximately eighty units of affordable rental housing and low-income senior housing in Avondale.[90]

Unlike Penn or Cincinnati, Yale has never made poverty reduction an explicit goal, but its community revitalization efforts continue to evolve in a direction that may hold promise for poverty reduction nonetheless.[91] In particular, a new area of focus at Yale has been sustainability. In 2005, Yale committed to reducing its carbon emissions by 43 percent by 2020 (10 percent below 1990 level). By 2008, it had achieved a 17 percent reduction. To date, much of Yale's effort has focused on improving building energy-efficiency and transportation. Ironically, sustainability is often disconnected from community development, but in some areas the push for sustainability may lead to new opportunities to link the two. For example, Yale has an $11 million dining services budget. Because of its sustainability goals, it has brought its dining services in house and is now seeking to have 60 percent of its food locally sourced. If implemented, this would mark Yale's first significant foray into local purchasing. Another significant development is the formation of First Community Bank, a local for-profit community development financial institution. Bill Placke, CEO of the bank, says that Yale has been a major backer of this effort, contributing $2 million in capital and providing major in-kind technical assistance. Yet Placke also sees Yale playing an even more critical role in the future by leveraging its investment capacity. "We need businesses to shift money from big banks to our bank. And one of those businesses is Yale," Placke said. "So that's one other area where I am counting on Yale's help."[92]

University as Convener: Syracuse, Minnesota, LeMoyne-Owen, and Emory

The four schools reviewed in this chapter—Syracuse University; University of Minnesota, Twin Cities; LeMoyne-Owen College; and Emory University—are marked by their strategic choice to engage in collaborative community development efforts. Not faced with an immediate safety threat (as were Penn, Cincinnati, and Yale), but still embracing the service component of their institutional mission, these schools have had greater flexibility to focus partnerships and resources on the broader community. With a vision of comprehensive neighborhood revitalization, the institutions described here have chosen to adopt a place-based strategy as a part of a larger community engagement agenda, focusing resources on non-adjacent neighborhoods, where issues of poverty and economic decline are most acute. (LeMoyne-Owen is the notable exception, as the college is located within its community of need.) This investment in a focused place-based strategy sets these schools apart from the facilitator model, while their participatory and coalition-based approach to engagement and community-based agenda-setting marks a clear contrast with the university-directed leadership model.

Critically, these institutions have all worked to forge liaisons—both human and physical—to more closely align themselves with the needs and voices of the community. As conveners, these schools bring in community organizations and residents as co-participants in planning and operations, and ultimately as "owners" of neighborhood revitalization. In a similar fashion, these universities help to build capacity among residents and community institutions. Project-based partnerships in health and education are seen at each of these institutions, often in support of the broader community development agenda.

Support from top administration, as well as some degree of institutional alignment, has helped focus university-wide resources on key community initiatives. However, unlike the efforts of Penn, Yale, and Cincinnati, direct corporate investment has been more limited. Instead, these institutions have relied on leveraging public and private funds in support of their community development agendas. The logic of these four schools' strategies is explored in further detail below.

Syracuse University

> This is our identity as an institution. Our areas of excellence are completely compatible with the future opportunity of these neighborhoods, so it really is mutually beneficial.
>
> —Nancy Cantor, president and chancellor, Syracuse University, interview by Rita Axelroth Hodges, Syracuse, NY, May 29, 2009

As a private research university that literally sits up on a hill overlooking downtown Syracuse and its surrounding neighborhoods, Syracuse University could easily exist in its distant ivory tower. Indeed, in the early 1990s, Chancellor Shaw made an intentional move to consolidate the university on its main campus. His thinking was that, if the city failed, Syracuse University could survive. When Chancellor Nancy Cantor—a social psychologist and leader in the higher education engagement movement—arrived on campus in 2004, however, she viewed the university as "an incredible test bed of how a private university, as a place-based

---

Figure 9. Syracuse Anchor Approach

Comprehensive Neighborhood Revitalization
- Near West Side Initiative: revitalizing neighborhood through property acquisition and renovation of existing homes, with a focus on arts and culture, in 11-block area
- South Side Initiative focuses on economic and community development

Community Economic Development through Corporate Investment
- Support to minority- and women-owned businesses through trainings and mentorship, as well as exclusive bid opportunities (8% of total purchasing)
- Convey economic inclusion principles to contractors
- Home Ownership Grant and Guaranteed Mortgage Program extend to Near West Side

Local Capacity Building
- Near West Side Initiative established as independent 501(c)3 with shared leadership
- SouthSide Innovation Center supports women and minority entrepreneurs (assisted in development of 45 new businesses and profitable turnaround of 58 others)
- South Side Initiative working to develop food co-op and other community-owned businesses

- Partnership with local foundation for resident training in Near West Side

Public Education and Health Partnerships
- Say Yes to Education, in partnership with Syracuse City School District, provides comprehensive services and promise of free college tuition

Academic Engagement
- "Scholarship in Action": more than 400 students and 75 faculty involved in Near West Side Initiative alone
- Tenure and promotion changes to support engaged scholarship
- Imagining America (housed at SU): public scholarship in the arts, humanities and design
- Entrepreneurship Initiative through the Kauffman Foundation

Multi-Anchor, City, and Regional Partnerships
- Connective Corridor: multisector partnership creating cultural strip that connects University Hill to downtown
- Leader of Say Yes to Education consortia of more than 100 private and public higher education institutions

institution, could play a role in the public good."[1] Cantor has defined the university's neighborhood as the city of Syracuse. At the same time, the university has demonstrated its commitment as an anchor by engaging in intentional partnerships with two particular neighborhoods in need of revitalization.

The most visible of these efforts has taken place in the Near West Side. In 2007, when the state of New York agreed to forgive universities' loans if the money were invested in an urban economic development project, many institutions simply used the money to build new campus buildings. Cantor instead made the decision to invest in the Near West Side. Syracuse gave all $13.8 million of its Debt Reinvestment Funds (i.e., forgiven loans from the state) to begin a comprehensive neighborhood revitalization effort that seeks to use the power of art, technology, and innovation, *in keeping with neighborhood values and culture,* to revitalize the ninth poorest census tract in the United States. Specifically, $8 million was dedicated for property acquisition and renovation; $2.5 million was allocated for architecture, including engaging Syracuse students in urban redesign; and $2.5 million was given to Syracuse's Center of Excellence to improve home energy and environmental performance. An additional $5 million was acquired from the Syracuse Neighborhood Initiative, Restore New York Communities grants (awarded by the state to the City of Syracuse), and private sources.[2]

Community revitalization efforts are being directed through the Near West Side Initiative (NWSI), a nonprofit corporation formed as a collaborative network of business, educational, and nonprofit leaders, neighborhood residents, and development professionals. NWSI's board president, Marilyn Higgins, also serves as the vice president for community engagement and economic development, appointed to this new university position by Cantor in 2007. Higgins has been responsible for acquiring seventy-four abandoned properties in the Near West Side as well as strip of abandoned warehouses. She hopes that her $8 million will leverage another $50 million needed for full construction. For example, debt reinvestment funds have been combined with grants from Restore New York to rehabilitate the Case Supply Warehouse, a 200,000-square-foot, turn-of-the-century structure, to house the region's public broadcasting station along with artist condominiums and the international literacy organization Pro-Literacy International. This rehabilitated warehouse—partners hope—will serve as an anchor project for neighborhood revitalization. Although Syracuse provided significant seed funding and is responsible for much of the oversight of the initiative, the university has tried to remain out of the spotlight. "When Nancy [Cantor] came to the first NWSI board meeting, she said very clearly that this is *not* a university initiative," reflects Kathy Goldfarb-Findling, former executive director of the Rosamond Gifford Charitable Corporation (2000–2010), and a member of the NWSI board. "This provided clarity from the beginning that partnership was key." It also meant that Syracuse wasn't going to provide ongoing financial support but rather encourage NSWI to become a self-sustaining entity.[3]

The Gifford Foundation is responsible for leading the neighborhood capacity building effort in the Near West Side. This has seen its challenges: with two competing minority populations in the area, some in the Latino community view the university's and NWSI's efforts as marginalizing. Rita Paniagua, executive director of the Spanish Action League and an NWSI board member, comments, "There is still a long history of distrust and disinvestment. We have a really poor Latino community here. They need to see tangible change—the new houses are a start, but there is a long way to go." A new Latino Cultural Center, which aims to bring university staff, faculty, students, and the Latino community together around culture, arts, and education, is being planned for the Near West Side. Faculty leaders hope this permanent site will signal university commitment to engagement with and access for the Latino community.

Another key member of the NWSI network is Home HeadQuarters, a nonprofit that provides mini-grants to homeowners for green renovations, constructs new homes, and provides apprentice training for low- and moderate-income individuals from the neighborhood interested in the construction trade. Syracuse's Center of Excellence facilitates home audits to determine where the mini-grants could have the most impact, and students help design groundbreaking green technology for the homes. "Centers of Excellence are usually traditional science think tanks; here, we're having a real impact on the neighborhood," comments Ed Bogucz, associate professor and Center director. The Center is largely focused on the 17 percent of existing homeowners in the community. "This neighborhood has been very discriminated against and underserved, so trust with the homeowners is huge," says Bogucz. "We have to keep them strong and engaged, so we can attract new homeowners." A Syracuse graduate student, employed as an "Engagement Fellow" with the NWSI, has visited the small businesses in the Near West Side to explain the initiative, evaluate their assets and challenges, and invite them to be involved. "We're building on what's there now," Bogucz comments. The dean of the Law School has also urged its Center on Property, Citizenship, and Social Entrepreneurism to help design resident-owned business models for the Near West Side.[4]

Syracuse's second focused revitalization effort is in the South Side. The South Side Initiative formed in 2005 to connect the resources of the university with the community-identified needs of this neighborhood. "The litmus test for all our partnership projects is, when Syracuse University is no longer there, [can] the community sustain the business or project?" says Associate Vice President Linda Littlejohn. For example, Syracuse matched state funds to develop the South Side Communications Center. It will house a community technology room and a new community newspaper, where both Syracuse students and residents will be trained. Ownership and operation will eventually be turned over to the community in an effort to retain talented residents in the neighborhood. The South Side Initiative is also working toward a cooperatively owned grocery store. In addition, the university's Whitman School of Management operates a South Side Innovation Center that supports women and minority entrepreneurs in the area through one-on-one counseling, workshops, and incubator space. This is part of the South Side Entrepreneurial Connect Project, which, since 2006, has assisted the development of forty-five new businesses and in the profitable turn-around of fifty-eight others.[5]

Another key revitalization effort led by Syracuse University is the Connective Corridor. This cultural strip aims to connect University Hill with downtown Syracuse, stimulate economic development, and showcase art, technology, and sustainable designs. A Community Working Group, representing the city's neighborhoods, arts community, businesses, and nonprofit organizations, has been engaged in all the important steps along the way. "We're looking at all the arts and cultural organizations in the city and finding ways that SU can support them, particularly through leveraging the intellectual resources on campus," comments Eric Persons, Syracuse's director of engagement initiatives. A student artist team from the College of Visual and Performing Arts, for example, developed the innovative Urban Video Project, which projects artwork and other cultural video displays daily in three public venues. Another key partner is the Chamber of Commerce, which is steering the business development side of the corridor, including setting up a revolving loan fund for hospitality businesses. Persons says, "We've shied away from development opportunities that do not directly serve an institutional need." The corridor will extend to the Near West Side, helping to stimulate the revitalization of that neighborhood as well.[6]

Also tied into the Connective Corridor development, and extending to the Near West Side, is Syracuse's Guaranteed Mortgage Program, through which the university has provided support for over 100 individuals since its beginning in 1994. The Home Ownership Grant Program—providing a $1,000 university grant matched by $1,000 from Home Head-Quarters—also encourages faculty to live in the area.[7]

Syracuse's business office has undertaken deliberate efforts to support disadvantaged minority- and women-owned business enterprises (MBE/WBE), including training opportunities provided by major contractors and university staff. Contractors are strongly encouraged, but not mandated, to support the institution's goals of inclusion. "We really go above and beyond to assist women and minority business owners," comments Eric Beattie, director of campus planning, design, and construction. "We invite them to bid; if they're not successful, then we sit down afterward and explain how they missed the mark . . . we're trying to get them to a level playing field so they can be competitive." In 2008, 8 percent of Syracuse's purchase orders were issued to MBE/WBE vendors or suppliers. In the last three years, seventeen different firms were successful in bidding and being hired to perform work on twenty-four different projects that were set up with opportunities exclusively for MBE/WBE firms.[8]

Internally, Chancellor Cantor aims to further institutionalize community engagement efforts through embedding collaborative, cross-sector partnerships in every school and college. These efforts are being substantially supported through a five-year, $3 million grant from the Kauffman Foundation for a Campus-Community Entrepreneurship Initiative. Notably, Syracuse has made several policy changes, including alterations to its tenure and promotion guidelines, to encourage engaged scholarship. Cantor knew that she had to face, head on, the policy and practice implications: "The work can't just be on the back of dedicated staff and faculty. It needs to be embedded in the reward structure, and the mission." Today, "Scholarship in Action" is the bold vision of the entire institution. Put simply, Cantor defines this as "intellectual capital focused outward in a mutually beneficial way."[9]

Higgins emphasizes the leadership of the deans and the role of faculty/student engagement in making the chancellor's vision "come to life" and sustaining the initiative: "As courses and projects are developed, and students become regularly engaged in this work, the community realizes that this is not a temporary effort but an integral part of the university's culture, and something they can depend upon."[10]

University of Minnesota, Twin Cities

Perhaps our greatest challenge—and the greatest opportunity—is to strengthen the connection between our research and education missions and the needs of our society.

—Robert H. Bruininks, former president, University of Minnesota (2002–2011), *Inaugural Address: Advancing Knowledge: A Partner for the Public Good,* February 28, 2003, http://www1. umn.edu/pres/00_images/pdf/inaugural_address.pdf (accessed March 27, 2011).

As one of the nation's public land-grant universities, and one of the few located in a major metropolitan area, the University of Minnesota has been officially committed to "service" for over a century. Yet, like many land-grant institutions, the University of Minnesota developed an academic culture that often ran contrary to the idea of playing a public role. Overcoming organization inertia has proved challenging. Peer faculty interviews conducted at the University of Minnesota by Edwin Fogelman and Harry Boyte in 2001 and 2002 found that the "desire for public engagement in scholarly and other activities was widespread. But an equally widespread comment went something like: 'I could never discuss this with my colleagues.' We found strong norms of silence about that. We also found administrators that

---

Figure 10. Minnesota Anchor Approach

Comprehensive Neighborhood Revitalization
- University Northside Partnership and Urban Research and Outreach/Engagement Center (UROC) focus on education, health, and economic development in North Minneapolis

Community Economic Development through Corporate Investment
- Minimum 10% of base contracts to minority- and women-owned business enterprises; 34% inclusion in $2.8 million UROC construction
- Hiring policies for contractors to recruit 29% minorities/women/disabled workers from unions, and local partnerships for apprenticeship training

Local Capacity Building
- Management and technical assistance programs for small businesses and nonprofits through Office of Business and Community Economic Development
- FIPSE grant aimed to enhance capacity and collaboration of existing organizations
- CURA Northside seed grants have linked more than 20 community-identified projects to university resources

- New Business and Technology Center in UROC (includes training and incubator space)

Public Education and Health Partnerships
- 500 Under 5: early childhood intervention program for 500 North Minneapolis children and families
- Medical School Program in Health Disparities Research
- Urban Area Health Education Center designed to introduce youth to health careers

Academic Engagement
- Estimated 100 service-learning courses each year partner with more than 200 nonprofits in and around Twin Cities
- Participatory action research with faculty, students, and community residents
- Community Engagement Scholars Program (20 students/year)

Multi-Anchor, City, and Regional Partnerships
- Leading new Regional Higher Education Consortium

were supportive, in part because university support from the state was declining. We had a feeling there was a lot to build on."[11]

Inspired both by a Kellogg Commission for land-grant institutions in the 1990s and by internal activists such as Boyte and Fogelman, the University of Minnesota began rethinking its role as an engaged land-grant institution. The university's shift toward a vision of itself as an "urban land-grant university" was solidified with a strategic planning process in 2004 that called for an "urban agenda." This process also established Minnesota's goal of becoming one of the world's top three public research universities by 2014.[12] Although these objectives are complementary in an ideal future, wherein public engagement is used to advance the university's research goals, the country's current academic culture (which remains centered on the publishing of papers in academic research journals) creates some tension between Minnesota's two goals.

Subsequent to establishing its urban land-grant vision, structurally, the University of Minnesota took a number of administrative steps to advance its engagement work. One of these was to create the position of associate vice president for public engagement, established in 2006, responsible for promoting and aligning engagement strategies across the university's five campuses and further institutionalizing public engagement across the research, teaching, and outreach functions of the university. Associate Vice President Andrew Furco works to transform the university culture in ways that embrace community engagement as a strategy for producing research of significance, conducting quality teaching, and meeting the needs of the local and broader society. Guiding this position is Senior Vice President Robert J. Jones, who has been deeply invested in the university's comprehensive engagement plan and strategic urban agenda.

Across the campus, there are several dozen units and centers that support this new direction. For example, the university's Office for Business and Community Economic Development (OBCED) has an explicit focus on leveraging university assets and resources to improve economic opportunities for underserved minorities. Established in 1999 by the board of regents "to advance the University's interests in promoting economic development and training opportunities for historically underrepresented groups," it combines business and community development in a single office—something found in few universities. What guided the office's formation, according to its director, Craig Taylor, was the university's acknowledgment that simply relying on undirected university spending to spur community improvement was proving inadequate. "[The university] realized that a focused, intentional, and strategic effort was needed that leverages resources to do much more."[13]

To comply with the Regents' Policy, Taylor created a Small and Targeted Business Program, which, more than a decade later, now requires 10 percent of all base contracts to go to minorities and small businesses. Taylor also established formal policies and procedures to make sure these goals became an integral part of the bidding process. For several of the recent, large capital projects the university has set higher goals. Its new football stadium, for example, saw 23 percent of the $300 million project go to women- and minority-owned businesses.

These efforts paid off when the university decided to establish its first place-based urban research center in North Minneapolis. The targets for the renovation of the Urban Research and Outreach/Engagement Center set a new standard in this area of compliance; the university's usual bottom line of 10 percent was tripled. By the completion of renovation in September 2009, targets for inclusion of women- and minority-owned business enterprises and for women and minority participation in the workforce had exceeded all expectations at 34 percent.[14]

On the purchasing side, the university has become more creative in negotiations with large contractors. For example, when Time Warner approached the university to bid on cable services for student housing, OBCED negotiated that Time Warner provide (1) $50,000 in scholarship funding for students of color; (2) $100,000 toward a Management and Technical Assistance Program for Small Businesses; and (3) hire three women or minority interns every year. Taylor says, "We believe that if the contractors can't hire minority people [directly], then we can use seed capital they provide to create programs that will build capacity and provide technical assistance." The university now uses this strategy with many of its preferred vendors: IBM has committed computers and other hardware, software, and financial support to provide training and technical assistance to small businesses and nonprofits. In fiscal year 2008, $75 million of the $700 million that the university spent on goods and services went to women- and minority-owned businesses. According to Jones, Taylor and OBCED have "really invoked a different way of doing business for the university," including innovative thinking on minority participation, process transparency, and bidding opportunities.[15]

One of the most strategic elements of the university's urban-focused engagement approach was the creation of the University Northside Partnership. This grew out of the university's new urban vision and a series of town hall meetings wherein the residents of North Minneapolis expressed their concern over the university's recruitment of a very high profile researcher who wished to work in their community (the "Northside"). While there was substantial support for the university's presence, there was a small but vocal minority who felt they had not been consulted enough, resulting in a number of protests that grew into a series of difficult dialogues in community meetings with the university. "People were really nervous that the university was going to come in and then leave once they got what they needed," reflects Sherrie Pugh, executive director of the Northside Resident Redevelopment Council.[16] After much discussion, and with the support of a community vote, the University Northside Partnership was formed to not only convene community residents and organizations of North Minneapolis with university faculty and staff, but also to bring representatives from city and county government to the table.[17]

Out of this set of relationships, President Bruininks and Senior Vice President Jones proposed to the university's governing board the idea to establish the first Urban Research and Outreach/Engagement Center (UROC), mentioned above, as a way to anchor the university's presence in the community and to deliver on its mission as an urban research university. UROC focuses on three core areas identified through community discussions and votes: education, health, and community and economic development. Underpinning the university's approach is participatory action research, through which community residents are engaged as collaborative partners working alongside university faculty and staff. This approach has begun to build new, respectful, reciprocal, and sustainable relationships between the university and the North Minneapolis community.

The university administration made a significant financial investment through its purchase of a 21,000-square-foot shopping center to house UROC. Using money from the university's general funds, they purchased the building at fair market value of $1.25 million from the Northside Resident Redevelopment Council. The university invested an additional $2.8 million to renovate the facility and provides an annual operating budget (inclusive of salaries) for UROC of $900,000. UROC also attracted external support before it opened. In fall 2007, a three-year, $750,000 grant from the U.S. Department of Education's Fund for the Improvement of Postsecondary Education (FIPSE) supported the creation of UROC by fostering partnerships in the areas of health, education, and economic development. In addition, OBCED received a $300,000 Empowerment Zone grant in fall 2007 to establish the Business Tech Center now located in UROC.

The establishment of UROC in the Northside takes the university's urban mission formally and physically to the community. Irma McClaurin, who served as UROC's founding executive director (2007–2010), envisioned the building itself to represent a commitment to collaboration. In an early interview she stated, "With UROC we are forging new terrain, [facing] a new frontier if you will, and we're trying to figure out the best way to do that. . . . We can't just replicate the university's Research and Outreach Centers that serve rural Minnesota. And we're not a social service. We are truly trying to establish a partnership where we can be good neighbors. We believe in this place [the Northside] and we're here to stay."[18] The university hopes that its physical presence in North Minneapolis will continue to leverage both public and private investment in the area.

UROC opened its doors in October 2009, with a grand opening in May 2010, and currently houses new and existing university-community partnership programs, including the Center for Early Education and Development's "500 Under 5" early childhood intervention program; the School of Medicine's Center for Health Equity (funded by the National Institutes of Health and significant resources from the university); the first Urban Area Health Education Center designed to introduce youth to health careers; extension programs in urban youth development, nutrition education, and family development; and the University Northside Partnership Community Affairs Committee. OBCED's new Business Tech Center is also located in UROC and provides programs in youth entrepreneurship, small business training, and computer training and refurbishing. The programs at UROC are intended to eventually reach all urban corridors throughout the Twin Cities area. In the words of Senior Vice President Jones, "Since North Minneapolis is where these issues are most acute, we are introducing best practices for our urban engagement here."[19]

Minnesota is also looking to other partners to help drive development in the Northside. "The university wants to inspire, support, and make sure all of the issues are addressed, but not do all of the addressing itself," comments UROC's strategic plan consultant, Reynolds-Anthony Harris of the Lyceum Group. In agreement, Jones says, "We will need support from our partners—city and county government, business, and the philanthropic and nonprofit communities—to sustain these efforts." One such partner, Erik Hansen of the City Department of Community Planning and Economic Development, observes, "UROC is a physical presence that signals commitment, and there is great potential for the programming to really make a difference in the community. . . . There is a nice rapport happening with organizations working in [North Minneapolis] right now—community, city, university, philanthropic—this area hasn't seen that type of commitment in a long time. . . . But you can't undo forty years of neglect in a three-year project. Only time will tell."[20]

Looking toward long-term collaboration, individuals across the university are beginning to better appreciate how community and cultural knowledge can complement academic knowledge. One faculty member described the desired interaction as "vital involvement," with the goal of meaningful engagement where all participants are open to change. There is also a strong sense of having all partners involved in framing the research questions and providing an opportunity for the community to "own the data." Faculty member Sarah Axtell, who holds the relatively new position of community-campus health outreach liaison, speaks about the need for universities to think about the capacity for internal transformation: "In five to ten years, how will the campus be different? Unless there is reciprocal transformation, it is not a true partnership."[21]

LeMoyne-Owen College

> We knew that the college was going to go through changes. As people saw community buildings go up [through the work of the CDC], it has kept hope alive that LeMoyne-Owen wasn't going to close. Most people didn't know they were separate entities. The LeMoyne-Owen CDC is something that the college can be proud of, because it's attached to it and it brings credibility.
>
> —Minister Suhkara, community activist, Soulsville, TN, interview by Rita Axelroth Hodges, Memphis, October 13, 2009

LeMoyne-Owen College is situated in the heart of south Memphis, Tennessee, and is tied closely with the identity of its local community now known as Soulsville. Like many historically black colleges and universities (HBCUs) across the country, LeMoyne-Owen College has provided critical educational and economic opportunities for thousands of African Americans. Indeed, for over one hundred years, the overwhelming majority of Memphis's black leadership came from LeMoyne. Through the realization of integration, particularly at public institutions, however, many HBCUs are struggling to find their niche today. In the early 2000s, LeMoyne-Owen came close to losing its accreditation due to decreased enrollment numbers and significant financial difficulties. The work of the LeMoyne-Owen College Community Development Corporation has played no small part in this HBCU's survival.

LeMoyne-Owen has always been a strong partner with its community, providing needed resources and outreach in K-12 education and public health programs. In 1989, the college established the LeMoyne-Owen College Community Development Corporation (LeMoyne-Owen CDC) to institutionalize its commitment to community investment and improvement. However, it was another ten years before the CDC hired its first executive director, Jeffrey Higgs. From 1999 through 2009, Higgs helped the college secure seven HBCU grants from the Office of University Partnerships at the U.S. Department of Housing and Urban Development (HUD), raising over $150 million total in public and private funds. The CDC has an annual budget today of nearly $5 million and serves as the leader of revitalization efforts in the Soulsville community.

Figure 11. LeMoyne-Owen Anchor Approach

Comprehensive Neighborhood Revitalization
- Establishment of the LeMoyne-Owen College CDC, which focuses on housing, community, and economic development

Community Economic Development through Corporate Investment
- Modest efforts to direct purchasing to support local supply chains

Local Capacity Building
- CDC's revolving loan fund supports emerging small businesses
- CDC's Business Development Institute has graduated 800 people and created 75 businesses and 183 jobs
- CDC's Career Express Program has trained 502 people in highway construction, with a job placement rate over 70%
- Neighborhood residents hired for an estimated 80% of local development projects through CDC
- Homebuyers' training for residents by CDC

Public Education and Health Partnerships
- CDC's Family Life Center provides after-school programs and social services
- Health and Wellness program engages college students as health ambassadors and community peer educators (e.g., delivering asthma education series to more than 200 parents in public or low-income housing)
- Student teachers work with local schools
- Public high school on campus that provides college credit

Academic Engagement
- Small service-learning program and efforts for community-based participatory research
- Community service included in faculty evaluation

Multi-Anchor, City, and Regional Partnerships
- CDC partners with city for low-income housing development

As local neighborhood association president and former LeMoyne-Owen CDC employee Eric Robertson explains, the CDC was established as "the branch to extend the college's arm to the community. We were out there doing education and workshops to the community; we brought the college to the people and made it seem more accessible."[22] Indeed, LeMoyne-Owen College has developed a strong reputation for community development because of the work of its affiliated CDC. The CDC, in turn, has led the effort to rebrand the community—formerly known as LeMoyne Gardens after a large public housing development in the area that was torn down in 1997—as Soulsville, marketing the community's rich cultural history and assets.

Since the hiring of an executive director in 1999, the LeMoyne-Owen CDC has become increasingly independent. In 2001, the CDC began acting as its own fiscal agent, and in 2004, it completely took over management of its accounts. "We think we have a model that works well," says Higgs, "because it insulates the college from a lot of stuff—exposure, liability, and so on—and the community benefits from a lot of things that the college might not otherwise want to be involved in, because they are focused on their mission of education."[23] The CDC's programs and activities, meanwhile, have been concentrated in three core areas—housing, community development, and economic development.[24]

Taking on its first major real estate development—and elevating its work to "an entirely new level of sophistication"—in 2003, the CDC began acquiring properties for the four acres of land where the $11.5 million Towne Center at Soulsville project is now located. The building, completed in 2010, is 77,000 square feet and is aiming to attract a 30,000 square-foot grocery store to the newly built complex. Roughly 30 percent of the remaining space is to be reserved for community residents to have storefronts. Retail and mixed-use commercial space is planned for the first floor, including clothing stores and a food court. "We hope to have goods and services at the Center for residents and visitors that rival anywhere in the county," says Higgs. A one-hundred-seat call center is planned for the second floor, established by the Veterans Corp and National Economic Opportunity Fund. This will provide opportunities for veterans and local residents to start at entry-level jobs and be trained for more advanced skills and salaries. In the spring of 2010, the CDC staff moved to the new space, and the regional health clinic will soon follow. All in all, the CDC expects the Towne Center to create over 200 jobs. The CDC is working on a façade program with existing small businesses in the area to be able to compete with the new retail.[25]

The Towne Center aims to be an anchor in bringing sustainable, mixed-use, and mixed-income development back to Soulsville. An eleven-house subdivision is being built adjacent to the Towne Center to be sold at market rate for middle-income families. With the model home presold for $250,000 in 2007—in a neighborhood with an average sales price of around $33,000 in 2000—the CDC's efforts certainly seem to be catalyzing the market. Investment in the project includes $2 million from the CDC's own equity, $500,000 from a federal appropriation, $2 million in new markets tax credits, and another $5 million in personal debt from Wachovia Bank, private funds, as well as other federal, city and county resources. The LeMoyne-Owen CDC will retain 100 percent ownership of the building. "This is truly a public-private partnership," comments Higgs. "It is also the first major development in the area, so it is important for us to see it through."[26]

To support local entrepreneurs, the LeMoyne-Owen CDC runs a Business Development Institute. An average of thirty students enroll every quarter in the ten-week course that is offered free to residents in Soulsville and throughout Memphis. This program is directed by the CDC's chief financial officer, Austin Emeagwai, who also serves as an assistant professor of accounting at the college. (Emeagwai teaches two courses at LeMoyne-Owen but receives release time to serve in this capacity at the CDC.) Emeagwai, who also has a private CPA practice, and other professionals from across the city teach the business courses. Funded through a Small Business Administration (SBA) Program for Investment in Micro-Entrepreneurs (PRIME) grant, at least 50 percent of the grant dollars must go to low-income individuals. The LeMoyne-Owen CDC's program exceeds these expectations, serving approximately 75 percent low-income, 70 percent females, and 90 percent minorities. Since 2002, 800 people have graduated from the program, and seventy-five businesses and 183 jobs have been created. The CDC hopes to offer incubator space for seven emerging small businesses within the new Towne Center.

As part of their SBA grant, the CDC is also a micro-lender for West Tennessee. In its early years, the CDC's revolving loan pool experienced an 80–90 percent repayment rate. As of February 2007, the CDC had made thirty-three loans valued at roughly $830,000. Over time, however, some entrepreneurs went out of business. By 2009, the CDC had $700,000 in outstanding loans, and thus, they have not been able to make many new loans in recent years.[27]

Since 2005, LeMoyne-Owen CDC has been collaborating with the Tennessee Department of Transportation on a statewide job-training program. In 2009, the program received additional funding through a grant from the American Recovery and Reinvestment Act. Working in the Soulsville neighborhood in Memphis, and in three other cities across the state (with local CDC partners), LeMoyne-Owen CDC provides a sixteen-week program in life skills and on-the-job training in highway construction. The program is geared toward recipients of Temporary Assistance for Needy Families, high school dropouts, and ex-offenders. In its first four years, the program served 502 individuals, with a job placement rate over 70 percent; in 2009, the placement rate exceeded 80 percent statewide.[28]

Higgs hopes to create wealth for Soulsville residents through homeownership. To date, the LeMoyne-Owen CDC has built fourteen new affordable homes in Soulsville, and rehabbed seven others (with most of this work completed from 2002 to 2004). The CDC provides extensive homebuyers training with residents to prepare them for ownership, and thus, according to the CDC leadership, the recent foreclosure crisis has been less acute for their "clients." The neighborhood as a whole has been unable to avoid this national trend. Community input—formalized through the Community Action Coalition—has helped shape the CDC's activities. For example, the CDC initially intended to build multifamily rental development, but when the Coalition indicated that the community instead wanted more single-family homeownership opportunities, the CDC heeded this request. The CDC's next real estate initiative will likely involve redevelopment of eighteen lots, many of them vacant, at the entrance to the neighborhood from downtown.[29]

Within the college, service-learning courses and other scholarly activities engage LeMoyne-Owen students and faculty from multiple disciplines. A Health and Wellness Program, for example, engages college students as health ambassadors who conduct community-based participatory research. Students also serve as community peer educators through the Partnership for Asthma Trigger-Free Homes, a program in partnership with Abt Associates to provide educational workshops to families in public and low-income housing. "We create leadership opportunities for our students and set expectations for their involvement in the community," says sociology professor Femi Ajanaku.[30]

The CDC is looking to further institutionalize its collaboration with the college, partly by expanding its student internship program—through which students participate in a semester-long paid internship with the CDC or another local community group while often receiving service-learning credit—as well as developing a stronger community development curriculum to be offered at the college. For now, there remains great opportunity to more strategically align the college's outreach efforts (and its existing capital expenditures) with the community development work of the LeMoyne-Owen CDC; however, many of these outreach programs have weakened in recent years because of financial and staffing limitations at the college. As LeMoyne-Owen implements its 2008 Transformation Plan, the college is looking to increase its community engagement efforts and "claim a leadership 'niche' in urban higher education by building on our expertise in teaching urban students and catalyzing urban community development."[31] First, however, the college must continue to build its enrollment and guarantee survival. Meanwhile, the LeMoyne-Owen CDC seems well positioned to help gradually transform Soulsville into the vibrant, mixed-income community it was fifty years ago.

Emory University

> What we have done is select five to six communities that are our focus areas, where we can pair community-based [scholarship and learning] with our investments to better meet the needs of our neighborhoods. Not in two years, not in five years, but over a decade or more, then we'll have a long enough longitudinal set of data to know if we are succeeding. [So far], no one has had the patience to stay the course long enough to know what works or what doesn't.
>
> —Earl Lewis, provost, Emory University, interview by Steve Dubb, Atlanta, June 17, 2009

Emory might seem an unlikely case to be included in a study of community-university partnerships. Traditionally, Emory has been home to Atlanta's *white* elite. So much is this the case that Emory still sometimes finds itself having to downplay its old reputation as the "chill on the hill."[32] Nonetheless, Emory has gradually moved to prioritize minority and low-income areas of Atlanta in its community development strategy and, precisely because of its traditional role as an elite southern private school, Emory has the capacity to bring significant resources to the effort. As of 2009, Emory's endowment ranked sixteenth in the nation and stood, even after the 2008 financial crash, at \$4.3 billion.[33]

To date, Emory does not have signature multi-million-dollar projects. The one major exception came as a crisis response. Recognizing the critical role that Atlanta's publicly owned Grady Hospital (at which roughly a third of Emory medical faculty work) plays in providing health care for Atlanta's least fortunate, Emory agreed in December 2008 to forgive \$20 million of the \$62 million in debt it was owed from the hospital as part of a community effort to restore the hospital to fiscal health. Emory's action is particularly remarkable

---

Figure 12. Emory Anchor Approach

Comprehensive Neighborhood Revitalization
- Office of University Community Partnerships moving toward place-based strategy in five low-income neighborhoods of Greater Atlanta

Community Economic Development through Corporate Investment
- Focus on sustainability: 48% of produce purchased locally
- \$20 million debt forgiveness to help maintain the viability of Grady Hospital, Atlanta's leading charity hospital

Local Capacity Building
- Support to existing community development organizations, with continuity provided through OUCP
- OUCP hires from within the community development community
- Community Building and Social Change Fellows Program involves multiyear ongoing partnerships

- Resource development in immigrant communities, such as immigrant radio station (Sagal Radio)
- Neighborhood indicators and data provision for community development initiatives

Public Education and Health Partnerships
- Individual faculty projects, loosely coordinated

Academic Engagement
- Service-learning participation high: 24% campus-wide; 100% School of Nursing; 87% Theology; 85% Public Health

Multi-Anchor, City, and Regional Partnerships
- Community development partnership effort led by community foundation in formation
- OUCP hosts Equity Atlanta (now Partnership for Southern Equity), a public policy and foreclosure mitigation coalition
- Developing urban health initiative with local place-based foundation coalition

considering that it came just months after the September 2008 world financial panic had sent endowment values tumbling.[34]

At Emory, the notion of service has a strong echo, in part because Emory comes out of a Methodist tradition. Although highly secular today—theology professor David Jenkins claims that most students would ask, "What's Methodist?" if one mentioned Emory's religious denomination—Emory remains home to the Candler School of Theology, which enrolls approximately 425 divinity students in its three-year program. The Candler School itself requires all of its first-year divinity students to do eight hours a week of a non-church ministry, which involves a mix of pastoral and social service work. Service sites include three area hospitals, Metro State Women's Prison, the Poverty Rights Center, and the Decatur Cooperative Ministry, a homeless shelter.[35]

The Candler School is hardly unique in its service work. The School of Nursing at Emory requires that all students, be they undergraduate or graduate, have "a service-learning experience at least once in their academic career." Campus-wide, 24 percent of Emory College undergraduate students engage in "community-benefiting activities" as part of their coursework. At some of the professional schools, these numbers are much higher. Participation in the School of Nursing, of course, is 100 percent since community learning is a requirement, but numbers are also high in theology (87 percent) and public health (85 percent).[36]

While Emory's service numbers are impressive, the path from "presence" to "impact," as Emory's Associate Vice Provost for Academic and Strategic Partnerships Alicia Franck puts it, has been complicated.[37] Indeed, Emory has pursued two paths that have operated largely independently of each other. One, the Clifton Community Partnership, aims to improve relations with Emory's immediate, largely middle-class neighbors. Meanwhile, Emory's community outreach and partnership center has focused on building relationships in low-income neighborhoods.

The Clifton Community Partnership, as Emory's Associate Vice President of Finance David Hanson explains, was prompted by the fact that Emory for years "had not had the best relationship with the community." The Clifton initiative, which focuses resources within a three-mile radius of Emory, was formally established in spring 2006. The partnership has helped plan an 870-unit housing project (with 20 percent of the units set aside to be sold at below-market rates), has conducted planning charrettes that have resulted in many neighborhood streetscape projects, and coordinates an advisory council that oversees Emory partnership programs with the local schools. Hanson estimates the initial annual cost to Emory at close to $1 million a year. Now, Hanson says, the need for expensive planning consultants has diminished, but the university continues to pay about $500,000 a year for core staff.[38]

While the Clifton Partnership has focused on Emory's immediate neighborhood, the Office of University Community Partnerships (OUCP) has concentrated on the more impoverished sections of metro Atlanta. Founded in 2000, in its early years OUCP was a small center with three full-time staff and one part-time employee. In 2002, OUCP began to run an innovative program directed at community building and social change. The exact shape of that program has changed over time, but the basic theme of having a small, dedicated groups of students, guided by faculty and graduate students and working in teams on intensive summer projects, has stayed fairly consistent. Community Building and Social Change fellows now receive a stipend of $3,500 to work thirty-two hours a week during the summer (an effective wage rate of roughly nine dollars an hour) as well as free housing and a summer tuition waiver.[39]

The fellows' projects vary, but they are designed in close consultation with community partners—indeed, the three 2009 project teams each worked in one of the three priority areas identified by Atlanta's place-based funders (including the Community Foundation of Greater Atlanta and three foundations that have concentrated grants in these neighborhoods). One year's projects at Emory build on previous years. Kate Grace, OUCP's director of the Community Building and Social Change Fellows Program, notes, "In the first few years, there were open calls for proposals. Now we have shifted to longer-term partnerships with community groups. This has benefits for the students—they can see how they fit into a longer continuum—and it also better matches the needs of the organizations." Indeed, two of the three focus areas in 2009 were also focus areas in 2002. As Nathaniel Smith, OUCP's director of partnerships and research for equitable development, puts it, "It is how we operate at OUCP . . . We build relationships with the community."[40]

In 2006, Emory's administration committed to invest $12 million over five years to boost OUCP's ability to link Emory with the community. This has enabled OUCP to expand its staff from three-and-a-half to thirteen positions. With this opportunity, OUCP has given priority to hiring employees who have worked with community groups and thus are able to serve as effective liaisons or translators between the university and the community.[41]

Adding staff has allowed OUCP to boost its capacity in two key areas: (1) data analysis, such as the ability to use geographic information systems (GIS) mapping tools, which enables OUCP to be a key data supplier for community groups, nonprofit organizations, and government agencies working in Atlanta neighborhoods; and (2) convening and community outreach. For example, in 2008, OUCP agreed to act as the host of "Equity Atlanta," a regional alliance of community groups, nonprofit organizations, and government agencies that are working with the national group PolicyLink on regional equity and equitable development in metropolitan Atlanta. In 2010, Equity Atlanta (now Partnership for Southern Equity) helped spearhead efforts to ensure that funds provided by the 2009 economic stimulus bill reached disadvantaged neighborhoods.[42]

The level of trust OUCP has built up among community groups is impressive and has enabled OUCP to play a broker role that few universities are positioned to provide. "People are showing a greater willingness to coordinate their activities," notes OUCP director Michael Rich. "Our role is to provide research, data, and try to work as a matchmaker. Where are the communities in most need? Can we find a way to develop a holistic coordinated approach? Can we help build local capacity for planning and action?"[43]

At the same time, Emory faces broader challenges as it struggles to implement a new, more focused, place-based approach. Rich notes that, in 2008, Emory "had school projects involving forty-two school districts and 350-plus schools across Georgia. We are now trying to adopt a place-based strategy that better aligns Emory's resources with [specific communities and schools] that need help and assistance." In particular, Emory has chosen to focus on five geographic areas: Edgewood, East Lake, Pittsburgh-Mechanicsville (or, more broadly speaking, Neighborhood Planning Unit V),[44] Northwest Atlanta, and Clarkson in central DeKalb County. The first three neighborhoods correspond with areas of focus of Atlanta's place-based funders (two family-based foundations and the Annie E. Casey Foundation's Atlanta Civic Site), while Northwest Atlanta and Clarkson represent two other neighborhoods where OUCP has been engaged since nearly its founding. The Emory administration is on-board with the approach. David Hanson notes that these days, when one talks about community at Emory, "We are normally talking about Greater Atlanta. It is a balanced approach. In the early years, we focused a lot on the immediate community relationships [in the Clifton Corridor], which were not great. Now we think more broadly."[45]

Looking across the Cases

Creating an Engaged Community

Syracuse, Emory, and Minnesota are immediately surrounded by middle- to upper-middle-income neighborhoods. Yet all three have chosen to focus university resources in non-adjacent, underserved, and impoverished communities as a part of their broader engagement agendas. Syracuse University has taken on the entire city as its "neighborhood," most visibly seen through its leadership in the Connective Corridor, while maintaining focused neighborhood initiatives in the South Side and Near West Side. Minnesota also takes on a view of the larger community. As Andrew Furco puts it, "We are the only research university in all of Minnesota, and a public institution—ultimately, we have responsibility to address issues across the state."[46] Minnesota also partners with the neighborhood organizations and business associations directly surrounding its campus, through the University District Partnership Alliance. Minnesota's urban efforts, on the other hand, are being manifested through its work in North Minneapolis—a community located six miles from campus that is one of Minneapolis's most diverse and most economically challenged. Whereas Syracuse has intentionally designed the Connective Corridor to extend to the Near West Side, as well as expanded its employer-assisted housing programs to the area, the University of Minnesota's homebuyers program is focused exclusively in the University District, and until the recent construction of UROC in North Minneapolis, there had been no efforts to physically connect the campus and the Northside community.[47]

For many years, Emory has engaged in partnerships with the surrounding upper-middle-class Druid Hills and Clifton Corridor neighborhoods, which has absorbed considerable time and energy. Emory, especially through OUCP, however, has begun to direct its mission—and resources—to target specific low-income neighborhoods in Greater Atlanta. Unfortunately, Emory's failure to do this before 2009 has reduced the impact of interventions, as well as limited opportunities for institutional resources to be strategically invested.

LeMoyne-Owen College stands alone among this group, as the work of the LeMoyne-Owen CDC is focused almost exclusively on revitalizing the community surrounding the campus now known as Soulsville. As Bob Fockler, president of the Community Foundation of Greater Memphis, puts it, the college is "in and part of this" historically underserved neighborhood, which has a strong African American heritage and soul music legacy, and is located just a couple of miles from downtown Memphis.[48] Therefore, the connection between the welfare of LeMoyne-Owen College and its community is more immediate than at Syracuse, Minnesota, or Emory.

Establishing Partnership Programs and Goals

Syracuse, Minnesota, and LeMoyne-Owen are reaching toward comprehensive neighborhood revitalization, while Emory's efforts are more focused on neighborhood capacity building. Education and health partnerships are strong at all four of these institutions, as is some degree of service-learning or academic engagement. Some of these curricular and project-based partnerships are in support of the larger community development agenda; others are only loosely connected. Neighborhood and nonprofit capacity building is prioritized among all institutions in this cluster.

Syracuse University's engagement initiatives, in particular, maintain strong principles and rhetoric of sustainability and community ownership. The Near West Side Initiative in Syracuse builds on the strengths of each member organization and the assets of the neighborhood. "NWSI has strong institutional partners, with their own missions and their own tools," comments Higgins. "Instead of the traditional process of setting up a 501(c)3 (hiring a director, etc.), we decided, no, let's make sure the resources are really going into the neighborhood. So the five main entities each dedicate staff to work on this effort." The university marches forward with real estate development, home renovations, and student and faculty engagement, while the Gifford Foundation has taken on the process of community capacity building. "There is a constant tension trying to keep residents' voices heard, while keeping the engine going around real estate development," says Goldfarb-Finding. "You have to really balance the capacity needs of the neighborhood with very real economic needs. Neighborhood development takes a long time; real estate development, relatively, takes no time at all."[49]

Syracuse has also taken on the largest education initiative among this cluster, through its partnership with Say Yes to Education and the Syracuse City School District. In this district-wide program for public school students, university volunteers and interns provide mentoring, curriculum, and even legal support, according to Rachel Gazdick, executive director for the Say Yes to Education Syracuse Chapter. Syracuse also leads a network of twenty-three private institutions and nearly one hundred New York public institutions to offer a free college education for any student who graduates through the Say Yes program. By building stronger schools and a stronger workforce, Syracuse Say Yes to Education intends to serve not only as a model of urban education reform but also of urban economic development.[50]

Prior to the establishment of the University Northside Partnership or the Urban Research and Outreach/Engagement Center, the University of Minnesota's Center for Urban and Regional Affairs (CURA) had been involved in North Minneapolis for forty years. CURA is the university's oldest center for institutionalized community engagement efforts, founded to match community requests with university resources, particularly responding to the "demands" from low-income and minority communities, many of which were located in the Northside.[51] The launch of the University Northside Partnership (UNP) in 2005 signified the first university-wide, administrative-led, collaborative effort with the community. After much discussion with the community, the Urban Research and Outreach/Engagement Center (UROC) was then established to serve as the anchor mechanism through which university resources could be coordinated in North Minneapolis.

Minnesota's commitment to an urban vision is manifested through UNP and UROC and is focused on three key areas identified by the community as priorities—education, health and wellness, and community and economic development. Those involved in UROC, and others like CURA with its deep connections to North Minneapolis, hope that matching community-identified priorities with university resources will enable them to strategically see solutions to the complex and most pressing issues facing North Minneapolis and other urban communities in the Twin Cities, and track measurable outcomes. This alignment is not always easy; according to a report prepared by consultants from the Lyceum Group, faculty have their own agendas, and when establishing new university-wide centers, there is sensitivity as to who was doing what first. Some programs have chosen to keep their distance from the effort to coordinate urban engagement at an institutional level because they have already established their own relationships and partners in the community and believe they would not necessarily benefit from greater university alignment.[52] On the other hand, the Lyceum report also suggests that the community would like to see greater coordination of the university's efforts, and have better access to the reports and findings that result from individual research projects.[53]

Emory's community development partnership efforts have had transformational effects on partner organizations. Andy Schneggenburger, executive director of the Atlanta Housing Association of Neighborhood-based Developers, the city's association of community development corporations, explains the reasons for Emory's high standing. "The ability to have access to the resources of Emory through OUCP is a tremendous help," Schneggenburger notes. "They are very aware of the resources that they have and the importance of not enforcing an approach or attitude toward community work. They are very congruent in the need to let the community's voice be heard and play a primary role in the decision-making process."[54] But while Emory's OUCP office has strong connections to community groups, OUCP is just beginning the process of coordinating partnerships in specific regions to achieve more concentrated impact. At present, many Emory health and educational partnerships, for example, are individual faculty projects that are loosely coordinated, rather than strategic interventions.

LeMoyne-Owen College's community development efforts are directed through its affiliated CDC, while the college oversees opportunities for students to be engaged in service-learning, health and education outreach, and urban leadership. In addition to its housing and economic development activities, the CDC runs a Family Life Center, providing after-school programs and social services, particularly for boys with behavioral problems. With a strong teacher education program, the college also provides tutoring and student teaching to local schools as well as operates a public high school on campus that provides minority students an opportunity to earn both a high school diploma and two years of college credit.[55] Because of the focus on the Soulsville community, these efforts present a holistic approach to neighborhood revitalization; however, the outreach activities of the college and the CDC remain largely distinct.

Institutionalizing an Anchor Vision

To a large extent, Minnesota and Syracuse have aligned their institutional priorities for engagement, from top administration through partnership centers to faculty and staff. Due in large part to its size and broad land-grant mission, however, Minnesota continues to have urban-focused partnership efforts that remain diffuse and disconnected; the establishment of UROC as a coordinating entity is an attempt to correct this situation and invest strategically in local urban communities. Emory's community partnership center and the LeMoyne-Owen College CDC, on the other hand, have strong support from their respective administrations, but remain largely "siloed" in their focused missions and activities.

When Nancy Cantor became president and chancellor of Syracuse University, she pushed a new philosophy throughout the university: that scholarship in action was critical to a vibrant local community and economy, and mutually beneficial for the institution and its partners. This took Syracuse to a new level, although many throughout the university were already committed to community engagement and economic inclusion. "This has always been a belief of ours; no one had to sell this to us, but it did take on a new emphasis with Cantor. It became more of a priority for the entire institution," comments Louis Marcoccia, Syracuse's executive vice president and chief financial officer. Marilyn Higgins's role as Syracuse's vice president for community engagement and economic development puts her in a critical position of power for bringing the university's resources to bear on key community initiatives. And as chair of the Near West Side Initiative board Higgins provides critical oversight of the real estate development in this community, as well as engages faculty, staff, and students in the comprehensive revitalization efforts. "Our students are deeply engaged in the NWSI . . . in real problem solving—feet on the ground—engaged scholarship. I would estimate that over the past three years the number [of students involved] is close to 400."[56]

Minnesota's administration is committed to public engagement and to its urban vision in particular. "It's not enough to be a land-grant . . . we have to more strategically focus our resources and expertise with the community and with others' resources and expertise," says Senior Vice President Jones. Jones was appointed by university president Bob Bruininks, who served in this position from 2002 through 2011, and whose scholarly work in child psychology made him a strong leader for community engagement.[57] Central to a new policy adopted by the board of regents in 1999 governing university purchases was creation of the Office of Business and Community Economic Development (OBCED). The administration's no-tolerance policy on discrimination has further supported the OBCED director in creating innovative and sustainable initiatives. Probably the most significant change at the university, which has not been replicated elsewhere, is the board of regents' approval of changes to the tenure and promotion policy to now include scholarship that promotes "ideas of significance and value to society" and teaching that is "not limited to classroom instruction" among its criteria for tenure and promotion.[58]

Emory's Office of University Community Partnerships has significant support from the administration and a growing budget, despite university-wide cutbacks. The Center's director, however, is not an associate vice president (as at many of the other institutions in this study), which inherently limits some institutional alignment. Moreover, at least until this was clarified in 2009, there had been some conflict and confusion in Emory's strategic direction with respect to the community between those who emphasize relations in the narrow three-mile radius around campus and those who see a mission to serve the needs of the disadvantaged neighborhoods of Greater Atlanta.

When then-president Burnett Joiner established the LeMoyne-Owen CDC in 1989, it was originally staffed and operated by the college dean and faculty on a part-time basis. Although the initiative received strong support from top administration, little was achieved without dedicated staff. Now a distinct entity from the college, the CDC maintains a leadership team of at least six full-time staff. The college president and two vice presidents sit on the LeMoyne-Owen CDC's board of directors. "One of the big advantages is that the CDC doesn't have to wait for our college board to meet to move its ideas and projects forward," remarks college President Johnnie B. Watson. Beyond board representation and limited involvement of faculty and students in CDC programming, there is no formal structure in place through which the college is involved in the CDC's community development work.[59]

Securing Funding and Leveraging Resources

Financial commitments toward community development from the four institutions in this cluster, while limited in comparison to Penn, Yale, and Cincinnati, are not insignificant and have attracted major public and private investments. University trustees have also played a strong role. According to Chancellor Cantor, Syracuse's trustees "get the idea of a place-based institution, both the pragmatic and ethical responsibility." They were excited about the $13.8 million loan repayment being redeployed to the Near West Side Initiative (NWSI), which has attracted significant public and private investment. Trustees also raised $350,000 in tuition scholarships for Say Yes to Education when the state fell through on providing these funds. Cantor has learned, however, that "in an economic crisis, you have to hone in on the rhetoric about why this work is good for the institution. When we're talking about salary freezes, but still carrying out our neighborhood initiatives, I have to explain." Although significant in-kind support will continue to filter through Higgins's office, the Center of Excellence, and other faculty, the NWSI hopes to be self-sustaining.[60]

Minnesota made a significant financial investment of over $3 million to purchase and renovate the new UROC building and an additional $900,000 annually for UROC's operations. Half of the Office of Business and Community Economic Development's $1.5 million budget also comes directly from university administration (with the other half coming from grants and contracts). In 2009, Minnesota used over $700,000 of its resources to serve as a match to a federal grant proposal and became the only university to receive funds through the Department of Commerce Broadband Technology Opportunity Program. The $2.9 million, three-year grant will be administered through UROC in collaboration with OBCED and a community partner, Minnesota Multicultural Media Consortium. It will provide for nine existing public computer centers in empowerment and enterprise zones in Minneapolis and St. Paul to receive new equipment, furniture, training, and staffing, and for two new centers to be established, including one in a public housing facility. This "demonstration model" also will result in job creation for community members as UROC broadband apprentices.[61]

LeMoyne-Owen College began the work of its CDC with modest operating funds nearly twenty years ago. From 1999 through 2009, it received seven HBCU grants (most recently, $800,000 in 2009) and raised nearly $150 million total in private and public funding. Starting in 2001, the CDC has acted as its own fiscal agent, with the college serving as the conduit through which HUD HBCU funds could be accessed. "The HBCU funds still have the least restrictions, which is a major advantage," says Emeagwai. "They've allowed us to acquire, demolish, build, and purchase assets." The CDC's largest real estate effort, the $11.5 million Towne Center project, has brought in numerous public and private resources, including a $7.3 million loan from the Wachovia Community Development Finance group using new markets tax credits and federal grants through the Economic Development Administration, Office of Community Services, and Office of University Partnerships. "It is still a challenge that it requires so much public investment to attract the private sector," comments Robert Lipscomb, director of the City of Memphis Division of Housing and Community Development and executive director of the Memphis Housing Authority, as well as chair of LeMoyne-Owen College's board of trustees. The college's financial support for the CDC has primarily involved in-kind donation of office space, utilities, and technology support. Regarding the college's direct investment in community development, Lipscomb adds, "We would like to see the college even more involved: more technical assistance to small businesses, more summer programming for kids and families . . . But it's a matter of resources— how to identify the dollars to do that. The trustees have bigger concerns right now—mainly, can we sustain this business model for the college? It's about survival."[62]

Emory's community partnership center has support from the administration and a growing budget. Staff has grown from three-and-a-half to thirteen since 2002. Its budget has also grown to over $2 million a year, and, in 2009, when other departments got cutbacks, the administration reaffirmed its support and held funding nearly constant, though small cuts did occur.

Building a Culture of Economic Inclusion

Both Syracuse and Minnesota have taken very deliberate efforts toward economic inclusion and are using their economic and purchasing power to create opportunities for local, minority, and women business owners. "When utilizing small, inexperienced contractors and vendors for the first time, the university is required to provide significantly more supervision," says Marcoccia of Syracuse. "Until practices and processes are fully understood by both parties, the chance is greater for error or misunderstanding. By increasing communication and physical supervision efforts, practices and processes become routine. . . . We had concerns in the past of whether [economic inclusion programs] would work, but now we are pretty confident."[63]

Also inspired by a positive track record and the university's new urban vision, Minnesota's Office of Business and Community Economic Development has created unprecedented policies and goals for the university's capital projects, purchasing/supply chain, and job creation. Director Craig Taylor aims to leverage additional university assets and resources— intellectual property, research, and technology transfer—to impact the quality of life in local communities as well as shift the university's business practices. The unusually high targets (over 30 percent) set for the renovation of UROC, in particular, can serve as a model for how the university can be inclusive—every aspect of UROC's development involved community engagement.

Emory University, on the other hand, has not given much focus to the impact of its business practices on local or underserved populations. There are some institutional efforts to buy food locally, but (like Portland State) the university largely focuses on sustainability—an important issue at a campus that has the most square feet of LEED-certified buildings of any university in the United States—rather than community economic development. Ciannat Howett, Emory's director of sustainability, notes, "We are trying to flex our muscles in the marketplace in relationship to food to influence what supply is available. We certainly aren't to our 75 percent goal yet, but we have a written plan, we are working with our food vendors . . . It is in process—we've increased our purchases of local food significantly—48 percent of produce is locally purchased." But Howett concedes that purchasing is "one of the areas we have done the least at Emory historically." Ozzie Harris, senior vice provost for community and diversity at Emory, also acknowledges that Emory is still at the early stages of aligning its business practices with its partnership work, but wants to move in this direction. "Hiring, recruitment, procurement—we should at least take the easy steps," Harris says.[64]

Because LeMoyne-Owen's community development efforts are directed through its CDC, all related activities are geared toward creating local economic opportunities. Its new Towne Center, for example, plans to create over 200 new jobs, incubate new businesses, and provide services for all residents. "We've said to the tenants that we expect you to hire locally. It's in the language to [our funders]. Urban economic development is about hiring locally—that's what we do," says Higgs. Through agreements with contractors, the CDC has also helped employ residents from the neighborhood on an estimated 80 percent of local development projects. The college itself now owns a decent amount of property in the neighborhood, including a recent purchase of a vacant lot for new student dorms, which was turned over to the CDC to develop and manage—a $5 or $6 million project. Although the CDC has reached great measures of success in building economic opportunities, local leaders agree that more must still be done to build community wealth through workforce and business development.[65]

Sustaining Participatory Planning and Robust Community Relationships

All four of these institutions have spent time developing relationships with their local neighborhoods as well as involved residents and other stakeholders in the planning of their community development initiatives. At Syracuse and Emory, in particular, the institutions have strived to be invisible leaders in their partnerships—the focus is on the partner and the community, not the university. For example, Nancy Cantor's first year at Syracuse was called "Discovering the Soul of Syracuse." She spent her first sixteen to eighteen months on campus going to church dinners and neighborhood gatherings and listening to the voice of the community. "She told them, 'Where we have excellence and can have impact, we will work with you. It's good for us, and it's good for you, and we want it to be sustainable,'" reflects Bogucz.[66]

"We've seen in other cities that when the university is the gorilla in the room, people are just habituated to go with what they want. Not here. [In Syracuse], there is a healthy give-and-take. The university provides a fulcrum through which strategy and vision can be catalyzed through resources they have that wouldn't otherwise be available," comment Frank Caliva and Kevin Schwab from the Metropolitan Development Association of Syracuse and Central New York.[67]

As discussed previously, the University of Minnesota spent over two years in dialogue about the potential of having a physical presence in the community before UROC was agreed upon. Although the community's desire to establish a community benefits agreement has yet to be realized, the university has established several activities that have provided ongoing opportunities for communication and collaboration. UNP work groups, FIPSE work groups, the Community Affairs Committee, and participatory action research groups are four specific initiatives that engage community residents, who work alongside university faculty and staff on focused neighborhood projects. Most significantly, UROC's strategic planning process to set direction for its first three years was inclusive of community voices from beginning to end. Guided by a Futures Conference model, led by the founding executive director Irma McClaurin and Erline Belton of the Lyceum Group, the strategic planning process included a two-day conference attended by over fifty community residents, leaders, and elected officials to envision what UROC might be in the future. Afterward, an Action Planning Team comprised of fifteen members (the majority of whom were from the community) crafted six goals, a set of belief statements, and the guidance partnership principles that are the cornerstone of UROC's three-year strategic plan. In draft form, the plan has been shared with those who attended the original conference, focus groups, and faculty. At every stage, a draft of the plan was available online for everyone to follow its development. "Transparency is what we have aimed for, in the building (which has glass windows in the front and back) and throughout the strategic planning process," says McClaurin.[68]

Critical to effective communication and trusting relationships is having "translators" on staff. In this vein, LeMoyne-Owen College perhaps has the most direct relations with its community. President Johnnie B. Watson grew up in the LeMoyne Gardens housing project, across the street from his current office. He and his five sisters all attended LeMoyne-Owen. Minister Suhkara A. Yahweh, who has played a significant role in the evolution of the college's community development initiatives, has been a community activist for several decades. Managed expectations and strong communication have helped keep residents content. "This community understands that development takes time," says the minister. "I also let them know about roadblocks. They feel they have input, and it keeps our efforts visible. After forty-one years here, I've got my fingerprints on all changes. I have a reputation and respect in this community."[69] Although the LeMoyne-Owen CDC director himself is not from the neighborhood, Higgs spent his first months on the job meeting all the leaders from the community and establishing relationships. He also formalized the Community Action Coalition, a group of resident stakeholders who advise and guide the work of the CDC. Over his ten years at the CDC, Higgs has established deep trust throughout the community.

Notably, Emory's Office of University Community Partnerships has always valued the role of translators. With its expanded budget and staff, OUCP has hired from within the community development community. It also ensures continuity in its partnerships and has been very effective in building nonprofit capacity. The fellows program, for example, involves small teams of undergraduates working with three nonprofit partners each year, providing ongoing connections with many of these community-based organizations. Guided proposals for students and faculty, rather than open calls, have also helped ensure continuity and increase impact. This has helped establish Emory's OUCP as a trusted partner with Atlanta-area CDCs, a phenomenon unknown to many universities, even if Emory as a whole still has not fully lived down its reputation as the home of the Atlanta elite.

The University of Minnesota has several liaisons with community organizing back-grounds. One of these people is Makeda Zulu-Gillespie, university-community liaison for the University Northside Partnership and UROC, whose involvement started when she was working as a community organizer for a CDC in North Minneapolis. When the university approached the CDC about working together, she helped initiate critical meetings between the university and the larger community. Along with a community resident, Zulu-Gillespie now co-chairs the Community Affairs Committee, which serves as the working body of the UNP. The UROC building has also begun to serve as a "physical translator" between the university and the North Minneapolis neighborhood.

Another physical translator is Syracuse's "The Warehouse," a former furniture ware-house at the western edge of downtown and neighboring the Near West Side, which the university purchased and renovated in 2005—an action driven by the vision of Mark Robbins, dean of the School of Architecture. The Warehouse now serves as a multiuse facility that brings 600 students, faculty, and staff into the central business district on a regular basis. Syracuse's Office of Community Engagement and Economic Development (overseeing the NWSI and the Connective Corridor) and COLAB (a new interdisciplinary initiative based in the College of Visual and Performing Arts) are housed at the Warehouse. In addition, 20 percent of the building space is reserved for community activities, including a gallery for local artists and a lecture hall for public events. Robbins also initiated an international design competition that has led to construction of three of the nation's most innovative green homes in the Near Westside.[70]

Meeting the Needs of Low-Income Residents and Neighborhoods

With goals of comprehensive neighborhood revitalization, these institutions have had to be patient with their desires for change in the quality of life and economic opportunities for local residents. The LeMoyne-Owen CDC's perseverance and leadership over the last ten years has begun to realize tangible impacts. "I measure our success by per capita income. In 1999, it was $8,000 in this neighborhood," says Higgs. "Now, it is $13,500 and climbing." Tk Buchanan, senior research associate for the Center for Community Building and Neigh-borhood Action at the University of Memphis, confirms that "the 'poorest of the poor' [in the zip code containing Soulsville] have also made progress: in 2009, 47.3% of tax filers made less than $10,001; yet, in 2000, that figure was higher, at 68%." The CDC continues to work to increase homeownership and support workforce and business development in Soulsville. "The goal is to be self-containing, self-sustaining, and self-maintaining," says Minister Suh-kara. However, the community has not been able to escape national trends resulting from the subprime mortgage and foreclosure crisis. Buchanan observes, "Before the foreclosure crisis, the LeMoyne-Owen CDC was among the most proactive, effective CDCs in our city and did great work creating homeownership opportunities for their service area. Post-housing-disaster, they're bailing water as fast as they can, but this knocks them (and their homeownership agenda) back a few decades." Despite these setbacks, significant community development and rebranding efforts led by the CDC have caused attitudes toward Soulsville (and, by default, LeMoyne-Owen College), both within and outside of the community, to slowly but significantly improve.[71]

This reputation change in Soulsville is something that UROC hopes to create in North Minneapolis. The building and investment in UROC signals new levels of commitment from the university; however, the potential is yet to be fully realized. According to UROC's strategic plan consultant, Reynolds-Anthony Harris, one challenge is that the need in North Minneapolis is so great and that the university must focus on just a couple of attainable goals that can be realized within the first three years of UROC's opening. "The university has to remind itself to go slow to go fast," says Harris. University leaders hope that their physical presence in the Northside will build community infrastructure, stimulate commercial development, and attract other organizations to set up satellite offices. They made a strong initial investment by having more than 30 percent of their $2.8 million renovation for UROC be awarded to women- and minority-owned businesses. The university is now beginning to leverage this opportunity to meet broader social and economic challenges of the community.[72]

Syracuse's work throughout the city, and particularly the Near West Side, is also young, although the university has made great strides in only a couple of years. "Through the Connective Corridor, we're already seeing development by private developers. But we have to be patient for change. . . . The university is playing an increasing leadership and catalytic role," say Caliva and Schwab. In the Near Westside, new homes have been built, old homes have been greened, abandoned warehouses are being renovated, and residents are being engaged in the efforts. A city agreement has allowed for a seven-year tax exemption for the vacant lots being redeveloped with subsidized funding through NWSI; this is an effort to protect current homeowners. Of course, some are concerned about the sustainability of using public dollars to subsidize new development. The hope is that, in seven years, revitalization will create greater economic prosperity for everyone in the community through newly created jobs and greater real estate values. "You can never underestimate how much patience and persistence this work takes," comments Daniel Queri, a private developer and consultant to NWSI. "We can't go just to go. We have had to execute our plans with real discipline."[73]

Emory's work so far has been more process- than outcome-oriented—as well as less geographically focused—and hence difficult to measure. On the one hand, the strong relationships that OUCP has built with community-based organizations, particularly in the East Lake, Edgewood, and Mechanicsville-Pittsburgh neighborhoods, have enabled it to take a leadership role in convening a number of Atlanta community forums, particularly geared to foreclosure issues, equitable development, and the 2010 census. But while OUCP's efforts are increasingly focused on specific neighborhoods, the greater university's community work has not yet gotten there. Emory's strong relationships leave it well positioned but still aware of the challenge ahead. "You need internal change agents," Emory provost Earl Lewis observes. "Major movements of institutions require these. Ten years from now we are likely to be part of the way to where we would like to be."[74]

PART 3

Best Practices

Given the financial restraints cities are facing, anchor institutions are central. . . . We need to assess what's working and what's not working, but also to put the emphasis on what are the *possibilities*, and where we can point to great things that are happening that can be leveraged in other universities.

—Ted Howard, founding executive director, Democracy Collaborative at the University of Maryland

Promising Practices and Lessons Learned

The literature on university-community partnerships is extensive. We are hardly the first to highlight best practices. For example, Dwight Giles and John Saltmarsh of the University of Massachusetts–Boston, along with coauthor Lorilee Sandmann of the University of Georgia, identify five key best practices that they found among the initial group of seventy-six colleges and universities qualifying for the Carnegie Foundation for the Advancement of Teaching's community engagement classification in 2006. In particular, Giles, Saltmarsh, and Sandmann emphasize the importance of (1) executive leadership, including by key faculty members, backed by supportive infrastructure; (2) purposeful advancement strategies (i.e., sustaining work over time); (3) longitudinal assessment plans; (4) rewarding community engagement among the faculty and including community partners in the peer review process; and (5) having a clear focus and direction in the community-campus partnership efforts.[1]

As the case studies in the previous chapters make clear, we concur that university administration leadership and supportive infrastructure—in particular, a "partnership center" that can coordinate university activity and is empowered to do so—is critical for a university or college to successfully implement an anchor institution strategy. And faculty support has also played a key role, both in generating and in sustaining university leadership backing for community partnership work. We have also argued throughout for the necessity of having a clear focus and direction in partnership efforts and the need to sustain efforts over time. We have, however, put comparatively little focus on such common topics in the literature as longitudinal assessment of postcollegiate student engagement or reform of the faulty tenure evaluation process. This is not because we believe these matters to be unimportant, but this distinction does point to a difference between our focus on the pursuit of an anchor institution mission by selected universities and the perhaps more common discourse of "community engagement."

As Randy Stoecker and Bo Hee Min of the University of Wisconsin and coauthor Mary Beckman of Notre Dame University have noted, civic engagement in higher education has often "focused on student development rather than community development." By contrast, the anchor institution approach, while not discounting the favorable impacts for faculty research and student learning, places a greater emphasis precisely on the community development effects of the partnership work. As Carol Coletta, head of CEOs for Cities, notes, a critical question facing universities that seek to pursue an anchor institution mission is, "Can colleges and universities play a more significant role in the revitalization of inner cities of America through focused strategies?"[2]

We believe the evidence presented in this study indicates clearly that although universities have often fallen short in these efforts, the *potential* for universities to have a powerful impact is great. Thus, it has been our intent to emphasize the *possibilities* of focused anchor efforts in this work. In particular, in this chapter, we attempt to identify "best practices" that we found among our ten profiled universities for key anchor institution strategies aimed at community development in the following areas:

- Comprehensive neighborhood revitalization
- Community economic development through corporate investment
- Local capacity building
- Public school and health partnerships
- Academic engagement
- Multi-anchor, city, and regional partnerships

We also describe best practices in navigating through several of the major challenges faced when implementing this work:

- Institutionalizing an anchor vision
- Securing funding and leveraging resources
- Building a culture of economic inclusion
- Sustaining participatory planning and robust community relationships

It is worth noting that a few themes, in addition to serving as stand-alone features, cut across many of these areas—for example, many community leaders have emphasized the importance of universities engaging in the work of building community capacity, a theme that also came up prominently among our own research and that is reflected in many of the best-practice summaries below and particularly highlighted in Emory's example.[3] We also second the emphasis that Penny Pasque of the University of Oklahoma places on the importance of "boundary crossers" who can interact comfortably with both "community" and "university" partners in making successful partnerships happen.[4] These individuals play critical roles in the success of the practices described below.

At the same time, we also wish to emphasize the value of leveraging universities' corporate practices for direct community *economic* benefit. The importance of universities' roles as economic institutions is increasingly widely recognized. For example, Lou Anna Kimsey Simon, president of Michigan State University, points out that the idea of the university as "economic engine" dates back to the origins of the land-grant college itself in 1862.[5] Nancy and Timothy Franklin, two administrators at Penn State University—like Michigan State, a land-grant institution—go even further in their remarks, arguing that today's universities increasingly "have adopted economic development as a fourth mission."[6] Unfortunately, too often this important university economic development work is not aligned with universities' community partnership work. We hope, however, that this study provides some tools for addressing this challenge.

In the pages that follow, we have chosen to highlight a number of different best practices, drawn from our interviews and site visits of the ten cases that we have studied, in "capsule" form. Such capsule summaries are, by necessity, oversimplifications. Each "best practice," of course, is embedded in the broader strategic approaches that we highlighted in part 2. Nonetheless, by presenting short summaries in this format, we hope to highlight and thereby make more accessible some of the key principles and practices that make community partnerships work—not just for universities but for the communities in which they form a part.

Comprehensive Neighborhood Revitalization

Penn: An Institution-Wide, Multipronged Approach

For more than twenty years, the University of Pennsylvania has partnered with its West Philadelphia neighbors to improve the community surrounding campus, beginning during the administration of President Sheldon Hackney in the mid-1980s. Much of this collaboration has been led by the Netter Center for Community Partnerships, which directs resources from across the university—particularly the academic and human resources of its faculty and students—to improve the quality of life in its local community, and the University City District, a business improvement district organization that focuses on promoting public safety, streetscape and façade improvements, and retail development. Community development efforts peaked in 1996 when President Judith Rodin launched the West Philadelphia Initiatives, a university-led, multipronged approach to restore and revitalize the neighborhood.

The West Philadelphia Initiatives sought to simultaneously address five critical areas: safety, housing, commercial and real estate development, economic development, and education. As stated in Penn's *Anchor Institutions Toolkit: A Guide for Neighborhood Revitalization*, "To address and tackle the challenges of the community, a tactic of Penn's strategy was simultaneous action of addressing all of the most pressing issues facing the

---

Figure 13. Comprehensive Neighborhood Revitalization at Penn

Strategy
University City District and Netter Center for Community Partnerships: coordinated hubs and tools to transform neighborhood surrounding campus

Key Features
- Enlist leadership from the top
- Create institution-wide engagement (academic, corporate, human resources) in focused geographic area
- Simultaneously address all critical community issues
- Use public schools as centers for community development efforts

---

community. Success depended upon mitigation in all areas, as ignoring any area could potentially undermine all other areas."[7]

Notably, this multipronged approach committed the university, as an *institution,* to revitalizing the surrounding neighborhood by linking its academic and research expertise with significant financial commitment and policy changes. Penn collaborated with neighborhood residents and businesses as well as other anchor institutions to determine mutually beneficial goals for revitalizing West Philadelphia. Still, the university took a clear leadership role in driving the initiatives forward. As Lewis Wendell, former executive director of University City District, puts it, "Penn is not the only game in town, but Penn's the leader. It's the engine of the region." The West Philadelphia Initiatives became a top university priority, with responsibility delegated across all of Penn's major administrative departments. Within each of the five focus areas, Penn and its partners established innovative and efficient tools to achieve its goals, many of which are still in effect today, such as University City District and "Buy West Philadelphia," a supplier diversity program to support locally owned businesses. At the same time, Harkavy recognizes that the university's role in broader West Philadelphia (i.e., both the neighborhoods that were and those that were *not* part of the initiative) still has much further to go to address "the still deep, pervasive poverty and highly-inadequate schooling that characterize much—if not most—of West Philadelphia."[8]

Penn's work has continued to evolve under the leadership of President Amy Gutmann. For example, the Netter Center for Community Partnerships has received growing support under Gutmann—to the tune of nearly one million dollars in annual operational funds as well as a $10 million endowment from a Penn alumnus. Each year, the Netter Center supports nearly fifty Penn faculty in teaching academically based community service courses, which engage over 1,500 students in solving universal problems of education, health care, and poverty as they are manifested locally in West Philadelphia. The vast majority of these students, along with hundreds of community work-study students and student volunteers, work with the Center's university-assisted community school programs, which reach nearly 5,000 low-income children, youth, and families each year. The university-assisted community school strategy assumes that "public schools can function as environment-changing institutions and can become the strategic centers of broadly based partnerships that genuinely engage a wide variety of community organizations and institutions." As Cory Bowman, associate director of the Netter Center puts it, "What we're really interested in is systemic university-community change."[9]

Penn has also worked with the University City District, the William Penn Foundation, local elected officials, and community organizations to stimulate commercial and economic development on two commercial corridors, Baltimore Avenue and Lancaster Avenue. Revitalization on Baltimore Avenue includes a five-block area where partners have done façade improvement, business recruitment, and pedestrian lighting. Wendell comments, "It's a real success . . . Baltimore [Avenue] is all ma-and-pa businesses. The African community is quite strongly represented." As of 2007–2008, 98 percent of University City's available retail space was leased or committed (compared to 75 percent in 2003–2004). West Philadelphia residents have filled more than half of the jobs created by Penn's retail planning and development.[10]

In examining the lessons learned from Penn's comprehensive approach, a few key factors stand out. First, leadership from the top is critical to linking the different initiatives as well as actively engaging the full resources of the university (corporate, academic, human, and cultural); second, linking academic work to focused community work provides the legitimacy to have staying power even as administrations change; third, the public school provides a valuable focal point to locate efforts in the community; and, fourth, focusing retail and commercial development on supporting local business can have a powerful job creation impact.

Syracuse: Revitalization through Coalition Building and Using Institutional Strengths

Building on the specific strengths of its institution and region, art, culture, and green technology are at the forefront of Syracuse University's partnership efforts. Syracuse's projects "are large in scale and complex in partners; engage faculty and students in work that furthers their disciplines while addressing pressing issues of the community; and draw collaborators from all sectors including business, neighborhood, government, schools, and not-for profit organizations," as chancellor and president Nancy Cantor described in a 2009 article.[11] Syracuse has tried to stimulate neighborhood revitalization in a way that directly enhances community capacity. This is seen, for example, in its collaboration to establish the Near West Side Initiative as the vehicle for neighborhood transformation. "We're all committed to the initiative becoming part of the neighborhood; neighborhood leaders will eventually be running the show," says Kathy Goldfarb-Findling, who served as executive director of the Gifford Foundation from 2000 to 2010.[12]

The Near West Side Initiative (NWSI)'s activity was jump-started through a financial commitment from President Cantor in 2007: $13.8 million from the state, which the university had received for "debt forgiveness," was reinvested directly in the effort. Although the university is a lead partner, NWSI operates as an independent nonprofit network of community organizations, institutions, and businesses. Other lead partners include the Gifford Foundation, Home HeadQuarters, the City of Syracuse, the Syracuse Center of Excellence, National Grid, and local residents. "We are a team," says Marilyn Higgins, vice president of community engagement and economic development. "I chair the board, but it is full of strong leaders. We all assign staff to volunteer for the initiative."[13]

The NWSI strategy is focused on commercial, residential, and mixed-used economic development in an eleven-block area. The university's $13.8 million, for instance, was used

---

Figure 14. Revitalization through Coalition Building at Syracuse

Strategy
Near West Side Initiative and Connective Corridor: nonprofit network of community organizations, institutions, and businesses investing in 11-block mixed-use development effort, and cultural strip connecting university with downtown

Key Features
- Draw collaborators from all sectors (business, government, neighborhood, schools, nonprofits)
- Build on strengths of institution and community (e.g., arts, culture, technology)
- Focus on community capacity building and ownership

to acquire and renovate seventy-four abandoned properties and a strip of abandoned warehouses. The university raised $2.2 million in federal funds and asked housing partner Home Headquarters to use it to purchase and renovate the residential properties while the university concentrated on the commercial buildings. The university's Center of Excellence is also engaged in home rehabilitation through implementation of sustainable green technology, including rain gardens and super-insulated walls. Redeveloped warehouses are being designated for mixed-use facilities, including a green technology incubator and artist live-work space. These efforts are aimed at restoring the residential and commercial vibrancy of the neighborhood while keeping with community values and culture. Much of the development is also focused on building schools as community centers. The Gifford Foundation has helped promote inclusive planning and community capacity building, including through residents' meetings and leadership trainings.

A second part of Syracuse's strategy that focuses on community and economic revitalization through art, culture, and technology is the Connective Corridor, "a signature strip of cutting-edge cultural development" connecting University Hill to the city below, which Syracuse is developing with local, state, and federal partners. The Connective Corridor aims to demonstrate the interdependency between campus and community by featuring art, technology, and sustainable designs developed by Syracuse faculty and students working in partnership with community artists and residents.[14]

Though comprehensive in nature, Syracuse's revitalization efforts are young and much of the impact remains to be seen. In the meantime, Syracuse must continue to nurture its inclusive practices. Jan Cohen-Cruz, director of Imagining America and a member of the Connective Corridor Working Group, comments, "Syracuse's campus-community partnerships are grounded in genuine recognition that people whose knowledge comes from different sources bring different assets to the table. Like anchor institutions everywhere, we face the built-in challenge of keeping the partnerships equitable even as [the university is] perceived as bringing more financial resources." "It is definitely a balancing act," echoes Eric Persons, associate vice president of government and community relations at Syracuse. "So much is about building relationships. We have to use SU's weight strategically."[15]

Syracuse's approach to comprehensive neighborhood revitalization offers a number of innovative ideas that could benefit other universities embarking on similar work. Two of the most notable features include, first, creating an independent network of community organizations, institutions and businesses to lead the effort, which allows for reciprocity, shared ownership, and greater accountability; and, second, building on the existing strengths and assets of both the university and the community, which allows limited resources to be used more effectively and efficiently.

Community Economic Development through Corporate Investment

Minnesota—Leveraging Contracting Dollars

The University of Minnesota has partnered with city government, community-based organizations, unions, and general contractors to implement innovative strategies for

Figure 15. Leveraging Contracting Dollars at Minnesota
Strategy Office for Business and Community Economic Development: dedicated office that oversees local, minority, and women inclusion
Key Features • Align practices with institutional urban agenda • Require general contractors to establish levels of participation for targeted businesses, and raise targets when opportunities arise • Set inclusion requirements for union construction workers • Provide apprenticeship opportunities, with help of local partners

minority and women inclusion in all university construction projects. Established by the board of regents in 1999, the Office for Business and Community Economic Development (OBCED) oversees these initiatives, and with the more recent establishment of Minnesota's urban vision and its first Urban Research and Outreach/Engagement Center (UROC), these practices have become increasingly focused on *local* economic inclusion. In conjunction with Capital Planning and Project Management, OBCED requires general contractors to establish levels of participation for targeted businesses at the start of every project. Director Craig Taylor's "boilerplate for all bid packages" requires 10 percent of base contracts to go to minority and small businesses. "This is a goal-based program [with] strong compliance—we have had a 96–97 percent success rate, and we probably have one billion dollars in construction going on now," comments Taylor. This effort is facilitated and monitored by a monthly compliance report all contractors must submit to OBCED.

The Office for Business and Community Economic Development also works with general contractors to employ minority and women construction workers on university capital projects. Most of the projects are unionized, so Minnesota has set inclusion requirements for specific groups from the union: 15 percent unskilled minorities; 8 percent skilled minorities; 4 percent women; and 2 percent disabled. "This forces construction groups to move past the hierarchy of unions," notes Taylor. OBCED and UROC have recently teamed up with a number of local trade schools and workforce development programs to provide apprenticeship opportunities for minorities. "The fact is that there are a minimum number of on-the-job hours to become journeyed, and then become unionized, and many minorities haven't been able to meet that. By setting inclusion requirements [for our capital projects], they can log those hours on the job," says Taylor.[16]

With Minnesota's recent focus on urban engagement, efforts have begun to far exceed Taylor's "boilerplate." For example, the university's $300 million stadium dedicated 23 percent of the contract toward women- and minority-owned business enterprises (WMBE). "We also gave a contract to Summit Academy [a nonprofit educational and vocational training center] to train fourteen to sixteen apprentices. Once they matriculated through, we hired them," says Taylor. The $2.8 million renovation of the first Urban Research and Outreach/Engagement Center (UROC) in 2009 then raised the bar, with a minimum target of 30 percent for WMBE construction services. By the completion of renovation in September 2009, targets for WMBE inclusion and for women and minority participation in the workforce had exceeded all expectations at 34 percent. Notes founding executive director Irma McClaurin, "UROC's presence and President Bruininks's support [for an urban vision] has allowed for the 'usual ways' of university business to be changed dramatically."[17]

Although Minnesota has had economic inclusion principles for university construction in place for some time now, its recent experience points to the new possibilities afforded by a university-wide commitment to urban engagement. In addition, the university's success demonstrates the importance of setting specific goals and targets for levels of participation and ways to benchmark the progress. Finally, by focusing locally and enlisting other local partners, the university has demonstrated promising efforts toward community economic development objectives, including its new workforce development program.

Penn: Local Purchasing

Penn launched its Buy West Philadelphia program in the 1980s. Since then, local procurement has grown from roughly $1.3 million a year to $100.5 million. "What we have made is an institutional decision that economic inclusion is one of our top business priorities. Each year we have set goals institutionally. Our sourcing managers, in part, are compensated by how well they do," says Ralph Maier, who served as associate director and then director of Penn Purchasing from 1990 through 2010.[18]

Tracking the impact of local purchasing, however, is difficult. Steven Williams, executive director of Partnership CDC, located in West Philadelphia, offers a skeptical assessment, claiming that the "community is not tapping into the economic benefits." To be sure, "local" purchasing as measured by Penn includes seven zip codes, a region that includes nearby Southwest Philadelphia, which has a higher concentration of business activity. Maier identifies two major restrictions to the program's impact specifically on West Philadelphia: "West Philly is largely a residential community. Small mom-and-pop businesses don't have the capacity to handle the kind of products we buy. The other major restriction is, because of technology and the priority of cost containment, we needed to shift focus to doing business from small to larger business. How do we match contracting opportunity with qualified suppliers?"[19]

Nonetheless, the initiative has had a major impact. D. L. Wormley, a local nonprofit leader and former Penn employee, has been critical of Penn for not doing more to encourage purchasing specifically within West Philadelphia (as opposed to the broader seven-zip-code region), though she concedes that Penn's focus on local purchasing has brought some

---

Figure 16. Local Purchasing at Penn

Strategy
Buy West Philadelphia: supplier diversity program promoting procurement of goods and services from local vendors

Key Features
- Establish robust local purchasing goals and compensate staff on performance
- Mentor local vendors to help become "first tier" suppliers on large contracts
- Leverage results by working with other anchor institutions
- Work with nonprofit organizations to meet local and minority vendors "where they are"

benefits to the community. "Telrose is probably the biggest success story," Wormley says. As Maier explains, "Office Depot had a minority partner [Telrose] doing delivery and customer service. We negotiated a flip on ownership of our existing office supply contract with Office Depot and created an opportunity for this partner to become a national tier one supplier. In the 1990s we did a similar flip with Staples."[20]

Maier estimates the Telrose contract alone is worth $4.8 million a year; Penn has also worked with nearby Drexel University to shift $1.8 million of its orders to Telrose. Wormley notes that Alpha Office Supplies, University Copy Services, and several West Philadelphia catering businesses have also benefited from Penn's local purchasing initiative. Maier adds that some efforts, such as promoting minority purchasing in research departments, are less visible but provide tangible benefits; he estimates that these efforts alone boosted Penn purchasing from African American–owned businesses by $5.5 million.[21]

In recent years, Penn has looked to partner with nonprofit organizations. Maier reflects, "We realized that supplier representatives were intimidated by coming into the purchasing office." In response, beginning in 2007, Penn Purchasing has worked with the Pennsylvania Minority Business Enterprise Center, which hosts an event with twenty to twenty-five of their certified suppliers. University purchasing staff attends and goes through a series of interviews. "It creates a more productive environment for negotiating purchasing agreements," says Maier. "Vendors are more at ease. It also creates greater awareness of what's going on in the community and greater awareness of the university in the community. We expect greater results going forward."[22]

Penn's local purchasing initiative, which has been sustained for more than two decades, offers a number of lessons. First, setting local purchasing goals and tying rewards to achieving these goals is essential. Second, to succeed requires a long-term vision that mentors local vendors by, for example, starting them as "second tier" suppliers that can later move up to "first tier." Third, institutions can leverage results by working in concert with other universities and anchor institutions. And, fourth, partnering with nonprofit organizations can help meet local vendors "where they are" and hence extend the program's overall impact and success.

Local Capacity Building

Emory—Supporting Community Organizations

Community development corporations (CDCs) in Atlanta did not have much of a presence until the late 1990s, at which point they had "a very scattered history of capacity and performance," according to Michael Rich, director of Emory's Office of University and Community Partnerships (OUCP). "Emory by choice does not have a CDC of its own, but supports existing CDCs," notes Rich. For example, since 2002, OUCP has run a Community Building and Social Change Fellowship Program. Each year approximately fifteen student fellows are selected for the yearlong program that combines study in the classroom with real work in the community. As program director Kate Grace explains, "It begins in the fall. There's a foundation course open to all students. This is done for two reasons. First, it's tough for students to make a yearlong commitment and sign on to a specific community partnership sight unseen. And, second, it's tough for us to identify students who are

Figure 17. Community Capacity Building at Emory
Strategy Office of University and Community Partnerships: use of students, faculty, and staff to build capacity of community organizations through partnerships and research
Key Features • Develop yearlong fellowship program for continuum of engagement • Engage partners in extensive front-end planning • Be proactive in designing collaborative interventions at critical moments • Hire staff with backgrounds in community organizations

appropriate for the program." In the spring, there is a second course, open only to those students who have applied and have been accepted to continue in the program, that is focused on developing the work plan students will use during the summer for their collaborative community building project. "During the summer practicum, the third course in the sequence, the fellows [perform] thirty-two hours a week of project work in collaboration with their community partners, with input from faculty, staff, and grad students."[23]

While the program began with open calls for proposals from community partners, OUCP soon began cultivating potential projects with community partners in order to ensure activities that would provide a variety of neighborhood contexts and issues as learning opportunities for students, were feasible for students to complete over the summer, and would advance the work of the host partner organizations. The program also began mapping out specific partnership goals in the spring. "We start that negotiation early, so the students are already three months into their relationship with their community partners before they start the summer project," says Grace. In 2009, one student team worked with community members in the East Lake Terrace neighborhood to develop a comprehensive neighborhood action plan. A second team worked with two public schools in the Edgewood neighborhood, conducting focus group research to help the schools and their community partners address the causes of enrollment decline. A third team worked on compiling a profile of a group of five neighborhoods near Turner Field (including Mechanicsville and Pittsburgh) to assist their community partners in gathering the data needed to bring a green job-training site to the area.[24]

Emory has also provided more direct assistance to building the capacity of Atlanta's small network of CDCs. Andy Schneggenburger, executive director of AHAND (Atlanta Housing Association of Neighborhood-based Developers), comments, "We enjoy the collaborative nature of working with OUCP. . . . They are very congruent in the need to let the community's voice be heard and play a primary role in the decision-making process as opposed to imposing a structure." In 2008, OUCP worked with AHAND to conduct interviews and listening sessions with Atlanta CDCs to help the CDCs identify their strengths and weaknesses during a very trying time financially. "The survey allowed us to get our heads around how bad the [financial] crisis was for the nine to twelve CDCs theoretically still functioning. We needed to figure out a way to partner in an ad hoc situation. We conducted the survey in August 2008. It allowed CDC leaders to anonymously share where their funding was pre-2007, and now, and how many staff members were going unpaid. It was an important profile for the industry, and a very appropriate role that Emory could play," says Nathaniel

Smith, OUCP's director of partnerships and research for equitable development. "We could then let the leadership of AHAND deal with the information. The result has been many facilitated conversations regarding what the industry might look like in the future."[25]

The strong relationship between existing CDCs and Emory's OUCP is notable, particularly because the rationale often given at other schools for *not* working with existing CDCs— that is, lack of CDC capacity—was obviously not absent in Atlanta. Emory's work over the past eight years, however, shows that a sustained effort to build CDC capacity can achieve results. Key factors have included, first, a willingness to engage in highly detailed, front-end design work in developing community partnerships; second, keeping the university's "ear to the ground" and taking a proactive role in designing collaborative interventions at critical moments, such as with the foreclosure crisis; and, third, hiring staff who have experience working with community groups. For example, both Grace, the fellowship program director, and Smith, who worked on the foreclosure-response effort, hail from community organizations themselves.[26]

Public School and Health Partnerships

IUPUI: Supporting Community Schools

IUPUI's work with local community schools launched in January 1998, when the university's Office of Neighborhood Partnerships received a COPC (Community Outreach Partnership Centers) grant, in collaboration with the Westside Cooperative Organization, to focus on several areas of community revitalization. Education was a clear priority. At this time, the neighborhood high school had been closed for academic failure. The newly formed Westside Education Task Force—comprised of residents and leaders of community and faith-based organizations, along with IUPUI faculty, staff, and students—visited model schools across the country, planned collaboratively, and presented the Indianapolis Public Schools superintendent with a proposal—to reopen Washington High School as a community school.

The community school began with middle school grades and slowly phased back in high school grades. In 2001, IUPUI became one of twenty schools to receive a replication grant from the University of Pennsylvania to adapt its university-assisted community school model. The partnership grew from there: George Washington Community School teachers took graduate-level classes at IUPUI to implement service-learning into their classrooms; IUPUI students begin serving as math and literacy tutors through the federal America Reads/ America Counts program; and undergraduate scholars began mentoring students through a

---

Figure 18. Supporting Community Schools at IUPUI

Strategy
Westside Education Task Force: multi-constituency collaboration to develop community schools in neighborhood

Key Features
- Participate in inclusive stakeholder group with ongoing dialogue
- Adapt programming to fit needs and interests of students, families, and broader community
- Demonstrate loyalty during adversity (e.g., school closings, principal turnover)

college preparatory curriculum. Today, the school has forty-eight community-based partners in addition to IUPUI.[27]

IUPUI continues to adapt its programming to fits the needs and interests of the community. For example, the university recently held a bilingual predatory lending forum and financial literacy workshop series at George Washington Community School for nearly 200 residents. It also launched the Fit for Life program, a partnership between the Schools of Nursing and Physical Education, to offer physical fitness programming for youth and their families at the school. IUPUI physiology students fulfill their service-learning placement at the Fitness Center and serve as personal student trainers for community residents for just twenty dollars for an entire year.[28]

The Office of Neighborhood Partnerships (ONP) and Westside Education Task Force have begun to build relationships with other Near Westside schools that are attempting to adopt the community school model. Lana Coleman, a longtime resident and retiree after thirty-seven years with Indianapolis Public Schools, observes, "IUPUI has been instrumental in helping us get the things we need for [Wendell Phillips Elementary] School 63. The nursing department sent student nurses to the school as we were getting established. We serve as a site for English-as-a-second-language classes, and IUPUI's language department helped translate documents. Dental students provided free care on-site—they gave sealants to all of the kids!" When asked about the common challenges of teacher and principal turnover, Starla Officer replies, "ONP and our community partners are clear that we're there *as partners*. When the principal turned over at School 63, we met with the new principal before she even started. We made it clear that we're not going anywhere." Since 2008, ONP has also coordinated the Central Indiana Community Schools Network—an informal regional network of those engaged in community school initiatives. And, in 2011, it was designated as a regional training center for university-assisted community schools through funding from the Netter Center for Community Partnerships at Penn.[29]

Today, the partners at George Washington Community School have helped local students achieve dramatic success. As the principal reported in spring 2009: two years ago, student attendance was 88 percent; this year, student attendance reached 96.2 percent, exceeding the district goal of 95 percent; an incredible 100 percent of 2009 graduating seniors were accepted into postsecondary education; and, in fall 2008, Washington community partners received the first federal Full-Service Community School funding to the tune of $2.4 million out of a national total of $4.9 million (the other $2.5 million was divided between nine school communities across the country).[30]

Key factors behind IUPUI's community school partnership success include taking advantage of the window of opportunity to develop strategic university-community-school partnerships; an inclusive stakeholder group that builds upon existing community leadership while embracing diversity; and flexibility to adapt programming to fit the evolving needs, strengths, and interests of the community.

Yale: Using Human Resources to Focus on Science Education

Yale has particularly close relationships with two area high schools. One long-standing partnership is at Hill Regional, a magnet school with over 700 students that focuses on science and technology. Michael Ceraso, principal at Hill Regional since 2007 and a member of the school faculty and administration since the school's founding, notes that when partnership efforts began in the mid-1990s, "There was great fear that the folks from the university would come in and be very prescriptive . . . But the people sent from the university were genuinely interested in their role of being resource people, not prescriptive."[31] Ceraso says a formal partnership agreement with Yale was worked out in 1998. "Since we were a magnet school, we were given an opportunity to make a program that might attract students from the sub- urbs outside New Haven. The whole concept was really radical," Ceraso emphasizes. One sign of success, according to Ceraso, is that roughly 40 percent of Hill Regional's students come from outside the city limits today, compared to less than 20 percent when the magnet school began. This in turn has played a major role in stabilizing the funding base of the New Haven public school district.[32]

More broadly, Yale works less intensively with about twenty New Haven public schools. However, this collaboration did not happen without putting the right communication—and people—in place. According to Claudia Merson, director of public school partnerships at Yale, who taught in New York City in the 1970s, "The university people didn't speak school. The school people didn't speak university. My work was pretty easy. I spoke both. That's why this partnership is still standing." Each partner school is assigned a student intern. These interns are on-site six hours a week and may bill the Office of New Haven and State Affairs for an additional four hours a week of prep time. Their main role is to act as a conduit of Yale volunteer assistance, so that volunteers meet school needs and arrive in a coordi- nated fashion. Abie Benitez, principal at the bilingual (English/Spanish) K-8 Christopher Columbus Family Academy, notes that Yale assistance for her school has ranged from field trips to Yale museums, to Yale students tutoring K-8 students in math or helping with the school's gardening project, to professors doing guest lectures and demonstrations in science classes.[33]

Yale's science program reaches out in other ways as well. Merson notes that federal prod- ding was key: "Beginning in 2002, the National Science Foundation (NSF) said every basic science grant had to have a broad impact, a K-12 component." To meet this need, in 2007, Yale combined grant funds (two-thirds) and internal provost funds (one-third) to create a full-time K-12 high school science coordinator position. Yale has also sought to step up its contact with communities of color in New Haven through the Yale Peabody Museum. Since the mid-1990s, the museum has developed an annual Martin Luther King, Jr. poetry slam

---

Figure 19. Science Education Partnerships at Yale

Strategy
Public School Partnerships: support to more than 20 New Haven schools, primarily through student vol- unteers and interns

Key Features
- Provide educational and human resources, rather than prescriptive model
- Build sustainable partnerships through trust, in-kind resources, and creative leveraging of external funds
- Put effective coordinators in place, both in management positions and as student liaisons

competition (attended annually by 5,000) and an annual Fiesta Latina event. In 2006, David Heiser, head of education and outreach at the Peabody, notes that the museum also began a mobile outreach program to attend community events. This program, Heiser estimates, now reaches 3,000–5,000 people a year.[34]

Yale's science partnerships with K-12 schools, which have been sustained on a formal level for over a dozen years, illustrate a number of key features that other universities seeking to undertake such an initiative might want to consider. First, the history of Yale's educational programs highlights the importance of establishing and maintaining trust, particularly if the anchor institution has been viewed with suspicion in the past. Second, Yale's effort emphasizes the importance of staff who can act as "translators" between the K-12 and academic worlds. And, third, its evolving work illustrates how federal programs, such as grant requirements for "broader impact" by the National Science Foundation, can spur new efforts and indeed help leverage external support that can buttress already existing community outreach programs.

Academic Engagement

IUPUI: Aligning Academic Resources with Community Development Goals

IUPUI's Office of Neighborhood Partnerships was founded in the mid-1990s to restore relationships with the Near Westside community. The office became part of the university's Center for Service and Learning in 2003, facilitating the concentration of academic resources in this community. More recently, through the university's engagement with the Great Indy Neighborhoods Initiative (GINI), these academic resources have been focused on the collectively identified target areas for community revitalization: housing, public safety, beautification, business and economic development, education, health, and civic engagement. Director Bob Bringle comments, "We encourage our faculty to work other places, too, but they have largely stayed focused on the Near Westside."[35]

While the GINI plan was being finalized in 2007, the Office of Neighborhood Partnerships was funded by Indiana Campus Compact to host several community dialogue sessions. One of the key activities developed as a result of these discussions was the Faculty Community Fellows program. Through this program, IUPUI's Center for Service and Learning committed to reallocate dollars for faculty engagement in the Near Westside community. To specifically create an impact in the focus areas of the GINI Quality of Life Plan, five faculty

---

Figure 20. Academic Engagement at IUPUI

Strategy
Faculty Community Fellows Program: three-year grants to engage faculty and their students in local neighborhood

Key Features
- Direct academic resources to collectively identified areas of need in community
- Promote interdisciplinary service-learning and community-based research through dedicated resources to faculty
- Develop a cadre of faculty experts in the scholarship of engagement

community fellowships were awarded in the 2008–2009 academic year, each linked with a specific community organization.[36]

Bringle says of the three-year grants to faculty fellows, "It's an interdisciplinary effort—we're trying to get them to work together on issues in the community." The fellows program is designed to deepen faculty and student practice in service-learning and community-based research by addressing community-identified needs in the Near Westside; increase departmental and campus support for partnerships with the Near Westside by developing a cadre of faculty experts in service-learning, community-based research, and the assets and needs of the Near Westside; augment the capacity of community organizations and residents to achieve community goals; and support faculty development by advancing the scholarship of engagement and documenting practices of engaged teaching and research.[37]

Faculty community fellow Darrell Nickolson speaks on the importance of applied scholarship and research: "The idea is that our Design Department should be using our skills and resources to directly impact the neighborhood most impacted by the university. Students see you involved and it gives them the impression that community development is something they should be involved in too—that architecture is more than just aesthetics. Residual impacts like this outweigh anything they learn about design."[38] More broadly, Bringle's Center promotes service-learning throughout the university, directing academic resources to more than 250 community partner organizations. In 2008–2009, an estimated 4,000 students contributed nearly 75,000 hours of service to these organizations.

IUPUI's recent approach to academic engagement through faculty fellows is remarkable particularly because of its alignment with broader community development goals. The university's experience points to the importance of several key factors in creating this connection: first, an increased focus of faculty and student academic work in a concentrated geographic area; second, the realignment of dollars for faculty engagement with community-identified goals; and third, a centralized unit on campus that helps to create opportunities for faculty to work together and sustain their community-based research.

Multi-Anchor, City, and Regional Partnerships

Portland State: Alignment with City Economic Development Goals

Portland State's motto, "Let Knowledge Serve the City," was adopted in 1994 under President Judith Ramaley. This mission shift stemmed largely from state pressure to assume an explicit urban focus and was accompanied by a curriculum overhaul centered on connecting students to the community. Fifteen years later, Portland State published *Economic Development Strategy: A 10-year Plan for Strengthening PSU's Contribution to Regional Economic Growth*. This 2009 document is a symbol of the deep and growing collaboration between the university as a whole and the City of Portland. As President Wim Wiewel writes in the introduction to this document, "Joint planning is the key to successful economic development . . . We will align our academic and research programs with regional economic development goals to assure that Portland State contributes strategically to the regional knowledge base, to innovation in technology and business practice, and to human capital creation."[39]

Figure 21. City and Regional Partnerships at Portland State

Strategy
Economic Development Strategy: 10-year plan for strengthening the university's contribution to regional economic growth

Key Features
- Align academic and research programs with regional economic development goals
- Collaborate with city departments on long-term real estate and economic development plans to leverage additional resources as well as achieve broader community goals

---

The university has worked particularly closely with the city's Bureau of Planning and its Portland Development Commission. Speaking of Portland State's *Economic Development Strategy*, Lew Bowers, Central City Division manager for the Portland Development Commission, says, "We crafted this with them over the last five years. It was done in conjunction with their Master Campus Plan and accompanies the citywide Economic Development Strategy [also completed in 2009]." Adds Senior Project Manager Lisa Abuaf, "They are becoming more institutionally aligned [with the city]. This plan adds more vigor to their efforts."[40]

Working with city partners encourages Portland State to keep broader goals in mind: "We want them to think about how they can become the spark plug—not just economic impact because they're a large institution," says Bowers. And, in some cases, the partnership mandates community development goals: "We work closely with the Portland Development Commission. They have their own agenda, put on in part by the city, which includes lots of regulations. For example, our real estate development in an Urban Renewal Area must include 30 percent affordable housing," says Mark Gregory, associate vice president for finance and administration.[41]

Wiewel is a leading expert in urban land use and the role that universities play in real estate development. Referring to Portland State's real estate activity, the president says, "Our development is primarily driven by our needs to accommodate our growth with students and faculty. That's why we do it ultimately. But we do it in a way that contributes to the vitality of the south end of downtown. We have mixed-use buildings, and all new developments have retail on the ground floor. Our own development is part of the city's overall development to keep it a vibrant area."[42]

Portland State's ten-year economic development strategy specifically commits the university and the city "to align their expertise and resources with those of the private sector and other regional public entities" to achieve several objectives, including creating new jobs in strategic economic clusters identified by the city; building on Portland's "reputation and commitment to sustainable development" by partnering on projects such as the new Oregon Sustainability Center and creation of an EcoDISTRICT on campus; strengthening Portland State's position as a workforce development provider; enhancing the university's capacity as the think tank for regional problem solving; and extending its contribution to physical development in the University City District in "a pattern that values partnership, mixed-use, and sustainability." Several of the specific tools to achieve these objectives are described in the plan, while others remain to be developed.[43]

Portland State's collaboration with the City of Portland offers several key lessons for universities trying to implement this type of anchor strategy. First, strategic, collaborative, long-term planning allows institutional partners to capitalize on each other's strengths and resources for broad objectives. Joint planning with city partners, in particular, can also help achieve mutually beneficial outcomes by securing funding for university real estate plans while directing university resources toward community development goals. Finally, focusing on mixed-use development can help gain public support (by keeping newly developed property on tax rolls) as well as contribute to the vitality of the university *and* community.

University of Cincinnati: Uptown Consortium

In 2003, the University of Cincinnati catalyzed a public-private partnership that led to the creation of the Uptown Consortium. The Consortium comprises the leaders of five of the largest employers in Cincinnati's Uptown neighborhoods: Cincinnati Children's Hospital, Cincinnati Zoo, UC Health (formerly the Health Alliance), TriHealth, and the university itself.[44] The CEOs of the Consortium first began meeting on an informal basis. They then hired a real estate finance and economic development consulting firm to help determine their shared needs and interests, as well as the needs and interests of the community. In 2004, they hired their first president, Tony Brown. "The chief executives hoped that group action, where members worked together and pooled common resources and experience, could have a greater impact than the disparate investments of individual organizations," writes Michael Romanos.[45]

Collaboration with the city is a notable feature of the Consortium's work. "After we raised our investment capital and local government saw us make sizable investments, we gained the respect and credibility of the city as a valuable community development partner, so much so that we now work closely with the city to coordinate our plans," said Tony Brown in a 2007 interview. For example, the Consortium recently consulted and assisted the city transportation division in the design of a new way-finding system for Uptown. Consortium partners provided the required 25 percent match in order to receive federal dollars for this initiative.[46]

From 2004 to 2009, nearly $400 million was invested in Uptown for neighborhood revitalization, primarily in real estate development. Gerry Siegert, Cincinnati's associate vice president for community development, speaks to the Consortium's progression: "The bricks-and-mortar development showed the community that the university and the other big employers were committed. Now, eight to ten years later, we're starting to see some good

---

Figure 22. Multi-Anchor Partnerships at Cincinnati

Strategy
Uptown Consortium: nonprofit collaboration among the leaders of the five largest employers in Cincinnati's Uptown neighborhoods

Key Features
- Work with other local anchors to pool resources
- Collaborate with the city to help achieve broader community development goals
- Provide opportunities for meaningful community participation and shared leadership

things happen as a result." Siegert recognizes the [often uneven] role that institutional preferences play in dictating the nature of many community efforts, which may "shoot higher than where the real problems lie." He stresses, "An important part of any community-directed program should begin with, and continue seeking, ongoing community input of what *they* see as the basic needs of the local populace as opposed to what the institution thinks is needed. We have recently begun using this approach and find striking differences in the perception of the problems, depending upon at which side of the table you sit."[47]

"We are at a point in the evolution of Uptown Consortium. It is very exciting," says Mary Stagaman, who served as Cincinnati's associate vice president for external relations and then presidential deputy for community engagement from 2002 through 2010. "Bringing the community to the table at an earlier point is an incredibly important lesson. It took a year of discussion, but everyone [the university, the Consortium, the community] now understands the importance. It has been a real transformation in the way the Consortium operates." In a similar vein, Bill Fischer, business development manager in the city's Department of Community Development, comments, "The Consortium laid out broad socioeconomic goals, but there were certain goals they had to accomplish first. They just invited the Community Council [representatives] to be on their board, so I think they will start tackling some tougher issues."[48]

The University of Cincinnati's leadership in the Uptown Consortium offers valuable lessons for those seeking to engage in multi-anchor partnerships. Chiefly, incredible resources can be leveraged when local institutions pull their assets and leadership together for community revitalization. This collective force can also hold significant weight as a collaborative partner with the city, working to achieve shared objectives. With such power, however, institutional preferences can often outweigh or overlook important community feedback; focused efforts are needed to ensure meaningful community participation and shared leadership.

Institutionalizing an Anchor Vision

Syracuse: Leadership for a Shared Vision

Since taking office as chancellor and president in 2004, Nancy Cantor has taken multiple steps to institutionalize community engagement at Syracuse University. Under Cantor's leadership, the university's vision, Scholarship in Action, represents "a commitment to forging bold, imaginative, reciprocal, and sustained engagements with our many constituent communities, local as well as global."[49] This vision entails a view of the university as an anchor institution in its community and is being manifested throughout the many community development initiatives spearheaded by Syracuse. "The chancellor's strategy is very multifaceted. We may have radically different strategies [to engagement] but there is *one* philosophy throughout the university," says Ed Boguez, director of Syracuse's Center of Excellence.[50]

Cantor shares her lessons from the past several years: "First, you have to have the stomach for doing the hard work of cross-sector partnerships. It shouldn't just be the institution. Large-scale projects take partnerships. They also take a long, long time." According to

Figure 23. Institutionalizing an Anchor Vision at Syracuse
Strategy   Presidential leadership: vision and actualization of university as an anchor in its community
Key Features   • Establish university-wide philosophy of engagement and communicate it internally and externally   • Enlist faculty leaders and embed work into student curriculum   • Institute supportive policy, both in academic reward structure and in business practices

Cantor, institutional engagement also requires getting as many faculty, schools, and colleges on board with the ambitious initiatives being undertaken by the administration, so that there is a breadth of representation. "We look for faculty leaders," says Cantor. Of course, some faculty were engaged in community initiatives long before Cantor's arrival: "We've been developing these efforts for many years from the ground up, supported by grants," says Marion Wilson, who serves as the director of community initiatives for Syracuse's School of Visual and Performing Arts. "Now that our work is validated through Nancy [Cantor]'s Scholarship in Action . . . this has really thrown the hierarchy of the university on its head."[51] Marilyn Higgins speaks of the work of faculty such as Marion Wilson and Stephen Mahan who partner with local high schools: "These programs have proven to be some of the most sustainable efforts between Syracuse and the community—faculty are committed to the work because they are advancing their own scholarship!" She also emphasizes the "important role of the deans in making the chancellor's vision come to life." Higgins, as Syracuse's vice president of community engagement and economic development and president of the Near West Side Initiative board, helps implement faculty ideas and academic resources in the neighborhood in a mutually beneficial way.[52]

Institutionalization also requires embedding engagement into student curriculum and life. *Enitiative* is a five-year, $3 million grant from the Kauffman Foundation that aims to infuse entrepreneurship across the curriculum and create productive campus-community partnerships. "The Kauffman *Enitiative* grant is helping to embed collaborative, cross-sector partnerships in every school and college. The grant provides course relief and backup dollars to faculty; lots of students are involved," says Cantor. Higgins estimates that the Near West Side Initiative engaged nearly 400 students and seventy-five faculty in revitalization of the neighborhood in its first three years alone.

Cantor notes that it is critical to take the policy and practice implications "head on," so that the work becomes "embedded in the reward structure and the mission" and not just "on the backs of dedicated staff and faculty. We're now rewarding tenure and promotion for more nontraditional kinds of scholarship," notes the chancellor. "After five years [of deliberation], we finally had a unanimous vote from the Senate." Policy changes for engagement have also occurred on the business and financial side of the university, though some of this spirit was also in place before Cantor. "[Economic inclusion] is part of our core values. We talk regularly about it. That's been key—it's driven down through the organization to all of our staff, and out to our contractors and subcontractors," say Douglas Freeman, director of purchasing and real estate, and Eric Beattie, director of campus planning, design, and construction, speaking about the university's local and minority purchasing and contracting programs. Cantor concurs that the university's business team, led by Louis Marcoccia, was "very on board from the beginning."[53]

Finally, Cantor elaborates on the importance of communication, both externally and internally. "I take, and took, too much for granted that students and faculty . . . would see the value [of scholarly engagement] and think [it] appropriate for the core of the institution. But it's hard to define, and the communication task is enormous! So many of us are doing this because we see it as the core of what we do; we forget that it needs constant justification to the world." More recently, the economic crisis has forced Cantor to "hone in on the rhetoric" of the mutually beneficial outcomes of community engagement, validating to the Senate Budget Committee the expenditures on neighborhood initiatives in the midst of salary freezes. Having deans and senior leadership on board is a necessary part of the equation. The chancellor also uses her personal capital to leverage city and political support for the university's initiatives, and she understands the importance of institutional commitment: "We're in it for the long haul, and it's going to be a long haul! Players do come and go, but the initiative stays strong."[54]

Syracuse's success in institutionalizing an anchor vision points to several critical factors: a unified philosophy throughout the university, and engagement of a breadth of faculty and students, to leverage the institution's full resources; policy changes on both the academic and corporate side of the university, rooting engagement into the rewards structure and the mission; and ongoing communication (internally and externally) to foster understanding and sustainability.

Securing Funding and Leveraging Resources

University of Cincinnati: Community Investment of Endowment Assets

The University of Cincinnati's Community Development Office is a separate department within the Finance Division. Under the direction of this office, the university has made significant financial commitments to community development in the Uptown neighborhoods through several methods: loans through investments of its endowment portfolio; operating grants through its general funds; and master leasing of selected spaces.

As of the fall of 2009, the University of Cincinnati had committed a total of $148.6 million out of its $833 million endowment to real estate development in Uptown. This comes from

---

Figure 24. Community Investment of Endowment Assets at Cincinnati

Strategy
Patient capital: investment of university endowment in community revitalization with long-term view of return

Key Features
- Create understanding of long-term financial and social return on investment
- Use endowment funds to leverage outside investors (e.g., other anchors, city government, banks, and private developers) and build community capacity
- Provide ongoing communication/transparency

a "commingled endowment" provided through the university's equity along with that of the university foundation. "We eventually learned to treat this investment separately [from the rest of our endowment]," says Monica Rimai, former senior vice president of finance and administration. "Of course there has been some questioning, in these difficult financial times, 'Should we have done this?' But I believe that universities, by design, are in it for the long haul, and they have to take a long-term view of all their investments. This is particularly true at an urban institution."[55]

University leaders refer to their investment as "patient capital"—at 4 percent interest rates, an investment that requires a deeper understanding of the long-term financial and social return. At the same time, this approach did create some mixed expectations. Rimai believes that more time could have been spent on the front end, educating the university, trustees, university foundation, and community at large about the intentions of Cincinnati's engagement and advocating the "long-term view" on investments. Over $80 million of the university's endowment loans remain outstanding as of 2009; yet the loans have leveraged significant additional funding from other public and private resources.[56]

Collectively, the seven community urban redevelopment corporations supported by the university have received an average of one million dollars in operating funds each year since the early 2000s, from the university's general funds. In the late 1990s, for example, the university and the City of Cincinnati each put in roughly $50,000 for a planning process to redevelop the Clifton Heights neighborhood. "Then, to make it actionable, they formed the Redevelopment Corporation in 2001, with three business association members, one community neighborhood association member, and one university representative. The university basically said, 'We'll fund you from an operational and developmental view, but we'll let you guys do the work,'" says Matt Bourgeois, director of the Clifton Heights Community Urban Redevelopment Corporation (CHCURC). "Our operations have been funded fully by UC since 2001, with the long-term goal being to reduce our reliance on these funds via project revenues as they come online," adds Bourgeois.[57]

Details of the first major development project in Clifton Heights sheds some light on the financing mechanisms through which the university has leveraged significant assets. This development, University Park, includes 291 units of student housing, 36,924 square feet of retail on the first floor, and a 1,118-space parking garage below. Funding for this project included $55 million in tax-exempt bonds, issued by the county and guaranteed by the Bank of New York/Citizens Bank LOC, and an $11 million university endowment loan for retail construction. In addition, CHCURC has joint use and retail use agreements with the university (e.g., the university must lease any retail spaces if retail revenues do not exceed $818,000 per year). "We're recognizing the risk, but also know we're building capacity among these community-based organizations," says Stagaman. CHCURC also used some of its operating funds to match city grants for a $1 million Façade Improvement Program in the neighborhood's old business district. As a result, Bourgeois notes, these businesses have also profited from the new retail and housing developments that have occurred down the street.[58]

Finally, the university and its partners in the Consortium funded a $52 million loan pool. This leveraging power brought in an additional $52 million from local banks through federal new markets tax credits (NMTCs) with which the Consortium created the Uptown Cincinnati

Development Fund to finance major Uptown redevelopment projects. In total, more than $400 million in public and private resources (including tax-exempt bonds, tax increment financing, and developer financing) have been invested in Uptown projects. The NMTC investors expect to see a faster return than some of the university's dollars that are being used as collateral, but the Consortium has not seen enough of these projects' mature to know how they are going to work. "Transparency is critical. Folks need to understand, in a very open way, why the institution is doing what it's doing, and what resources and limitations we have. New markets tax credits are very technical, so the university has to communicate in a way that people understand," says Rimai. The Uptown Consortium received an additional $45 million in NMTCs in 2009, which will allow partners to continue planned projects in the Uptown area, particularly in land assemblage and retail development.[59]

One lesson Rimai offers is that universities have to approach community development efforts "with a high degree of business acumen. You need to know what you're good at and what you're not good at . . . recognize your limitations. Part of the institutional investment has to be in [developing] partnerships as well . . . We didn't [initially] approach our investment with business discipline, which contributed to the inappropriate expectations that the community held."[60] Additional lessons from Cincinnati's experience include (1) university endowment funds invested in community revitalization efforts must be treated as "patient capital"; (2) when invested strategically, these funds can not only help build capacity within the community but also leverage significant outside investment; and (3) the intentions and limitations of the university's investment should be communicated properly from the beginning.

LeMoyne-Owen College: Leveraging Public and Private Dollars

From 1999 through 2009, LeMoyne-Owen College received seven historically black colleges and universities (HBCU) grants from the Office of University Partnerships at the U.S. Department of Housing and Urban Development (HUD). While the College was the actual applicant for the HUD HBCU grants, the CDC received these funds directly. The grants averaged $550,000 for each year and have provided core operating funds for the LeMoyne-Owen College Community Development Corporation to carry out its neighborhood revitalization activities on the college's behalf. Furthermore, this funding has supported organizational stability, including a staff of charismatic leaders at the CDC who have leveraged millions of dollars in additional public and private investments for programmatic activity.[61]

Figure 25. Leveraging Public and Private Dollars at LeMoyne-Owen

Strategy
Creative financing: HUD dollars used as core funding to operate an independent entity that could attract millions of dollars in public and private capital

Key Features
- Build on initial funding to first provide stability and then leverage additional resources
- Seek investment from a wide variety of public and private sources (e.g., new markets tax credits, federal appropriation, private developers)
- Invest in sustainable development (e.g., job creation, housing development and homeownership training)

One of the CDC's largest efforts to date is the $11.5 million, mixed-used Towne Center at Soulsville USA. This project complements the $20 million development of the new Stax Museum and Stax Music Academy in the Soulsville community, as well as the earlier transformation of the LeMoyne Gardens public housing development into a mixed-income development, College Park. The Towne Center project was largely made possible by a $7.3 million loan from the Wachovia Community Development Finance group using new markets tax credits. It was also supported through a half-million-dollar federal appropriation sponsored by a Tennessee senator. CDC director Jeffrey Higgs says of the senator's support: "We had a track record and people believed in our vision."[62] Additional grants were secured from the City of Memphis, Shelby County, the U.S. Economic Development Administration, the Office of Community Services, and the CDC's HBCU funding from HUD. (The city's contribution included funding for the demolition of existing structures on the four-acre property as well as an additional $250,000.) "We invested a lot of equity into [the Towne Center] on our own—about $2 million from our budget," adds Higgs. Indeed, at times the CDC has had to rely heavily on its own line of credit and cash reserves to cover development costs.[63]

Since Cincinnati and LeMoyne-Owen have taken advantage of new markets tax credits in their major redevelopment efforts, it is worth exploring this mode of financing a little further. The New Markets Tax Credit Program was established in 2000 as part of the Community Development Financial Institutions Fund of the U.S. Treasury Department. It allows institutions to invest in a community development project in a low-income neighborhood in exchange for a tax credit. The credit provided to the investor totals 39 percent of the cost of the investment over seven years: 5 percent in each of the first three years, and 6 percent in the final four years. In other words, it is a "shallow but not deep subsidy" that helps realize inner-city investments that are on the margins of being made. As Higgs puts it, "If it's a good deal from the start, [the tax credits] make it even better." Since higher education institutions themselves do not have tax liabilities, they cannot derive any tax benefits from the new markets tax credits. Private investors, such as local banks, however, can invest money in the development project for a portion of the tax credit, which they can then apply to any federal taxes they may owe. Meanwhile, the development organization now has capital to invest in its neighborhood revitalization activities.[64]

Putting the NMTCs to good use, the Towne Center is 100 percent owned by the LeMoyne-Owen College CDC, an ownership stake that is projected to rise in value to $15 million when the Center is fully occupied. It is also expected to provide more than 200 jobs, incubator space for emerging local businesses, and first-class goods and services for neighborhood residents, including many LeMoyne-Owen students. The CDC is also working on a façade program with existing small businesses around the Towne Center.

In addition to such large-scale projects as the Towne Center, the LeMoyne-Owen CDC has leveraged and directed significant funding toward housing development and home ownership in Soulsville. For instance, the CDC is a housing development partner in the city of Memphis's Neighborhood Stabilization Program, which is funded by $63 million in federal grants awarded to the city, county, and state. "We have built fourteen new homes and done seven rehabs [in Soulsville]," says Higgs. With the addition of homebuyers' training, this has "helped to increase homeownership among people who were renting in the neighborhood." The CDC also receives $500,000 from the city to do house repairs for seniors and low-income residents. "We have done at least one hundred repairs all over Memphis," adds Higgs.[65]

LeMoyne-Owen College's approach to community development is different from most other higher education institutions in several ways—chiefly in that the college allows significant federal funding to be deposited directly into the account of its associated CDC, which then carries out focused objectives independently from the institution. Operational and financial autonomy has permitted the CDC to react quickly and deploy resources as needed. This rarity in itself sheds light on an innovative approach to financing and carrying out an anchor strategy. At the same time, LeMoyne-Owen CDC's success points to several universally applicable lessons when leveraging resources for community development strategies: first, build on existing resources and reputation to provide organizational stability and create a strong, shared vision; second, seek a diversified portfolio of public and private investment to carry out programmatic activities; and third, use this investment strategically to guarantee not only the organization's sustainability, but also that of the neighborhood.

Building a Culture of Economic Inclusion

Miami Dade College: Creating Opportunity for All

Miami Dade College's commitment to personal economic development through education is seen clearly in its open-door policy and synchronization of its professional schools with the region's target industries. "The opportunity to learn and build workforce skills is the fundamental building block of city revitalization," claims President Eduardo Padrón. By way of example: 61 percent of Miami-Dade County public school graduates who attend colleges and universities in Florida attend Miami Dade College; MDC students represent 178 countries, and more than 50 percent report a native language other than English; more than half are the first in their families to attend college; 74 percent need college preparatory coursework; 61 percent are low-income, and 39 percent are below the federal poverty level; 68 percent of enrolled students are Hispanics, and 19 percent are black non-Hispanics; and MDC ranks second in the nation for the number of Pell Grants awarded to public colleges and universities.

Figure 26. Building a Culture of Economic Inclusion at Miami Dade College

Strategy
Opportunity for all: reach underserved populations through open-door policy, job training, small business development, and employment

Key Features
- Focus primary resources on support services to at-risk student body
- Provide workforce training to low-income residents and connect to actual jobs
- Support local economic development through micro-entrepreneurship training in minority business corridor
- Develop inclusive hiring policies

The College's support services to this unique student body are leading to results: 80 percent of 2006–2007 associate in arts graduates transferred to Florida colleges and universities immediately after graduation; 96 percent of associate in science graduates and vocational career certificate graduates were placed in jobs related to their studies within a year of graduation or chose to continue their education; and nine out of ten Miami Dade College students stay in the region and contribute to the local economy after graduating.[66]

Miami Dade College also connects low-income residents of Miami-Dade County to job opportunities and small business development, particularly through the work of its School of Business, School of Community Education, and the Carrie Meek Entrepreneurial Education Center. For instance, the college—with a $100,000 grant from a local community redevelopment agency—launched the Hospitality Institute "to specifically connect job opportunities in the local hospitality industry with Miami's inner city residents through customer service and job readiness training." The School of Business hosts the Institute in Overtown, one of Miami's oldest and poorest neighborhoods. "[The program] offers individuals a certificate of completion, gift certificates for professional attire from an area thrift store, and job placement services," says Geoffrey Gathercole, director of the School of Community Education. From January 2008 through December 2009, 628 individuals participated in the training and receiving completion certificates. The School of Business estimates that 223 graduates secured a job with 149 different employers in the area during these two years.[67]

Serving the African American neighborhood of Liberty City, a locale that has struggled to develop a thriving business center, the Meek Center is a "partner for renewal" by "equipping local business entrepreneurs with the skills and support to undertake the challenge of small business ownership." For example, the Meek Center offers a FastTrac Entrepreneurship course in collaboration with the City of Miami and NANA (Neighbors and Neighbors Association) that currently provides training for fifty-five micro-enterprise businesses in Liberty City.[68]

Finally, President Padrón takes pride in the fact that "the College's workforce very closely mirrors the larger community and our hiring efforts are very conscious of maintaining and furthering the diversity and equity that we value." Across its eight campuses, Miami Dade College employs 6,200 faculty and staff. Ethnic minorities account for 74 percent of full-time employees; 59 percent of full-time faculty are ethnic minorities, and 53 percent are female. The college's total payroll and benefits budget is approximately $240 million.[69]

Miami Dade College's experience creating "opportunity for all" points to several important aspects for higher education institutions seeking to promote economic inclusion. First, a multifaceted approach to creating education and workforce opportunities helps reach a greater population. Second, when dealing with an underserved student population, primary focus must be given to helping these individuals succeed in higher education. Once necessary resources and energy have been dedicated to this mission, additional funding (and in-kind resources) can be leveraged to support targeted programs/trainings to those most in need in the broader community. Critically, these programs should be connected to real job and business opportunities. Finally, existing institutional resources can be redirected to support economic inclusion, such as local and minority hiring policies.

Sustaining Inclusive Planning and Robust Community Relationships

Minnesota: Overcoming Mistrust through On-the-Ground Collaboration

The University of Minnesota has worked hard to overcome a history of mistrust with some of its Northside neighbors, and things still do not always go smoothly. When the university embarked upon its urban agenda in 2005, a number of community leaders said that they should have been approached earlier. For example, the university called its effort the "University Northside Initiative." "We challenged that name, and changed it to 'Partnership.' This meant it was going to be a participatory relationship," says Sherrie Pugh, executive director of the Northside Resident Redevelopment Council. Additionally, the university had recruited a world-renowned child psychologist to establish a child and family center that would focus on the community's large number of children in foster care. This action created concern among some community members, since past university research had rarely involved community members in project design. Instead, community members had primarily been treated as research "subjects" with little involvement in project goal setting, implementation, or assessment.[70]

The university spent over two years in dialogue with the community about the potential of having a physical presence in North Minneapolis. Though not always pleasant, this dialogue eventually led to a shared vision in which three focus areas were identified for collaborative research, outreach, and engagement: education, health and wellness, and community and economic development. In 2006, 65 percent of the community (who cast ballots) voted to allow the partnership to come into their neighborhoods.[71] As a way to deliver on its promises and demonstrate its commitment to sustaining the relationship, the university established the Urban Research and Outreach/Engagement Center (UROC) as the anchor through which resources could be coordinated in North Minneapolis. In 2006, a team of university students conducted community asset mapping, as the university made it explicit that they did not wish to compete with existing assets and resources. Although the community's desire to establish a community benefits agreement has yet to be realized, the university has established several activities that have provided ongoing opportunities for communication, on-the-ground collaboration, and capacity building.

For example, the University Northside Partnership encouraged the formation of the Community Affairs Committee (CAC) in 2006 to "inform the process, procedures, and practices of the partnership."[72] Beginning in 2008, UROC's executive director recommended

---

Figure 27. Sustaining Inclusive Planning and Robust Relationships at Minnesota

Strategy
Mutually beneficial partnerships: opportunities for ongoing communication, collaboration, capacity building, and shared ownership

Key Features
- Enter into genuine dialogue to reach a shared vision and engage stakeholders in strategic planning process
- Create opportunities for on-the-ground collaboration through focused work groups with shared leadership
- Invest in building capacity among existing organizations and partnerships

that the CAC be co-chaired by a university representative and a community representative. The CAC facilitated a series of meetings to identify potential collaborative projects in the previously identified themes of education, health and wellness, and community and economic development. Work groups in these three core areas, as well as the arts, now meet regularly to define goals, strategies, and timelines for these issues. More than sixty community individuals have signed up to participate along with one hundred faculty, students, and staff. Collaborative leadership oversees the work groups, who have been trained in participatory action research. Community leaders, in particular, play a critical role in bringing community knowledge to the table. "The work groups are partly to harmonize the fact that the university is about process, process, and process, and the community is about action, action, action," says Makeda Zulu-Gillespie, university-community liaison and CAC co-chair.[73]

The FIPSE (Fund for the Improvement of Postsecondary Education) work groups are another form of interdisciplinary teams, each led by co-chairs from the university and the community. Within the urban agenda's three focus areas, FIPSE projects are centered on out-of-school time, healthy foods, and youth entrepreneurship—subjects of shared interest where some level of partnership already existed. The FIPSE budget (two-thirds provided by the U.S. Department of Education, and one-third of which is an in kind match provided by the university) has primarily been invested in capacity building. "We knew that if we funded [new] programs, the money would run out. So instead, we build capacity for existing organizations and programs," says Geoff Maruyama, a university associate vice president and the FIPSE grant principal investigator. According to community leaders, this strategy appears to be working: "FIPSE has served as a real catalyst for out-of-school time groups to talk to each other. We are matching up resources, and I can now find support for other pieces of that continuum [of child and family support]. This collaboration has also brought legislators in, and we're talking about funding and policy best practices. University resources were able to provide for what we haven't been able to do alone," says Mary Fitzpatrick, executive director of the nonprofit Seeds of Change.[74]

The FIPSE grant was largely seen as a way to get the University Northside Partnership going, and UROC will also provide ongoing support for these activities. In addition, UROC has facilitated three participatory action research groups to focus primarily on healthy homes and issues of foreclosure. Within these groups, UROC has placed several community members in paid, part-time positions to work alongside a paid research assistant and a couple of faculty and staff. These research teams also consult with a larger stakeholder group. Efforts like these are beginning to address a key community concern: for research to be driven by what the community needs and wants.[75]

Finally, leading up to the development of the UROC building, Minnesota embarked upon a strategic planning process that deeply engaged community stakeholders. This has not always been easy, according to founding executive director Irma McClaurin: "Everyone wants community engagement without investing in it and recognizing that it's a process. It needs to be built into the timeline and the costs. Our budget did not include community engagement, so we had to get creative." She asked her architectural team to convene a community workshop to engage residents in the design of the UROC building. "We want the

143

space and the design to reflect the collaboration," says McClaurin. This includes having offices without doors, large and open shared workspace, community artwork on the walls, computers in the reception area for public use, and free coffee.[76] Following initial interviews with a number of key stakeholders by UROC's consultant group, more than fifty community and university representatives attended a strategic planning conference in February 2009 (before the building opened) around the theme of "Coming Together to Create a Shared Future for North Minneapolis." Both the workshop and the conference allowed residents to develop ideas for UROC that they are beginning to see come to fruition. McClaurin says this is helping residents take ownership of UROC's creation. "The university has made a 'good faith effort.' They're at the tipping point now, for an opportunity for change, and that's why I'm engaged," says Raymond Dehn, the community co-chair of CAC. "Our biggest concern now is how to have engagement and revitalization without displacement."[77]

The University of Minnesota's relationship with its North Minneapolis neighbors, particularly since 2005, holds several lessons for building mutually beneficial partnerships between anchors and their communities. First, ongoing opportunities for communication and on-the-ground collaboration are critical for gaining trust and community buy-in. Next, in a similar vein, participating in inclusive practices from the beginning leads to shared ownership of the process. Third, focusing on a few identified priority issues and drawing upon existing community strengths, organizations, and relationships helps build local capacity as well as revitalization efforts that are likely to be sustained.

As we discuss in the next, and concluding, section of this book, these best practices—taken together—form the building blocks to a comprehensive anchor institution strategy. Learning from the successes and limitations of current efforts, we hope, will provide valuable tools and practices to other universities implementing anchor-driven community development initiatives. To fully realize their anchor mission, however, will require universities to develop internal organizing strategies that consciously engage their comprehensive resources—human, academic, cultural, and especially economic—with their communities in collaborative and sustainable ways. It will also require significant support from funders and public policy.

PART 4

Envisioning the Road to Be Taken: Realizing the Anchor Institution Mission

We need to be . . . on the ground, strategically focused and understand the task of changing neighborhoods, but we have to be organically connected back up to administrative levels that will provide us with resources and support to help us develop our capacity—grow, strengthen, protect, and work with us.

—Henry Louis Taylor, director, Center for Urban Studies, University at Buffalo, phone interview by Rita Axelroth Hodges, April 16, 2009

Building Internal Constituencies for Partnership Work

In the fall 2009 issue of *The Presidency*, a journal of the American Council on Education, Chancellor Nancy Cantor of Syracuse University implores her colleagues to heed the call of President Barack Obama that higher education work to address the needs of urban communities. Cantor contends that universities today could play a role for twenty-first-century urban America as important as that played by land-grant colleges for rural America following the passage of the Morrill Act of 1862.[1]

In calling for a "New Morrill Act," Cantor posits, "One might think that a global financial crisis would be no time for college and university presidents to think expansively. Hunkering down is the more natural reaction to a threat of the magnitude that the economy continues to present. But expansive thought is exactly what we need right now—not necessarily the kind that grows our physical plant or our list of program offerings, but a fundamental reexamination of what American higher education is all about and where each of our institutions fits into that ideal."[2]

Like Cantor, we understand that although higher education institutions typically define their core missions around teaching and research, the positioning of universities and colleges in today's society opens up great potential to expand this narrow designation. We argue that universities can and should think of themselves as having an education mission, a research mission (if a research university), *and* an anchor institution mission. In many schools, especially land-grant institutions, "public service" has frequently been identified as the third mission, but the term is often left undefined. We have suggested that an anchor institution mission be defined as *the conscious and strategic application of the long-term, place-based economic power of the institution, in combination with its human and intellectual resources, to better the welfare of the community in which it resides.*

In her article, Cantor describes three critical elements for her university's efforts as an anchor institution in today's economy: (1) developing "reciprocal" partnerships that "constitute 'communities of experts' composed of scholars, professionals, and citizens from public, private, and nonprofit sectors"; (2) "building corresponding values into our institutional infrastructure, such as mechanisms to reward publicly engaged scholarship"; and (3) ensuring the university is "investing [its] time, resources, and intellectual capital optimally" by playing to institutional strengths and the strengths of its partners.[3] Imbedding these principles in any institution's engagement strategy, we argue, would help ensure that an anchor institution mission would be complementary to its teaching and research missions, rather than unrelated or competitive.

Even the most well developed examples of higher education institutions working with their communities—a number of them, of course, profiled here—have fallen short of the lofty goals we have described. Of course, context matters: the fact that universities have fallen short in developing fully effective and comprehensive approaches to community development reflects a broader national failure to address these issues. Harry Boyte of Minnesota observes that "'civic engagement in one university' is impossible—the fate of the university efforts are tied to much broader change, because the university is intricately embedded in systems and cultures across the world."[4]

At the same time, universities are not *merely* reflective of broader social trends either. Rather, they both reflect upon and can push back against their environment. As Boyte notes, Minnesota between 1997 and 2005 was able to achieve "notable cultural and institutional changes . . . that create[d] foundations for continuing civic innovation and leadership." According to Boyte and his colleagues, what is needed is "an institutional commitment to public purposes and responsibilities intended to strengthen a democratic way of life in the rapidly changing information age of the 21st century." Benson, Harkavy, and Puckett call for "democratically minded academics throughout the world [to] work continuously, collaboratively, and creatively" to help build "participatory democratic communities."[5]

One key area where creativity and commitment are required is in the coordination of universities' community engagement work with their corporate practices and broader institutional strategies. In particular, university hiring, real estate, purchasing, and investment strategies need to be more effectively linked to community partnership programs as well as academic engagement efforts. Sometimes, of course, the failure to coordinate community work with other university priorities has actually undermined the relationships that the community partnership programs helped to build. To cite a couple of prominent examples: expansion projects by Harvard in the Allston neighborhood of Boston and by Columbia in the "Manhattanville" section of Harlem have raised the ire of many community residents, effectively costing those universities a considerable part of the goodwill gained through their community partnership efforts.[6] This subject also points to the importance of building a commitment to an anchor institution mission throughout the university, which requires engaging faculty, students, and staff, in addition to presidents and administrators. Put somewhat differently, this requires having both an administrative commitment to engaged scholarship, as well as faculty buy-in on more corporate-focused (investment, hiring, purchasing, real estate) or administrative-led initiatives. As Rubin argues, "Often, the key faculty members [engaged in the community] have very different approaches, attitudes and community relationships than the administrators." One critical measure of impact when implementing anchor strategies, Rubin argues, must be "the strengthened connection of engaged scholarship and teaching to the overall university-community focus."[7]

As noted throughout, the ten institutions profiled in this study—and many others across the country—have demonstrated a variety of innovative ways universities can partner with their local communities, organizations, and government to *begin* to address problems of poverty, unemployment, inadequate schooling, affordable housing, crime, and other social issues. The specific building blocks, which can be integrated into a comprehensive model of an effective anchor institution strategy, are now available around the nation.

The question then becomes, provided a university acknowledges its role as an anchor, how does it achieve its *anchor institution mission*? We believe the answer, in part, lies in combining and building from university best practices, such as the ones described throughout this book and especially in the previous chapter. A number of specific steps that universities can take are outlined in figure 28. In particular, we are calling for a more conscious linking of the corporate and academic sides of the university in order to help solve significant urban problems as they are manifested locally. Further, to make significant contributions to their communities and cities requires higher education institutions to take their anchor institution mission seriously. As we described with our colleagues in the Anchor Institutions Task Force, universities poised to take on this mission are "working on multiple issues, such as housing, economic development, employment, education, and culture, that involve the corporate as well as academic sides of the university, including the significant commitment of senior leadership."[8] These "fully vested" institutions, as called by Perry and Wiewel, seek to "achieve the multiple interests of cities and communities, as well as universities, in ways that are mutually agreeable."[9]

We believe that this path must also lead to economic development in a way that benefits a broader swath of society. In other words, while successes in individual program areas are widespread, few efforts have had across-the-board success on such common community development challenges as poverty, health disparities, educational achievement gaps, and

---

Figure 28. Internal Steps to Build an Anchor Institution Mission

- Create a vice president position overseeing community and economic development initiatives to demonstrate high-level administrative commitment.
- Employ the university's resources fully and consciously—human, academic, cultural, and especially economic.
- Link university hiring, real estate, purchasing, and investment strategies to community partnership goals.
- Reward scholarship of engagement in promotion and tenure.
- Engage community residents and groups in mutually beneficial and respectful partnerships.
- Build networks across institutions so that they can share "best practices" and develop collaborative strategies.
- Adopt a strategic, place-based approach to capitalize on existing resources, even when limited.
- Leverage university economic power to support jobs for community members at the lower end of the socioeconomic scale.
- Ensure that Carnegie's "elective classification for community engagement" takes into account community-supportive practices in the corporate areas of purchasing, hiring, investment, and real estate.

affordable housing. "There are great examples of [university] investment—[but] this is [only] a *precursor* to wealth development," comments urban policy analyst Rosalind Greenstein.[10] The point is *not* that universities can, by themselves, bring about an end to poverty, but it *is* about universities exercising at least as much energy in generating jobs and wealth for community members at the *low* end of the socioeconomic scale (i.e., residents who lack college degrees and may not even have completed high school) as universities currently put into developing "biotech corridors," "technology parks," and the like. The challenge, in short, for twenty-first-century American universities wishing to pursue an anchor institution mission is to get back to the land-grant mission of economic development that benefits the greater society. In the words of Andrew Hahn and colleagues, for greatest impact, universities must "*think about these economic anchor roles in a cohesive and coordinated manner,* that is, as an integrated cluster of activities and practices, and not as piecemeal and separate phenomena." The specific economic roles Hahn refers to include purchaser, employer, workforce developer, real estate developer, incubator, advisor and network builder, community service partner, and advocate.[11]

The road map to a university achieving its anchor institution mission, then, requires putting together, piece by piece, a comprehensive community development strategy that engages the university's resources fully and consciously—human, academic, cultural, and economic—with its community in democratic, mutually beneficial, and respectful partnerships. It requires teasing out the best practices among existing initiatives, so that there is a clearer vision of what this model *could* look like. Building this road map is one of the objectives of this book. In other words, we believe that by linking the promising strategies found among the colleges and universities profiled in this study, a vision of a fully engaged anchor institution begins to emerge . . . Imagine a university with the local purchasing practices of Penn, the public education and health partnerships of Yale and IUPUI, the presidential leadership of Syracuse, the endowment-funded loan pool of Cincinnati, the leveraging power of LeMoyne-Owen College's CDC, the educational and job opportunities provided by Miami Dade College, the citywide collaboration of Portland State, the capacity-building efforts of Emory, and the participatory planning model of Minnesota.

Of course, building an anchor institution vision requires more thought than just adding together the best traits from each university's program. In this work, we divided the ten universities we analyzed into three clusters, in accord with the patterns we found as we examined their practices. Each set of schools has a mixture of strengths and shortfalls. Some, such as IUPUI, Miami Dade College, and Portland State (the "facilitators"), have a high degree of engagement with community groups, but have made relatively small investments on the corporate side and have undertaken only limited efforts toward strategically focused community development. Others, such as Penn, Yale, and Cincinnati (the "leaders"), have made impressively large corporate investments and have engaged in comprehensive community development efforts, but often these efforts have been limited in terms of their partnership aspect (i.e., while community groups have been regularly "consulted," they have rarely been true partners in university partnership program creation). Still others, such as Emory, Minnesota, Syracuse, and LeMoyne-Owen (the "conveners"), have been more thoughtful in building community capacity and involving community groups at the front end, but have relied heavily on commitments from outside public and private sources to achieve their objectives.

To be sure, the different approaches reflect the different nature of the institutions themselves. IUPUI, Portland State, and Miami Dade College are all large (and often largely underfunded) public institutions with limited resources. Their achievements through in-kind resources, such as the level of participation in community-based research at Portland State, the level of service-learning participation by students at IUPUI, and the success in diversity hiring at Miami Dade, are very impressive. Still, the corporate component and place-based nature of these efforts is rather limited. We argue that, even when resources are restricted, adopting a strategic, localized approach to community development can help ensure that existing resources have much greater impact. The power of doing so is illustrated by LeMoyne-Owen, a historically black college with very limited resources that, nonetheless—by creating an associated CDC that has leveraged significant external resources—has been able to effectively employ an approach similar to that of much wealthier schools like Syracuse, Minnesota, and Emory *because* of its very focused use of the limited resources it does have.

The patterns of the other six schools we examine provide an interesting contrast, since all of these schools have significant (albeit not equal) resources, yet have proceeded to follow two rather distinctive paths. Penn, Yale, and Cincinnati all initiated comprehensive community partnership efforts in response to threatening conditions. The "crisis response" framework helped galvanize the university leadership and broader university community to deploy large amounts of money, staff, and attention, but it also meant that many of their "university-community partnerships" were implemented quickly and were largely of the university's design. Often, too, such university efforts, while undoubtedly improving the lives of many residents, have had greater success at creating a safe shared corridor than at alleviating urban poverty or building capacity among community groups. By contrast, the partnerships at Emory, Syracuse, and Minnesota place more emphasis on building nonprofit capacity and mutual goal setting, but the resource commitment by these schools remains—relative to Penn, Cincinnati, and Yale—considerably less. We believe there is a chance for organizational learning on both sides of the spectrum. Universities that initiate programs in response to a crisis can become more collaborative. Indeed, Cincinnati, Penn, and Yale have all taken steps in that direction. Conversely, schools that have developed more collaborative approaches but have failed to align their institutional resources to support the community partnership objectives have much to learn from schools that have made more extensive use of the full gamut of available university resources. Again, Minnesota, Emory, and Syracuse have taken deliberate steps in this direction.

An anchor institution mission has implications in other areas beyond research, however. While we have only briefly mentioned faculty tenure and promotion in our case studies, if a university accepts that it has an anchor institution mission, then faculty that help it achieve that mission surely have to be rewarded in some way.[12] To be clear, an anchor institution mission demands that academic *and* non-academic resources be directly and strategically connected to improving the quality of life in the university's local community.

Thinking of an anchor institution mission as being part of what universities do also has implications for how those actively involved in studying community partnerships think

151

about their work. For example, in December 2006, the Carnegie Foundation for the Advancement of Teaching launched its elective "community engagement" classification, which represented a huge step forward for the field. For the first time, universities can compete to be nationally recognized for their community partnership work. In the third round in 2010, 296 schools ultimately received the "community engagement" classification, representing substantial commitments in the categories of both curricular engagement and outreach and partnerships. At the same time, the standards for "engagement" fail to take into account many of the corporate factors—hiring, purchasing, investment, and so on—that are part and parcel of an anchor institution approach. Adopting an anchor institution mission thus requires a rethinking by those evaluating institutions as well as those working in the field.[13]

Catalyzing Change with Philanthropy

The impact an integrated higher education anchor strategy might achieve over time cannot properly be gauged by focusing on academic institutions alone. A key matter is the nexus of funders, local and state governments, and the federal government, and how these groups can provide new incentives and motivations for higher education to engage in community building and economic development work. A summary of some of the key ways philanthropy can promote anchor institution strategies at universities is set forth in figure 29.

In our case studies, we have focused primarily on the *internal* dynamics that have led to the development of university-community partnership efforts. We think this focus is appropriate given the central role played by the actors involved—that is, community members, university staff and administrators, faculty, and students. However, this is not meant to obscure the important role played by external funders. For example, the Netter Center at the University of Pennsylvania in 2007–2008 received over $944,000 in funding from Penn, but had a total budget of $5.47 million, more than half of which ($2.86 million) came from grants (with the remaining third of the budget financed largely through the support of individual

---

Figure 29. Building the Anchor Institution Mission through Philanthropy

- Support information sharing and networks that promote the work (e.g., Coalition of Urban Serving Universities).
- Develop a funders' group that can support long-term, comprehensive, multi-modal initiatives at leading campuses.
- Create incentives to encourage structural changes, including policy amendments and internal collaboration that support an anchor institution mission.
- Provide pre-development and capital support for community job creation strategies linked to anchor institutions, as in Cleveland.

donors).[1] Clearly, the ability of the Netter Center to secure external resources is crucial to the success of its work.

But to extend the Netter Center example further and state the obvious, the $2.86 million in grants that Netter received in 2007–2008 came in a bunch of smaller packages. The messy process through which external funds are secured can complicate overall effectiveness. As Cory Bowman, associate director at the Netter Center, notes, "Every grant requires some form of evaluation: [metrics like] literacy, attendance, college acceptance. One school publicly held us responsible for achieving their 'Adequate Yearly Progress' targets from No Child Left Behind. So, 'slice by slice' we can show results. But what we're really interested in at Netter is systemic university-community change . . . [We would like to] identify the best way to advance teaching and research for real-world problem-solving."[2] Philanthropic funds, in particular, have the potential to emphasize such systemic change, especially because, unlike many government grants, they are relatively unburdened by specific targets and reporting requirements. Foundations thus have considerable influence over the direction of the community partnership movement.

A few years ago, the Democracy Collaborative at the University of Maryland surveyed university faculty, administrators, and staff, as well as some foundation leaders, regarding where interviewees believed that foundations could best contribute to leveraging universities to be effective in pursuing their anchor institution mission. Two themes stood out: (1) promoting networking by using the convening power of foundations to bring practitioners together to develop a common voice; and (2) promoting comprehensive, multi-modal initiatives to create engaged campuses or groups of campuses, which could then be emulated by others.[3]

In regards to developing a common voice, foundations can play an important role through support for networking organizations like the Coalition of Urban Serving Universities (USU). Elizabeth Hollander, former president of Campus Compact, notes that "foundations always do well when they invest in getting exchanges—developing the practice, getting the publications—trade association functions. This worked in service-learning. It started with connecting people at the bottom as well as at the top."[4] Broader convening of groups can also facilitate this organizing process. Harry Boyte highlights that one place "where foundations have a role, an important role, is as colleagues and peers of people in faculty positions . . . Foundation officials are public intellectuals and can help broaden the discussion."[5]

Comprehensive foundation initiatives, however, are also important. Several years ago, John Burkhardt, director of the National Forum on Higher Education for the Public Good at the University of Michigan and a former program officer for the Kellogg Foundation observed, "We have so many good examples out there. So the priority now is less about trying to fund new programs. It's more about structural and systemic changes that need to occur."[6]

Foundations have begun to support development in this direction. The Annie E. Casey Foundation, for example, made a small grant ($20,000) to USU to assemble information on partnership best practices, evaluate partnership impact, and support the development of advocacy work. In 2009, Living Cities made a larger investment of nearly $1 million supporting the replication of the "Strive" educational model from Cincinnati (profiled above) at four other schools: California State University, East Bay; IUPUI; University of Houston; and Virginia Commonwealth University in Richmond, Virginia. Living Cities in 2009 also provided a $250,000 capacity-building grant to USU to support "the advancement of universities as transformational community anchors."[7]

A funders' group committed to steadily advancing a coherent overall agenda could prove decisive in making such a comprehensive initiative possible and focusing the economic might of universities for the benefit of their communities. One model might be the original Living Cities consortium, which began as a ten-year commitment in 1991 by foundations and an insurance company to expand the work of community development corporations in twenty-three cities, and received significant support from the federal departments of Housing and Urban Development and Health and Human Services. Presumably, an anchor institution funders' initiative would have different players. (For example, one might expect the U.S. Department of Education to play a role.) The newly established Social Innovation Fund in the Corporation for National and Community Service, which was set up to fund intermediaries such as this kind of consortium, might also play a role. Regardless of the specific structure of a funders' group, it must be understood that this is no "quick fix" campaign: an initiative of this import and magnitude should not be undertaken unless understood as at least a ten-year effort.[8]

To be successful, a strategic philanthropic initiative would require adequate dedicated staff to organize the effort and to implement a two-track strategy working both within and outside of the higher education system: (1) a systematic, step-by-step strategy directed at developing and promoting federal and state policies that can provide the right mix of incentives to bring about a major reorientation in some of higher education's goals and (2) a parallel strategy aimed at building up the internal capacity of universities to fully realize their anchor institution mission.

Success would also depend on individual foundations giving consideration to what they can do in their own grant-making to influence and motivate university engagement. This need not depend on using limited community development grant funds. In 2009, only 3 percent of foundation giving went to community economic development; that same year, 23.3 percent of all foundation funding or $5.1 billion was disbursed to education.[9] Refocusing some of the latter to provide incentives for university engagement could have a substantial impact. For example, the Kellogg Foundation initiated the "Engaged Institutions" project in 2005, which seeks to discover how colleges and universities can more thoroughly integrate "civic engagement within their organizational structures and practices, and their research, teaching, and outreach activities." In partnership with PolicyLink (a national research and action institute based in Oakland, California), the Engaged Institutions project has supported university-community partnership efforts at four schools: the University of Texas, El Paso; Penn State University; University of Minnesota, Twin Cities; and the University of California, Santa Cruz. Each partnership is different, but all foster the goals of improving the lives of local youth and increasing civic engagement within their institutions through a focused project that has broad lessons.[10]

Organizational transformation also requires significant *internal* collaboration. Burkhardt describes the challenge here: "The funding basis that allows for this work is organized most frequently by disciplines, and doesn't really foster collaboration. Key faculty members working in the same community may even be competing." External funding, such as from foundations, may be able to support universities in organizing a more coordinated strategy toward community development.

Another innovative role foundations can play in helping universities leverage their assets toward community economic development is illustrated by the Cleveland Foundation, which is guiding the redevelopment of Cleveland's Greater University Circle neighborhoods. The Cleveland Foundation took the lead in convening stakeholders from the community's nonprofits, anchor institutions, and city government, as well as community development consultants—including the Democracy Collaborative—which led to the development of the Evergreen Cooperative Initiative. While drawing on precedents and experience gained in cities around the world, this is the first attempt to bring together anchor institution economic power to create widely shared and owned assets and capital in low-income neighborhoods. It is also the first significant effort to create green jobs that not only pay a decent wage, but also build assets and wealth for employees through ownership mechanisms (with a focus on worker-owned cooperatives). A central element of the Evergreen strategy has been to work closely with Cleveland's largest anchors (in particular, the Cleveland Clinic, University Hospitals, and Case Western Reserve University) to devise ways in which their business decisions, particularly procurement, could be focused to produce greater neighborhood and citywide benefit.

Leaders of the Evergreen Initiative made a conscious decision at the outset to pursue a model of economic development that would not require ongoing subsidy. Philanthropic dollars are used to provide *initial* seed funding for each cooperative business, but the businesses are then expected to be able to turn a profit and stand on their own. Importantly, foundation resources are also used to leverage additional sources of financing (e.g., bank loans, new markets tax credits, U.S. Department of Housing and Urban Development funds, U.S. Department of Energy funds, and State of Ohio renewable energy investments). By way of example, $750,000 in grant funds from the Cleveland Foundation leveraged a total of $5.7 million in public, private, and philanthropic dollars to launch the Evergreen Cooperative Laundry in October 2009. The Initiative's flagship effort, this laundry now operates with the smallest carbon footprint of any industrial-scale laundry in northeast Ohio while taking advantage of the growing laundry needs of the area's health industry.

To expand its scale and impact, the Cleveland Foundation also established the Evergreen Cooperative Development Fund, a nonprofit revolving loan fund. The fund was capitalized with $3 million in grants and expects to raise an additional $10–12 million. The fund hopes to use this money, in turn, to leverage as much as $100 million in further public, private, and philanthropic investment. To date, the fund has helped to launch two additional employee-owned businesses. One of these, Ohio Cooperative Solar, opened in the fall of 2009 and does weatherization work, including installation of solar panels on the roofs of the city's largest hospitals, universities, and government buildings. The third business to be developed, Green City Growers, broke ground in the fall of 2011 and is designed to be a 3.25-acre urban

156

greenhouse. Each cooperative that receives initial financing from the fund will repay the loan over time so that financing is available to other start-ups. Importantly, each of the Evergreen cooperatives is also obligated to pay 10 percent of its pretax profits back into the fund to help seed the development of new jobs through additional cooperatives. "Thus, each business has a commitment to its workers (through living wage jobs, affordable health benefits and asset accumulation) and to the general community (by creating new businesses that can provide stability to neighborhoods)."[11] Again, refocusing foundation dollars dispersed to higher education institutions in a way that provides incentives not only for coordinated, strategic engagement, but also for shared ownership of program initiatives with the community could significantly enhance the sustainability of anchor efforts.

Policy Support for the Anchor Institution Mission

W e believe that by engaging their resources fully, strategically, and collaboratively, universities can improve the quality of life in their local communities and build opportunities for individual and community wealth. We also believe that universities that respond to the broader economic needs of society may gain significant public support. As Henry Taylor puts it, "It's an inside-outside game. First, we need to make sure [government] understands the types of things the university is capable of doing . . . Then, they can put incentives into place to help universities move [further] in this direction."[1]

As described throughout this book, a number of universities have chosen to assume greater roles as anchor institutions, but most of this action has taken place in the absence of significant policy support. Of course, this is not to deny that universities receive very substantial levels of federal support. Not counting indirect federal support (e.g., U.S. Department of Education financing for student subsidized loan and grant programs), in fiscal year 2010, universities were the beneficiaries of over $24.99 billion in National Institutes of Health (NIH) grant funding, $6.532 billion in National Science Foundation (NSF) grant funding, and $1.358 billion in National Institute for Food and Agriculture (NIFA) or "land-grant" support. By contrast, federal funding of anchor institution strategies has been paltry. In fiscal year 2010, the Office of University Partnerships program at the U.S. Department of Housing and Urban Development, the leading federal program in this area, received an allocation of $23 million. In fiscal year 2011, this disparity continued. While NSF and NIH received 1 percent budget cuts, the land-grant budget was cut by more than 9 percent and the Office of University Partnerships' funding was completely eliminated.[2] Additionally, in the fiscal year 2011 budget, a related program in the Department of Education (Learn and Serve America), which had typically provided about $10 million a year in support for university service-learning programs, also saw its funding eliminated.[3] As we discuss below, narrowing this gap is a critical piece of promoting the anchor institution strategy.

The first element of a serious external strategy should be to identify specific state and federal opportunities for immediate action. Some opportunities may involve working within new government policy initiatives, such as the Obama administration's Choice Neighborhoods and Promise Neighborhoods programs, and, indeed, universities have been made eligible recipients for this funding. The Choice Neighborhoods Initiative, funded at $65 million in fiscal year 2010, seeks to integrate public housing revitalization and social service provision. The Promise Neighborhoods planning grants, funded at $10 million in fiscal year 2010, represent a small step toward federal efforts to replicate the highly touted Harlem Children's Zone program that applies a comprehensive "cradle through college" academic support system for children in targeted geographic zones as a poverty alleviation strategy. While the Obama administration proposed sizable increases in funding for both of these programs (original requests were for $250 million for Choice Neighborhoods and $210 million for Promise Neighborhoods), ultimately the FY 2011 budget Congress approved contained much more modest allocations—$64.9 million for Choice Neighborhoods and $30 million for Promise Neighborhoods. Another Obama administration initiative, the Sustainable Communities Initiative at HUD, funded at $150 million in fiscal year 2010 and at $99.8 million for fiscal year 2011, aims to integrate housing, environmental, and transportation planning; here, too, anchor institutions have an important role to play. This is not merely a matter of universities seeking out new sources of funding. Rather, the federal government has an incentive for universities to participate, since small amounts of federal investment can leverage considerable additional university resources. Given that the Harlem Children's Zone costs $70 million a year, federal funding alone is highly unlikely to achieve significant replication *without* anchor institution participation and investment.[4]

At the same time, while opportunities to promote an anchor institution mission within existing funding streams exist, this should not distract from the broader policy need to develop comprehensive longer-term legislation, based on the vision of a twenty-first-century anchor institution comparable to that of the land-grant institution. The emerging new model would be largely based on a collaborative approach to problem-solving—a two-way street in which practitioners and community members contribute to shaping the research, teaching, and service agenda of the university. Another critical element of this strategy is promoting and publicizing the best examples of community-building programs of universities, with priority given to the "economic engine" impact that universities are making on their communities. In addition, more case studies and training materials based on these models should be developed for use by other universities and policymakers. Ultimately, an anchor institution mission has the potential to become a core function of universities, just as community health clinics have become a mainstay at most nonprofit hospitals or service-learning has become a standard practice at our nation's high schools and universities. A summary of ways federal policy can foster anchor institution work by universities is provided in Figure 30.

As noted previously, after the election of Barack Obama as president in November 2008, Ira Harkavy and a team of community partnership practitioners, researchers, and university presidents came together to address how public policy could help leverage the existing movement within the university community to take on a more serious investment in

America's communities, cities, and metropolitan areas as anchor institutions. The task force's charge was to advise incoming Secretary of Housing and Urban Development Shaun Donovan, which gave the recommendations a HUD tilt. Nonetheless, in thinking about how public policy might strengthen and deepen universities' anchor institution mission work, the principles behind the recommendations are worth examining in more detail.

Figure 30. Policy Measures to Support the Anchor Institution Mission

- Support comprehensive programs through collaboration with new government policy initiatives (e.g. Promise Neighborhoods), expansion of current Office of University Partnership programs, and creation of an "Urban Grant" program.
- Fund specialized programs that match anchor resources to critical public objectives in specific areas (e.g., affordable housing, business development, K-12 education).
- Create anchor-based community development programs that leverage universities' economic power (e.g., purchasing, investment, hiring, real estate) for community benefit.
- Convene a multi-stakeholder group that can support cross-anchor institution collaborative efforts through a competitive grant program.
- Utilize local government to incentivize universities to invest in comprehensive community development efforts, as well as provide matching grants.
- Award prizes as NSF does to provide recognition for exemplary university efforts and help legitimize the work.
- Develop a national consultation team of faculty and staff from institutions that have been successful in their work with the community to aid in training and technical assistance.

A key principle behind the task force's work was that public resources are required to move faculty and university administrators to make the kinds of changes needed to embed and sustain an anchor institution mission across all components of the institution. Universities receive considerable federal support, but the federal funds received direct universities toward lab research, rather than fulfilling their anchor institution mission. As noted above, in fiscal year 2010, universities received over $6.5 billion from the National Science Foundation, roughly $25 billion from the National Institutes of Health, $1.358 billion from the U.S. Department of Agriculture's land-grant programs, and $25 million from the HUD Office of University Partnerships (OUP).

The federal allocation for university partnerships has been tiny, yet it is important to note that nine of the ten schools profiled here (all but Syracuse) have been OUP grant recipients.[5] At critical points, this federal support, limited though it has been (while grants vary in size, a standard amount has been in the $400,000–$700,000 range), has often proven catalytic in the development of the much larger initiatives profiled here. A 2002 study commissioned by HUD found that the typical $400,000 Community Outreach and Partnership Centers grant leveraged $475,000 in external funding. Moreover, if one considers that many partnership centers persist in their work for years or even over a decade after the initial grant has expired, the actual leveraging effect of federal investment has been far greater.[6]

Nevertheless, it is hard to imagine the funding disparities outlined above *not* influencing the allocation of university faculty, students, staff, and resources. A serious federal government strategy to encourage urban universities to adopt an anchor institution strategy needs to contribute appropriate resources to do so. A reasonable goal, the task force believed, would be to gradually increase federal "anchor institution" funds for urban universities to match the current level of support given "land-grant" programs. This would mean an annual allocation of $1.2 billion—an amount that is equivalent to $4 per U.S. citizen or 0.03 percent of total federal expenditures. Roughly speaking, these funds would be used in three key areas: (1) comprehensive "partnership" type programs, including reviving OUP programs, as well as creating an "Urban Grant" program, modeled after the USDA's "land-grant" and cooperative extension programs, but incorporating partnership principles (such as splitting funding between universities and community partners) and with an express focus on meeting the needs of urban areas—an idea originally promoted by the Coalition of Urban Serving Universities; (2) specialized programs that leverage anchor institution resources to meet critical public objectives in specific areas, such as affordable housing, workforce development, public health, K-12 education, culture-based development, and community-based research; and (3) anchor-based community development programs that systematically leverage universities' economic power (purchasing, investment, hiring, and so forth) for community benefit. (A more specific breakdown of how the Anchor Institutions Task Force envisioned the funds being used is provided in appendix 1.)[7]

For the last of these areas, one central idea is to convene a multistakeholder group, which the task force labeled an Integrated Community Anchor Network (I-CAN) that can support cross-anchor institution collaborative efforts such as the Uptown Consortium in Cincinnati profiled in this study. Partners at the federal level might include Health and Human Services, the White House Office of Urban Affairs, the Office of Social Innovation in the Corporation for National and Community Service, the HUD-DOT-EPA (Housing-Transportation–Environmental Protection Agency) Interagency Partnership for Sustainable Communities, and university and hospital associations.[8] Partners at the local level might include city government, local community development financial institutions (CDFIs), business development technical assistance groups, workforce development nonprofits, local public schools, community foundations, and area hospitals and universities. A competitive grant program that selected an initial slate of I-CAN cities might include the following as criteria in the initial request-for-proposal (RFP) document: (1) clear community building objectives in terms of local investment, local purchasing, hiring in low-income communities, business incubation, green job development, and wealth creation; (2) clear delineation of how economic development objectives will connect with core institutional programs—for example, education for universities; (3) indication of institutional support at the CEO/presidential level and of a commitment of internal funds and in-kind support; (4) evidence of state and local government matching support; (5) inclusion of community development corporations and other local community groups in the development of goals and objectives as well as implementation; and (6) clear metrics to track the impact anchor institution investments in community building have over time. To insure institutionalization of the process, the RFP might also require that a high-level unit for engagement be established in either the president's or provost's office and that a university-wide strategic planning process be undertaken with clear, measurable community-building outcomes.[9]

"HUD's approach has always been to provide seed money so that universities would continually seek their own money to sustain [partnership] programs. We have to find a comfort level for providing long-term support, so universities can continue the work, and not have to quit when they just get going," says Victor Rubin of PolicyLink (who also once served as director of HUD's Office of University Partnerships).[10] State and federal financing can continue to keep pushing universities forward, but, according to Rubin, they need to have criteria in place to prevent gentrification and encourage equitable development. PolicyLink defines equitable development as "an approach to creating healthy, vibrant, communities of opportunity. Equitable outcomes come about when smart, intentional strategies are put in place to ensure that low-income communities and communities of color participate in and benefit from decisions that shape their neighborhoods and regions."[11] David Cox also emphasizes the role of federal dollars for greatest leverage: "With federal funding, first, there is greater probability of [university-community partnerships] being sustainable and going to scale—they could support several hundred universities. Second, if we have a federal program, foundations can play an important role in providing funding that supports the spirit of engagement within the federal framework. The reality is that higher education, especially research universities, carries a cachet that it's important to legitimize this work." This legitimacy, Cox says, results in support for tenure and promotion policies that recognize knowledge produced from community engagement.[12] For this purpose, as proposed by the task force, prestigious national awards should be given to outstanding universities, and their community partners, that have embraced their anchor institution mission to improve the "quality of life in the community and the quality of research, teaching and service on campus." In addition, "a consultation team comprised of faculty and staff from institutions that have been successful in their work with the community" could help provide training and technical assistance for other universities and communities who are looking to develop anchor-based strategies for community economic development.[13] These efforts can promote more rigorous evaluation and monitoring of anchor strategies as well.

On the local level, universities can be part of a constellation of development, which city departments and elected officials should encourage. Rosalind Greenstein suggests that city government should "help guide universities' development initiatives" in ways that they can be successfully integrated with city wide "goals for jobs, real estate development, etc."[14] Henry Taylor at SUNY-Buffalo also talks about incentivizing universities to leverage their resources in ways that will support community development strategies: "We're in the early stages of this, so we'll see, but we're trying to get elected officials, especially at the state and city level, to buy into the central notion of [universities' role in] local development. They can then use every university lobbying effort to push back on the university to work in these areas. This is especially important if your state legislatures are working with you, because there are lots of state policies that the university needs in order to do what they want to do; so the elected officials are in a position to put external pressures on the university." As suggested by the task force, the federal government could "provide a pool of capital—grants and loans—that can supply matching funding" for state, regional, and local governments that "encourage anchor institutions to leverage their assets," such as credit enhancements that leverage university endowment funds. Taylor speaks about the federal level as well. "We have to arm HUD to push for some of these policies to get the *whole* university involved. . . . We've got to show the connection between building a prosperous urban region and redeveloping distressed areas. The secret to a vibrant city that can anchor urban regional development is transformation of the distressed areas, because distressed areas are a repellent, as long as there is crime, decaying house values, etc."[15]

One challenge for funders of university-community partnerships, whether foundations or government, is to provide support for the development of lasting infrastructure and not just programs. This includes both internal infrastructure (coordination and administrative support) and external infrastructure (engagement process and relationship building).[16] From some institutions' perspectives, pursuing the anchor institution mission, which has often gone by the name "the engaged university," seems almost like a social work or business development agency—with little or no relationship to its educational and research mission. We disagree, as do many of the higher education leaders interviewed in this study. Indeed, we think both the educational and the research functions of the university can be greatly enhanced by anchor institution work—if, that is, the concept is taken seriously.

Thinking Forward

In 1990, former president of Harvard University Derek Bok wrote, "In the constant interplay between universities and the outside world, neither side has done a satisfactory job of promoting the nation's long-term interests. University leaders have not worked sufficiently hard to bring their institutions to attend to our most important national problems. At the same time, neither trustees, nor the professors, nor foundation officers nor public officials, nor anyone else concerned with higher education has done enough to urge universities to make greater efforts along these lines or to help them mobilize resources sufficient for the task. There is good reason now to contemplate a fresh attempt to improve on this record."

In the twenty-plus years since this statement, higher education leaders have come a long way—as have funders and policymakers—in acknowledging universities' roles as anchor institutions with great potential to impact urban and regional development. Still, most colleges and universities have yet to fully realize their anchor institution mission and work to solve our nation's most pressing social problems. In the meantime, and particularly as our nation struggles to recover from the recent financial crash, Bok's words have only gained more urgency: "Observing our difficulties competing abroad, our millions of people in poverty, our drug-ridden communities, our disintegrating families, our ineffective schools, those who help to shape our universities have reason to ask whether they too have any time to lose."[1]

As America's urban and metropolitan communities continue to struggle, higher education institutions are at a crossroads where they must choose between leveraging their assets to improve the quality of life of their surrounding community, or retreating to their ivory tower. Actively pursuing a comprehensive anchor institution strategy will not be easy, but few would have imagined that universities would have gotten as far as they have today.

Perhaps in the years to come—by following a path such as the one illuminated in these pages—universities will begin to realize this mission. There is no time to lose.

In part 1 of this book, we underscored that historically such an effort for anchor-based community development is not unprecedented, but rather stems from the tradition of the land-grant colleges, first created in 1862. In part 2, we examined in depth the renewed movement over the past few decades by a number of universities from a range of different backgrounds (community colleges, historically black colleges and universities, state comprehensive universities, land-grant colleges, and private research universities) to adopt innovative anchor institution strategies, even in an environment characterized by a relative *lack* of philanthropic and public support. In part 3, we zeroed in on the promising practices, including specific tools used and lessons learned, from each of the ten profiled institutions, which have the greatest potential for building individual and community wealth in distressed neighborhoods. Figure 31 briefly recaptures these best practices.

Finally, in part 4, we have focused on the roles university leadership, philanthropy, and public policy can play to deepen and consolidate the idea that universities have an *anchor institution mission* as a key part of the work they do. These recommendations are summarized again in figure 32. To reemphasize our position, we argue that universities should think of themselves as having an education mission, a research mission (if a research university) *and* an anchor institution mission. We have suggested that an anchor institution mission should involve *the conscious and strategic application of the long-term, place-based economic power of the institution, in combination with its human and intellectual resources, to better the welfare of the community in which it resides.* In addition, we have advanced a series of proposals that outline an approach which promises to (1) achieve this shift, and (2) even more importantly, help universities fulfill their potential to improve the quality of life in communities across the United States. We firmly believe—and we believe the evidence in this study supports our contentions—that there is great potential benefit to adopting this approach.

At the same time, it is worth emphasizing that while philanthropy and public policy have a role to play, the university community itself must play the central role. In this book, we have purposefully not addressed many issues that have consumed considerable academic debate—the benefits to education of scholarly engagement and the efficacy of community-based participatory research being two obvious areas. This is not because such issues are unimportant. However, we felt it was important to make the case for an anchor institution mission, not, as is usually done, *solely* on the basis of how it helps universities realize their educational and research missions, but rather as being important *in its own right.*

This, naturally, poses a number of research challenges that extend beyond the scope of this study. One area where data is particularly lacking is quantitative community impact data. Here, it is important to highlight, however, what we are not calling for. These days nearly every university can cite the gross economic impact of its spending and purchasing, but as Chancellor Steven Diner of Rutgers University notes, "Economic impact data is *not* what anchor institution research is about. It's about the impact of partnerships." And here the data is, frankly, more limited. In 2009 and 2010, the Coalition of Urban Serving Universities conducted an initial survey of thirty-nine of its forty-six members—with promising

Figure 31. Best Practices among Anchor Approaches—Select Features

Comprehensive Neighborhood Revitalization at Penn	Establish institution-wide engagement (academic, corporate, human resources) in focused geographic area
Revitalization through Coalition Building at Syracuse	Draw collaborators from all sectors (business, government, neighborhood, schools, nonprofits) and build on existing strengths
Leveraging Contracting Dollars at Minnesota	Require general contractors to establish levels of participation for targeted businesses and raise targets when opportunities arise
Local Purchasing at Penn	Establish robust local purchasing goals and compensate staff on performance
Community Capacity Building at Emory	Engage partners in extensive front-end planning and be proactive in designing collaborative interventions at critical moments
Supporting Community Schools at IUPUI	Focus resources in neighborhood schools and adapt programming to fit needs and interests of students, families, and the broader community
Science Education Partnerships at Yale	Build sustainable partnerships through trust, in-kind resources, and creative leveraging of external funds
Academic Engagement at IUPUI	Direct academic resources to collectively identified areas of need in community
City and Regional Partnerships at Portland State	Collaborate with city departments on long-term real estate and economic development plans to leverage additional resources as well as achieve broader community goals
Multi-Anchor Partnerships at Cincinnati	Work with other anchors to pool resources for community investment
Institutionalizing an Anchor Vision at Syracuse	Create supportive policy, both in academic reward structure and in business practices
Community Investment of Endowment Assets at Cincinnati	Employ endowment to finance community development, and create understanding of long-term financial and social return
Leveraging Resources through an Independent Entity at LeMoyne-Owen	Seek investment from a wide variety of public and private sources (e.g., new markets tax credits, federal appropriation, private developers)
Building a Culture of Economic Inclusion at Miami Dade College	Provide "opportunity for all," including workforce training for low-income residents that is connected to actual jobs
Sustaining Inclusive Planning and Robust Relationships at Minnesota	Enter into genuine dialogue to reach a shared vision and engage stakeholders in strategic planning process

Figure 32. Recommendations for Realizing the Anchor Institution Mission	
University	• Create a vice president position overseeing community and economic development initiatives to demonstrate high-level administrative commitment. • Employ the university's resources fully and consciously—human, academic, cultural, and especially economic. • Link university hiring, real estate, purchasing, and investment strategies to community partnership goals. • Reward scholarship of engagement in promotion and tenure. • Engage community residents and groups in mutually beneficial and respectful partnerships. • Build networks across institutions so that they can share "best practices" and develop collaborative strategies. • Adopt a strategic, place-based approach to capitalize on existing resources, even when limited. • Leverage university economic power to support jobs for community members at the lower end of the socioeconomic scale. • Ensure that Carnegie "elective classification for community engagement" takes into account community-supportive practices in the corporate areas of purchasing, hiring, investment, and real estate.
Philanthropy	• Support information sharing and networks that promote the work (e.g., Coalition of Urban Serving Universities). • Create incentives to encourage structural changes, including policy amendments and internal collaboration that support an anchor institution mission. • Provide pre-development and capital support for community job creation strategies linked to anchor institutions (e.g., Cleveland Foundation's Evergreen Initiative). • Develop a funders' group that can support long-term, comprehensive, multi-modal initiatives at leading campuses.
Policy	• Support comprehensive programs through collaboration with new government policy initiatives (e.g., Promise Neighborhoods), expansion of current Office of University Partnership programs, and creation of an "Urban Grant" program. • Fund specialized programs that match anchor resources to critical public objectives in specific areas (e.g., affordable housing, business development, K-12 education). • Create anchor-based community development programs that leverage universities' economic power (e.g., purchasing, investment, hiring, real estate) for community benefit. • Convene a multi-stakeholder group that can support cross-anchor institution collaborative efforts through a competitive grant program. • Utilize local government to incentivize universities to invest in comprehensive community development efforts, as well as provide matching grants. • Award prizes as NSF does to provide recognition for exemplary university efforts and help legitimize the work. • Develop a national consultation team of faculty and staff from institutions that have been successful in their work with the community to aid in training and technical assistance.

indicators from the twenty-six respondents—but systemic collection of this data remains in its infancy. Case study data, as illustrated herein, is rich on the success of programs, but we readily acknowledge that quantitative cross-program, overall impact data remain very hard to come by.[2]

A June 2010 meeting of the Anchor Institutions Task Force outlined some additional research challenges. These include such questions as (1) Are there tensions between democratic and effective partnerships, and, if so, how can those challenges be addressed? (2) What are the effects of different partnership structures on outcomes? (3) How does the community agenda fit into anchor institution work? (4) How can universities make their assets and resources more accessible to the community? (5) How does university type—community college, state comprehensive school, land-grant, historically black college or university, liberal arts college, research university, and so on—impact the type of anchor institution work it can do? While we would like to believe this book makes a contribution to addressing all of these questions, we hardly claim to have the final word on these matters.[3]

In short, the challenge to achieve an anchor institution mission remains broad. As Benson, Harkavy, and Puckett acknowledge, "To become part of the solution, higher eds must give full-hearted, full-minded devotion to the painfully difficult task of transforming themselves into socially responsible *civic universities and colleges.*"[4] The obstacles are considerable, but the opportunities are also great. We hope this book deepens the discussion of how to overcome these obstacles—and sheds some light on the *road to be taken,* one in which urban universities actively pursue their anchor institution mission and work with city and community partners for the benefit of all.

Budget Documents from Anchor Institutions Task Force

Anchor Institutions as Partners in Building Successful Communities and Local Economies: Recommendations for HUD Action (2009); for supporting notes, see http://www.community-wealth.org/_pdfs/news/recent-articles/10-10/rht/axelroth-dubb_AppendixA.pdf.*

HUD Anchor Institutions Task Force Recommendations

The Anchor Institutions Task Force was guided in its budgeting by the following factors and principles:

1. HUD needs to make a bold commitment to leveraging anchor institutions to succeed in its community development mission.
2. Resources are required to move faculty and administrations and lead higher education to make the kinds of changes needed to embed and sustain civic engagement across all components of the institution. Universities are not starving for funds, but the funds received direct universities to lab research, not community development. For instance, in FY 2005, universities received $4.4 billion from the National Science Foundation, $16.8 billion from the National Institutes of Health, and roughly $33 million from the HUD Office of University Partnerships (OUP).
3. Although the total amount of money proposed ($1.21 billion) may seem large, it is almost exactly identical to the current level of USDA funding to support university work in (primarily) rural development through the National Institute of Food and Agriculture (NIFA). Of course, the majority of anchor institution capital is based in urban, not rural, areas.
4. The Task Force was also guided in its efforts by the groundbreaking work of the Coalition of Urban Serving Universities, a group of three dozen university presidents which has

---

*For further detail of the rationale behind the various items included in the budget, we refer readers to the published report: Ira Harkavy et al., "Anchor Institutions as Partners in Building Successful Communities and Local Economies," in Paul C. Brophy and Rachel D. Godsil, eds., *Retooling HUD for a Catalytic Federal Government: A Report to Secretary Shaun Donovan* (Philadelphia, PA: Penn Institute for Urban Research, 2009), 147–168.

proposed an Urban University Renaissance Act with a $700 million set of programs in HUD, as well as related programs in other federal departments.

5. The Task Force also wanted to expand the focus of OUP from an exclusively university-based focus to also encompass medical centers and hospitals and other anchor institutions. This effort to expand beyond typical partnership programs to leverage anchor economic assets also added to the cost figures.

6. **The Task Force recommends a first-year budget of $290 million, which would be ramped up over 5 years to the $1.21 billion amount in the full budget, as presented below.**

Year 1 and Full Budget Scenarios are provided below to demonstrate the potential impact of federal investment.

Budget Scenarios
Year 1 Budget Scenario

a. Office of University Partnerships: $105 million
  - "Phase 1" Community Outreach Partnership Center programs ($20 million)
  - "Phase 2" Community Outreach Partnership Center programs ($30 million)
  - Expanding OUP's other component programs ($50 million)
  - Awards, training, and program evaluation ($5 million)
b. Program Division of Anchor Institutions: $60 million
  - Integrated Community Anchor Network (I-CAN) program of cross-anchor partnerships ($35 million)
  - Seed grants for individual anchors, state/local matching grants ($15 million)
  - Anchor best practices website, awards, training, and program evaluation ($10 million)
c. White House Summit/Regional OUP HUD staff: $5 million
d. Community economic development programs: $120 million
  - Anchor institution-supported housing ($20 million)
  - Green housing workforce development ($25 million)
  - University-assisted community schools and school-centered community development ($20 million)
  - Community development staff continuing education and urban studies curriculum grants ($5 million)
  - Urban Revitalization Corps ($35 million)
  - Health Partnership Centers ($5 million)
  - Cultural economic development grants ($2 million)
  - Research grants ($8 million)

TOTAL: $290 million
Anticipated Impacts
  - 100 campuses dedicating a minimum of $1 million each to partnership work (half from anchor match)
  - Integrated Community Anchor Network modeled on successful HUD-supported Living Cities model, which has achieved a leverage of 29:1 per federal dollar invested

- 125 workforce development sites for greening of affordable housing
- Anchor institution employer-assisted housing programs in approximately 60 sites
- Anchor-subsidized housing for up to 10,000 AmeriCorps/VISTA employees
- 2,000 new Urban Revitalization Corps AmeriCorps/VISTA workers nationwide
- Health partnership centers at 25 anchor institutions
- Funding for urban research and urban studies curriculum development
- Cultural economic pilot initiatives at four anchor institutions
- 10 training and workforce centers for community development continuing education
- Dedicated funding for 40 campuses with K-12 partnership programs, particularly university-assisted community schools: based on conservative graduation figures, federal investment of $20 million would have an economic return of $52 million ($260,000 increase in lifetime earnings per high school graduate)

Full Budget Scenario

Total "ask" contained in the Task Force's report comes to **$1.21 billion in year 5**.

- Comprehensive "partnership" type programs ($455 million, see Strategy 1 below)
- Programs focused on leveraging anchor institution's economic power ($310 million, see Strategy 2 and items 1–6 of Strategy 3 below)
- Anchor institution programs related to workforce development, health, K-12 partnerships, culture-based development, and community-based research ($445 million, see Strategy 3, items 7–18 below)

Year 5 budget would add the following specific programs, in addition to those listed in year 1 budget above:

- Urban Grant program: extension-like outreach to urban communities
- HUD Urban Research Grants
- Community Economic Development Centers network to boost CED productivity
- Project-based Community Health Anchor Partnership Grants
- Civic engagement metropolitan planning grants to boost anchor partnership results
- Workforce training program to train new community development leaders

TOTAL: $1.21 billion

Anticipated Impacts

- Transformation of the role of anchor institutions in local community and economic development.
- Many programs listed above are on a 5-year grant cycle, meaning the full impact (and full cost) of the programs as "steady state" only occurs after year 5.
- Significant potential for tremendous gains. For instance, in 2008, 1.23 million Americans failed to graduate from high school. The cost to the nation of this failure at $260,000 per student comes to a total of $320 billion. With the schooling example above, the dedicated $100 million funding for university-assisted community schools could be expected to reach 200,000 K-12 students. A very conservative projection (1,000 more students graduating a year) would mean a return of $260 million for the federal government's $100 million investment.

- If 75 anchor institutions by year 5 had duplicated the results of Penn's purchasing program, it is reasonable to assume that these efforts would have generated 12,000 local jobs, $375 million in local wages, and nearly $1 billion in additional local economic activity. It is also reasonable to assume similar gains in the other anchor economic and community development efforts, partnership initiatives, and supporting programs.
- Budget outlined by the Anchor Institutions Task Force provides a mechanism for HUD to begin to think and act comprehensively and holistically in its role as facilitator and catalyst for leveraging anchor institutions for community and economic development in the 21st century.

Regarding the particular recommendations presented in the Task Force report, a chart outlining the recommended investment amounts follows:

Summary of Recommended Investment Amounts			
Strategy 1—Partnership Programs: Enhance the Current Office of University Partnerships	**Direct HUD Investment**	**Anticipated Anchor Match**	**Total Investment**
1. Revised Community Outreach Partnership Centers—Phase 1 grants	60,000,000	60,000,000	120,000,000
2. Revised Community Outreach Partnership Centers—Phase 2 grants	90,000,000	90,000,000	180,000,000
3. Increase funding and support for OUP's other component programs (for HBCUs, tribal colleges, community dev. work study, etc.)	50,000,000	50,000,000	100,000,000
4. Urban Grant University program	200,000,000	200,000,000	400,000,000
5. HUD Urban Research Assistance Grants	50,000,000	0	50,000,000
6. Awards, training, and evaluation	5,000,000	0	5,000,000
Strategy 2—Anchor Institutions: Joining Forces with HUD to Meet the Housing Need	**Direct HUD Investment**	**Anticipated Anchor Match**	**Total Investment**
1. Nonprofits House America	50,000,000	100,000,000	150,000,000
2. Universities Serving America	25,000,000	50,000,000	75,000,000
3. Housing Information System community housing data program	25,000,000	50,000,000	75,000,000

Strategy 3—Anchor Institutions: Promoting Community & Economic Development	Direct HUD Investment	Anticipated Anchor Match	Total Investment
1. Anchors Build Community	15,000,000	15,000,000	30,000,000
2. Integrated Community Anchor Network	35,000,000	35,000,000	70,000,000
3. Grant pool to supply loans or matching capital for state/local efforts	50,000,000	50,000,000	100,000,000
4. Community Economic Development (CED) Centers	50,000,000	50,000,000	100,000,000
5. Grant pool for CED Center projects	150,000,000	150,000,000	300,000,000
6. Awards, training, and evaluation for items 1–5 above	10,000,000	0	10,000,000
7. Youth Green America	25,000,000	25,000,000	50,000,000
8. Youth Rebuilding Communities	25,000,000	25,000,000	50,000,000
9. Health Partnership Capacity Grants—Phase 1 grants	25,000,000	25,000,000	50,000,000
10. Community Health Anchor Partnerships—Phase 2 grants	20,000,000	20,000,000	40,000,000
11. Awards, training, and evaluation for items 9 and 10 above	5,000,000	0	5,000,000
12. Continuing education for community development organization staff	25,000,000	25,000,000	50,000,000
13. Urban Revitalization Corps (2,000 AmeriCorps/VISTA positions)	35,000,000	0	35,000,000
14. High school urban planning curriculum development grants	10,000,000	0	10,000,000
15. University-Assisted Community Schools and School-Centered Community Development Center grants	100,000,000	100,000,000	200,000,000
16. Cultural-based anchor development grants	10,000,000	10,000,000	20,000,000
17. Action research metro/regional grants	40,000,000	0	40,000,000
18. Civic engagement anchor metro planning grants	25,000,000	0	25,000,000
TOTALS	1,210,000,000	1,130,000,000	2,340,000,000

Interview Subjects and Contributors

Section 1. Site Visit Interviews

Emory University/Atlanta, GA

- Frank Alexander, Professor of Law, Emory
- Rob Brawner, Program Director, Beltline Partnership
- Madge Donnellan, Associate Professor of Nursing, Emory
- Sam Marie Engle, Senior Associate Director, Office of University-Community Partnerships, Emory
- John Ford, Senior Vice President and Dean of Campus Life, Emory
- Alicia Franck, Associate Vice Provost for Academic and Strategic Partnerships, Emory
- Kate Grace, Director of the Community Building and Social Change Fellows Program, Office of University-Community Partnerships, Emory
- David Hanson, Associate Vice President of Finance and Special Assistant to the Executive Vice President of Finance and Administration, Emory
- Ozzie Harris, Senior Vice President for Community and Diversity, Emory
- Moshe Haspel, Director of Research and Evaluation and Adjunct Professor of Political Science, Emory
- Ciannat Howett, Director of Sustainability Initiatives, Emory
- Young Hughley, Executive Director, Reynoldstown Revitalization Corporation
- David Jenkins, Director, Faith and the City and Assistant Professor of Church and Community Ministries, Candler School of Theology, Emory
- Kathy Kite, Senior Associate Director, Lillian Carter Center for International Nursing and Administrative Director of Service Learning, Emory
- Bob Lee, Associate Dean, Multicultural Medical Student Affairs, School of Medicine, Emory
- Earl Lewis, Provost and Executive Vice President for Academic Affairs, Emory
- Kate Little, President and CEO, Georgia State Association of Neighborhood Developers
- Carlton Mackey, Assistant Director, Ethics and Servant Leadership, and Assistant Coordinator, Undergraduate Studies, Center for Ethics, Emory
- Crystal McLaughlin, Director of Student Development, Oxford College, Emory
- Emily Penprase, Coordinator of Community Service, Oxford College, Emory

- Alicia Philipp, CEO, Community Foundation of Greater Atlanta
- Edward Queen, Director, Ethics and Servant Leadership, and Coordinator of Undergraduate Studies, Center for Ethics, Emory
- Michael J. Rich, Associate Professor of Political Science and Environmental Studies and Director, Office of University-Community Partnerships, Emory
- Andy Schneggenburger, Executive Director, AHAND (Atlanta Housing Association of Neighborhood-based Developers)
- Nathaniel Smith, Director of Partnerships and Research for Equitable Development, Office of University-Community Partnerships, Emory
- Patti Owen-Smith, Director, Theory-Practice-Service Learning Program, Emory
- Denise Walker, Assistant Director of Community Affairs, Office of Governmental and Community Affairs, Emory
- Betty Willis, Senior Associate Vice President, Governmental and Community Affairs, Emory
- J. Lynn Zimmerman, Senior Vice Provost for External Academic Initiatives and Special Assistant to the Provost, Emory

Indiana University–Purdue University Indianapolis (IUPUI)/Indianapolis, IN
- Diane Arnold, Executive Director, Hawthorne Community Center
- Jennifer Boehm, Director, Government and Community Relations, External Affairs, IUPUI
- Richard Bray, Assistant Director, Office of Multicultural Outreach, IUPUI
- Robert Bringle, Executive Director, Center for Service and Learning, IUPUI
- Lorrie Brown, Associate Director of Civic Engagement, IUPUI
- Claudette Canzian, Associate Director, Office of Purchasing Services, IUPUI
- Lana Coleman, Near Westside Resident
- Patrice Duckett, Near West Coordinator, Great Indy Neighborhoods Initiative
- Richard Gordon, Event Consultant for NonProfit Solutions, Solution Center, IUPUI
- Jim Grim, Director of School/Community Engagement, George Washington Community High School
- Robert Halter, Director, Office of Purchasing Services, IUPUI
- Krista Hoffman-Longtin, Associate Director, Solution Center, IUPUI
- Ann Kreicker, Coordinator, George Washington Community High School
- Aaron Laramore, Program Officer, Local Initiatives Support Corporation, Indianapolis
- Libby Laux, Assistant Director of Development, Center for Service and Learning, IUPUI
- Laura Littlepage, Clinical Lecturer, Center for Urban Policy and the Environment, IUPUI
- Darrell Nickolson, Community Faculty Fellow, Engineering and Technology, IUPUI
- Starla Officer, Coordinator, Office of Neighborhood Partnerships, Center for Service and Learning, IUPUI
- Morgan Studer, Coordinator, Office of Community Work-Study, Center for Service and Learning, IUPUI
- Anne-Marie Predovich Taylor, Executive Director, Indianapolis Neighborhood Resource Center

LeMoyne-Owen College (LOC)/Memphis, TN

- Femi Ajanaku, Associate Professor, Department of Sociology, LOC
- Mairi Albertson, Division Administrator, Department of Planning and Development, City of Memphis
- Tk Buchanan, Senior Research Associate, Center for Community-Building and Neighborhood Action, University of Memphis
- Damita Dandridge, Instructor, Political Science and Program Director, American Humanics, LOC
- Austin Emeagwai, Assistant Professor of Accounting, LOC and Chief Financial Officer, LeMoyne-Owen College Community Development Corporation
- Bob Fockler, President, Community Foundation of Greater Memphis
- Cheryl Golden, Professor and Division Chair, Sociology and Behavioral Sciences, LOC
- Jeffrey Higgs, Executive Director, LeMoyne-Owen College Community Development Corporation
- Robert Lipscomb, Director, City of Memphis Division of Housing and Community Development and Executive Director, Memphis Housing Authority
- Eric Robertson, Chief Administrative Officer, Center City Commission and President, Soulsville Neighborhood Association
- Emily Trenholm, Executive Director, Community Development Council of Greater Memphis
- Johnnie B. Watson, President, LOC
- Melissa Wolowicz, Director of Grants and Initiatives, Community Foundation of Greater Memphis
- Suhkara A. Yahweh, Community Activist

Miami Dade College (MDC)/Miami, FL

- Alex Alvarez, former Director, Take Stock in Children, Miami
- Phil Bacon, Vice President for Neighborhood and Regional Initiatives, Collins Center for Public Policy
- Marilyn Brummitt, Director of Community Development, Miami Rescue Mission/Broward Outreach Centers
- Crystal Dunn, Program Manager, Meek Entrepreneurial Education Center, MDC
- Sheldon Edwards, Coordinator, Minority and Small Enterprise Office, MDC
- Geoffrey Gathercole, Director, School of Community Education, MDC
- Annette Gibson, Faculty, School of Nursing, Medical Center Campus, MDC
- Norma Martin Goonen, President of the Hialeah Campus and former Provost for Academic and Student Affairs, MDC
- Ossie Hanauer, Kendall Campus Director, Center for Community Involvement, MDC
- Daniella Levine, Executive Director, Human Services Coalition of Dade County
- Theodore Levitt, Director, Division of College Communications, MDC
- Michael Mason, Program Manager, Meek Entrepreneurial Education Center, MDC
- Elizabeth Mejia, Executive Director, Communities in Schools of Miami
- Eduardo Padrón, President, MDC

- Barbara Pryor, Staff, Meek Entrepreneurial Education Center, MDC
- Vivian Rodriguez, Vice Provost for Cultural Affairs and Resource Development, MDC
- Denis Russ, Director of Community Development, Miami Beach Community Development Corporation
- Linda Scharf, Program Manager, Working Solutions Program, MDC
- H. Leigh Toney, Director, Meek Entrepreneurial Education Center, MDC
- Joshua Young, Campus-Wide Director, Center for Community Involvement, MDC

Portland State University (PSU)/Portland, OR

- Lisa Abuaf, Senior Project Coordinator, Portland Development Commission
- Bob Alexander, Special Projects Manager, Portland Development Commission
- Lew Bowers, Central City Division Manager, Portland Development Commission
- Lara Damon, Director, Business Outreach Program, PSU
- Lindsay Desrochers, former Vice President for Finance and Administration, PSU
- Stephanie Farquhar, Associate Professor, School of Community Health, PSU
- Jill Fuglister, Co-Director, Coalition for a Livable Future
- Mark Gregory, Associate Vice President for Finance and Administration, PSU
- Diana Hall, Program Supervisor, School and Community Partnerships, Department of County Human Services, Multnomah County
- Brian Hoop, Manager, Neighborhood Resource Center, Office of Neighborhood Involvement, City of Portland
- Kevin Kecskes, Associate Vice Provost for Engagement and Director, Community-University Partnerships, PSU
- Lynn Knox, Program Manager, Economic Opportunity Initiative, Bureau of Housing and Community Development
- Roy Koch, Provost, PSU
- Paul Leistner, Neighborhood Program Coordinator, Office of Neighborhood Involvement, City of Portland
- Julie Massa, Portland Policy Coordinator, Oregon Opportunity Network
- Genny Nelson, Co-founder, Sisters of the Road
- Laurie Powers, Director, Regional Research Institute for Human Services, PSU
- Karen Preston, Manager, Purchasing and Contracting Services, PSU
- Ethan Seltzer, Professor and former Director, School of Urban Studies and Planning, College of Urban and Public Affairs, PSU
- Steve Trujillo, President, Downtown Neighborhood Association
- Robert Voica, Contracts Officer, Facilities and Planning, PSU
- Dee Walsh, Executive Director, Reach CDC
- Wim Wiewel, President, PSU
- Mark Wubbold, Special Assistant to the Vice President for Finance and Administration, PSU
- Diane Yatchmenoff, Director of Research, Regional Research Institute for Human Services, PSU

Syracuse University (SU)/Syracuse, NY

- Eric Beattie, Director, Campus Planning, Design, and Construction, SU
- Ed Bogucz, Director and Associate Professor, Syracuse Center of Excellence in Environmental and Energy Systems, SU
- Inmaculada Lara Bonilla, Assistant Professor and Faculty Associate, Latino-Latin American Studies, SU
- Allan Breese, Director, Business and Facilities Maintenance Services, SU
- Frank Caliva, Director of Talent Initiatives, Metropolitan Development Association of Syracuse and Central New York
- Nancy Cantor, Chancellor and President, SU
- Tim Carroll, Director of Operations, City of Syracuse
- Jan Cohen-Cruz, Director, Imagining America
- Dionisio Cruz, Community Consultant
- Ana Fernandez, Project Manager, Syracuse Center of Excellence in Environmental and Energy Systems, SU
- Douglas Freeman, Director, Purchasing and Real Estate, SU
- Rachael Gazdick, Executive Director, Say Yes to Education Syracuse
- Kathy Goldfarb-Findling, former Executive Director, Rosamond Gifford Charitable Corporation, Syracuse
- Marilyn Higgins, Vice President of Community Engagement and Economic Development, SU
- David Holder, President, Syracuse Convention and Visitors Bureau
- Linda Littlejohn, Associate Vice President, SU
- Stephen Mahan, Visiting Instructor, College of Visual and Performing Arts, SU
- Alys Mann, Senior Neighborhood Planner, Home HeadQuarters
- Louis Marcoccia, Executive Vice President and Chief Financial Officer, SU
- Chris McCray, Assistant Professor and Executive Director, COLAB, College of Visual and Performing Arts, SU
- Daniela Mosko-Wozniak, Administrative Specialist, University Arts Presenter, SU
- Rita Paniagua, Executive Director, Spanish Action League of Onondaga County, Inc.
- Eric Persons, Associate Vice President of Government and Community Relations, SU
- Daniel Queri, Real Estate Consultant
- Kevin Schwab, Director of Communications and Air Service Development, Metropolitan Development Association of Syracuse and Central New York
- Benjamin Sio, Economic Development Specialist, Syracuse Chamber of Commerce
- Steve Susman, Executive Director, Westcott Community Center
- Marion Wilson, Professor and Director of Community Initiatives in the Visual Arts, SU
- Jeff Woodward, Managing Director, Syracuse Stage

University of Cincinnati (UC)/Cincinnati, OH

- Jennifer Blatz, Director of Operations, Strive
- Matt Bourgeois, Director, Clifton Heights Community Urban Redevelopment Corporation
- Tony Brown, former President and CEO, Uptown Consortium

- Myrita Craig, former Executive Director, Agenda 360, Cincinnati USA Regional Chamber
- Thomas Croft, Chief Investment Officer, UC
- Kathy Dick, Director, Center for Community Engagement, UC
- Jeff Edmondson, Executive Director, Strive
- Bill Fischer, Business Development Manager, Department of Community Development, City of Cincinnati
- Tom Guerin, Associate Vice President, Purchasing and Material Management Services, UC
- Brooke Hill, former District Director of Southwest Ohio, U.S. Senator Sherrod Brown's Office
- Larry Johnson, Dean, College of Education, Criminal Justice and Human Services, UC
- Kathy Merchant, President, Greater Cincinnati Foundation
- Rob Neel, President, CUF (Clifton Heights, University Heights, Fairview) Community Council
- Eric Rademacher, Co-Director, Institute for Policy Research, UC
- Monica Rimai, former Senior Vice President of Finance and Administration and Interim President, UC
- Michael Romanos, Professor, School of Planning and Director, Center for Research in Urban Development, UC
- Michael Sharp, Director for Community-Engaged Learning, UC
- Gerry Siegert, Associate Vice President for Community Development, UC
- Cheryl Smith, Interim Director, Office of Contract Compliance, UC
- Mary Stagaman, former Presidential Deputy for Community Engagement and Associate Vice President, External Relations, UC
- Scott Stiles, Assistant City Manager, City of Cincinnati

University of Minnesota (UMN)/Twin Cities, MN
- Martin Adams, Project Coordinator, Fund for the Improvement of Postsecondary Education, UMN
- Sara Axtell, Community-Campus Health Liaison and Assistant Professor, UMN
- Harry Boyte, Senior Fellow, Humphrey Institute of Public Affairs, UMN and Founder and Co-Director, Center for Democracy and Citizenship, Augsburg College
- Jay Clark, Program Director, Minnesota Center for Neighborhood Organizing, Center for Urban and Regional Affairs, UMN
- Raymond Dehn, Community Resident Co-Chair of Community Affairs Committee, University Northside Partnership
- Mary Fitzpatrick, Executive Director, Seeds of Change
- Felecia Franklin, Principal Officer and Administrative Specialist, Office of Equal Opportunity and Affirmative Action, UMN
- Andrew Furco, Associate Vice President for Public Engagement, UMN
- Ed Goetz, Director, Center for Urban and Regional Affairs, UMN
- Erik Hansen, Principal Project Coordinator, City Department of Community Planning and Economic Development

- Reynolds-Anthony Harris, Urban Research and Outreach/Engagement Center, Strategic Plan Consultant, Lyceum Group
- Robert Jones, Senior Vice President for System Academic Administration, UMN
- Margaret Kaplan, Operations Director, Minnesota Center for Neighborhood Organizing, Center for Urban and Regional Affairs, UMN
- Helen Kivnick, Professor, School of Social Work, UMN
- Lauren Martin, Research Associate, Center for Early Education and Development, UMN
- Geoff Maruyama, Associate Vice President for System Academic Administration and Professor, College of Education and Human Development, UMN
- Irma McClaurin, former Associate Vice President and Executive Director, Urban Research and Outreach/Engagement Center, UMN
- Scott McConnell, Professor, College of Education and Human Development and Director of Community Engagement, Center for Early Education and Development, UMN
- Jan Morlock, Director, Community Relations for the Twin Cities Campus, UMN
- Kris Nelson, Director of Neighborhood Partnerships for Community Research, Center for Urban and Regional Affairs, UMN
- Makeda Norris, Program Coordinator, Minneapolis Urban League
- Beverly Propes, Community Resident
- Sherrie Pugh, Director, Northside Resident Redevelopment Council
- Craig Taylor, Director, Office of Business and Community Economic Development, UMN
- Makeda Zulu-Gillespie, Community Liaison, Urban Research and Outreach/Engagement Center and University Northside Partnership, UMN

University of Pennsylvania (Penn)/Philadelphia, PA
- Randy Belin, Senior Program Officer, Local Initiatives Support Corporation, Philadelphia
- Cory Bowman, Associate Director, Netter Center for Community Partnerships, Penn
- Glenn Bryan, Assistant Vice President of Community Relations, Office of Government and Community Affairs, Penn
- Tom Burns, Managing Director, Urban Ventures Group
- Jamie Gauthier, Program Officer, Local Initiatives Support Corporation, Philadelphia
- David Grossman, Director, Civic House, Penn
- Ira Harkavy, Associate Vice President and Director, Netter Center for Community Partnerships, Penn
- Hillary Kane, Director, Philadelphia Higher Education Network for Neighborhood Development
- Lucy Kerman, former Vice President, Policy and Planning, Greater Philadelphia Urban Affairs Council
- Ann Kreidle, Project Coordinator of Penn Partnership Schools, Graduate School of Education, Penn
- James Lytle, Director of Penn Partnership Schools, Graduate School of Education, Penn
- Ralph Maier, former Director of Purchasing (Chief Procurement Officer), Penn
- Rick Redding, Director of Community Planning, Philadelphia City Planning Commission
- Gretchen Suess, Director of Evaluation, Netter Center for Community Partnerships, Penn
- Eleanor Sharpe, former Associate Director, Netter Center for Community Partnerships, Penn

- Tony Sorrentino, Executive Director, Public Affairs, Penn
- Joann Weeks, Associate Director, Netter Center for Community Partnerships, Penn
- Lewis Wendell, former Executive Director, University City District
- Steven Williams, Executive Director, Partnership CDC
- D. L. Wormley, former Deputy Director, NeighborhoodsNow

Yale University/New Haven, CT

- Abie Benitez, Principal, Christopher Columbus Family Academy
- Michael Ceraso, Principal, Hill Regional Career High School
- Rose Evans, Librarian, Christopher Columbus Family Academy
- Florita Gonzales, Chair, Dwight Community Management Team
- David Heiser, Head of Education and Outreach, Yale Peabody Museum
- Suzannah Holsenbeck, Yale Partnership Coordinator, Co-op High School
- Jeannette Ickovics, Deputy Director for Community Outreach, Yale Center for Clinical Investigation
- Sheila Masterson, Executive Director, Whalley Avenue Special Service District
- William Placke, Chief Executive Officer, First Community Bank of New Haven
- Claudia Merson, Director of Partnerships, Office of New Haven and State Affairs, Yale
- Frank Mitchell, Chair, Board of Directors, Common Ground
- Michael Morand, Associate Vice President, Office of New Haven and State Affairs, Yale
- Colleen Murphy-Dunning, Director, Urban Resources Initiative, Yale
- Holly Parker, Director, Sustainable Transportation Systems, Yale
- Joanna Price, Coordinator of Community Programs in Science, Office of New Haven and State Affairs, Yale
- Abigail Rider, Associate Vice President and Director of University Properties, Yale
- Shana Schneider, Deputy Director, Yale Entrepreneurship Institute
- Sheila E. Shanklin, Director of Cooperative Management, Home, Inc.
- Jon Soderstrom, Director, Office of Cooperative Research, Yale
- T. Reginald Solomon, Program Director, Office of New Haven and State Affairs, Yale
- Deborah Stanley-McAulay, Chief Diversity Officer, Office of Diversity and Inclusion, Yale
- Linda Townsend-Maier, Executive Director, Greater Dwight Development Corporation

Section 2. Additional Background Interviews and Quoted Individuals

- John C. Burkhardt, Professor and Director, National Forum on Higher Education for the Public Good, University of Michigan
- David Cox, Executive Assistant to the President and Professor, University of Memphis
- Amy Driscoll, Consulting Scholar, Carnegie Foundation for the Advancement of Teaching and Senior Scholar, Portland State University
- Rosalind Greenstein, Urban Policy Analyst and former Senior Fellow and Chair, Department of Economics and Community Development, Lincoln Institute of Land Policy
- Laura Harris, Assistant Professor, Division of Public and Nonprofit Administration, University of Memphis

- Nick Harris, Assistant Vice President for Community and Economic Development and Executive Director, Dillard University Community Development Corporation
- Elizabeth Hollander, Senior Fellow, Jonathan M. Tisch College of Citizenship and Public Service, Tufts University and former Executive Director, Campus Compact
- David Maurrasse, President and Founder, Marga Incorporated
- Ruth Meyers, Director, Demonstration Projects for Community Revitalization, United Way for the Greater New Orleans Area
- David Perry, Associate Chancellor, Great Cities Commitment and Director of the Great Cities Institute, University of Illinois at Chicago
- Victor Rubin, Vice President for Research, PolicyLink
- Amber Seeley, Finance Program Director, Renaissance Neighborhood Development Corporation, a subsidiary of Volunteers of America, New Orleans
- Karl Seidman, Senior Lecturer in Economic Development, Department of Urban Studies and Planning, Massachusetts Institute of Technology
- Henry Louis Taylor, Professor and Director, Center for Urban Studies, University at Buffalo

Additional Resources

Anchor Institutions Task Force
c/o Marga, Inc, P.O. Box 4565
New York, NY 10163
T 212-979-9770   F 917-591-1547
aitf@margainc.com
www.margainc.com/initiatives/aitf
The Anchor Institutions Task Force, initially convened to advise incoming U.S. Secretary
of Housing and Urban Development Shaun Donovan in 2009, is now a permanent
organization that aims to develop and disseminate knowledge to help create and advance
democratic, mutually beneficial anchor institution-community partnerships. Bringing
together scholars, university presidents, and others, the task force aims to increase
cooperation and alignment among government, anchor institutions, businesses, schools,
community organizations, and philanthropy in order to improve communities.

Democracy Collaborative
6930 Carroll Avenue, Suite 415
Takoma Park, MD 20912
T 301-270-1554   F 301-270-4000
info@community-wealth.org
www.community-wealth.org
www.democracycollaborative.org
The Democracy Collaborative was established in 2000 to advance a new understanding of
democracy for the twenty-first century and to promote new strategies and innovations in
community development that enhance democratic life. The Collaborative is a national
leader in the field of community development through its Community Wealth Building
Initiative, which sustains a wide range of projects involving research, training, policy
development, and community-focused work designed to promote an asset-based
paradigm and increase support for the field. One of the Democracy Collaborative's current
flagship projects is the Evergreen Cooperative Initiative in Cleveland, Ohio. In partnership
with the Cleveland Foundation, the Ohio Employee Ownership Center at Kent State
University, and many of Cleveland's major anchor institutions, the Collaborative has

designed and is helping to implement a comprehensive wealth building effort in six low-income neighborhoods through community-based businesses that will employ hundreds of local residents through a worker cooperative model.

Netter Center for Community Partnerships
University of Pennsylvania
133 South 36th Street, Suite 519
Philadelphia, PA 19104
T 215-898-5351   F 215-573-2799
nettercenter@upenn.edu
www.upenn.edu/ccp

Founded in 1992, the Barbara and Edward Netter Center for Community Partnerships is the University of Pennsylvania's primary vehicle for bringing to bear the broad range of human knowledge needed to solve the complex, comprehensive, and interconnected problems of the American city so that West Philadelphia (Penn's local geographic community), Philadelphia, the university itself, and society benefit. The Netter Center's programs focus on local public schools, urban nutrition, and a range of community development initiatives. Academically based community service is at the core of the Netter Center's work, linking theory to practice, through community-oriented, real-world problem solving. Through these courses, Penn students and faculty work with West Philadelphia public schools and community organizations to solve critical universal problems in a variety of areas related to the environment, health, arts, and education as they are manifested locally. The Netter Center also aims to create and strengthen local, national, and international networks of institutions of higher education committed to engagement with their local communities.

Acknowledgments

Research for *The Road Half Traveled* began early in 2009, but this study has a much longer gestation. The Democracy Collaborative was founded in 2000 by a group of scholars at the University of Maryland, College Park, who saw the need for a center that could promote engaged scholarship that linked research to democratic practice. Maryland itself is a land-grant university, so the Collaborative has seen as one of its goals to examine what being a land-grant institution means in the twenty-first century.

In 2005, the Democracy Collaborative published an article outlining its engagement vision. Later, in 2007, the Collaborative produced a full report titled *Linking Colleges to Communities: Engaging the University for Community Development*. Several dozen people participated in interviews for that report, and their contributions helped frame the questions of this study. In *Linking Colleges*, author Steve Dubb outlined the history of university engagement and examined recent developments in policy and in the field, but with limited detail on any one school. Here, we wanted to examine fewer schools in greater depth, thereby enabling us to personally visit every school we selected—and helping us to generate a better understanding of both the challenges and opportunities for universities that seek to develop and realize an anchor institution mission.

There are numerous other influences, but two are particularly important to mention. One is the Netter Center for Community Partnerships at the University of Pennsylvania, which produced its *Anchor Institutions Toolkit* in March 2008 to provide a manual for universities seeking to expand their community partnership work in a responsible way. Author Rita Axelroth Hodges hails from the Netter Center, and was a student of Ira Harkavy's, and thus brings an inside perspective to this work on how community partnership centers function.

A second influence is the Anchor Institutions Task Force, a group created in December 2008 to advise incoming U.S. Secretary of Housing and Urban Development Shaun Donovan on how the federal government might leverage the intellectual and economic resources of universities to better conditions in low-income communities. Both authors participated in the task force and in writing its report. We gratefully acknowledge the contributions of Ira Harkavy and the two dozen original members of the task force.

Ted Howard, Executive Director of the Democracy Collaborative, has played a key role in framing the Democracy Collaborative's research. Financial support from the Annie E. Casey Foundation and the Kendeda Fund made this project possible.

In conducting this study, we relied on the goodwill and contributions of literally hundreds of individuals. A full list of interview subjects and their affiliations is included in appendix 2.

For interviews on the "university" side of the community-university partnership equation, we relied on having contact people who could help coordinate our site visits. Steve Dubb did the site interviews at Emory, Penn, and Yale and gratefully acknowledges the extraordinary logistical assistance and scheduling efforts of Sam Marie Engle at Emory, Joann Weeks at Penn, and Michael Morand at Yale. Rita Axelroth Hodges conducted the site visits at Cincinnati, IUPUI, LeMoyne-Owen, Miami Dade College, Minnesota, Portland State, and Syracuse. She gratefully acknowledges the remarkable coordination and communication efforts of Mary Stagaman in Cincinnati, Starla Officer at IUPUI, Jeffrey Higgs at the LeMoyne-Owen CDC, Joshua Young at Miami Dade, Irma McClaurin at Minnesota, Amy Spring at Portland State, and Marilyn Higgins at Syracuse.

We also gratefully acknowledge the help of the following individuals who reviewed sections of the original report and provided critical feedback. Ozzie Harris, Alicia Philipp, Michael Rich, and Nathaniel Smith reviewed the section on Emory. Tom Burns, Ira Harkavy, Eleanor Sharpe, and Lewis Wendell reviewed the section on Penn. Michael Morand, William Placke, Abigail Rider, and Linda Townsend-Maier reviewed the section on Yale. Matt Bourgeois, Gerald Siegert, and Mary Stagaman reviewed the section on Cincinnati. Bob Bringle and Starla Officer reviewed the section on IUPUI. Mairi Albertson, Jeffrey Higgs, Jeffrey Lowe, and Eric Robertson reviewed the section on LeMoyne-Owen College. Daniella Levine, Ted Levitt, Nicole Tallman, Leigh Toney, and Joshua Young reviewed the section on Miami Dade College. Raymond Dehn, Andrew Furco, Robert Jones, Deb Kran, and Irma McClaurin reviewed the section on Minnesota. Kevin Kecskes and Wim Wiewel reviewed the section on Portland State. Nancy Cantor, Kathy Goldfarb-Findling, and Marilyn Higgins reviewed the section on Syracuse.

A number of individuals also provided comments on other sections of the report or the draft as a whole. We gratefully acknowledge the valuable comments provided by Dan Apfel, Armand Carriére, David Cox, Evan Dobelle, Maurice Dorsey, Amy Driscoll, Elizabeth Hollander, Ted Howard, Kathryn Kravetz, Rex La More, Jeffrey Lowe, David Maurrasse, Victor Rubin, Henry Louis Taylor, Justin Wellner, and Kinnard Wright. While it is not possible to fully incorporate all of the valuable feedback we received, the final product is immeasurably improved due to the contributions of all of the above named individuals. All responsibility for errors and omissions remains, of course, our own.

A few individuals deserve special mention for their contributions. Michael Morand, in addition to providing very helpful comments on Yale, also called our attention to the broader analytic question of "who is the community" and whether (and when) the university itself should be considered separate from—or a part of—the community. Henry Louis Taylor and David Cox encouraged us to bring the discussion of what an anchor institution mission is to the beginning of our analysis. Amy Driscoll and Liz Hollander helped us rethink the organization of the best-practices section and called our attention to the importance of addressing the Carnegie engagement criteria. Ira Harkavy encouraged us to look at the significance of institution-wide engagement, as well as the challenge of effectively addressing poverty in the broader community. Kathryn Kravetz and Victor Rubin pushed us to rethink the organization of several sections of the report. Bob Bringle encouraged us to focus on an asset-based approach to community development. Maurice Dorsey encouraged us to address tenure and promotion. Justin Wellner provided invaluable information on the latest policy developments.

We are especially grateful to Hiram Fitzgerald, Associate Provost for University Outreach and Engagement at Michigan State University, for seeing the potential in our report and encouraging us to seek publication in MSU Press's series on Transformations in Higher Education, for which Hiram also serves as Editor in Chief. We also greatly appreciate the work of the two anonymous peer reviewers through MSU Press who provided critical feedback on our manuscript, and whose advice informed our final edits and organization for this book.

Lastly, we would like to thank our partners who watched us work on the project from beginning to end. Rita Axelroth Hodges would like to recognize the love, patience, and encouragement of Michael Hodges. Steve Dubb would like to acknowledge the love, friendship, and support of Barbara Berglund.

Notes

Introduction

1. Ira Harkavy et al., "Anchor Institutions as Partners in Building Successful Communities and Local Economies," in Paul Brophy and Rachel Godsil, eds., *Retooling HUD for a Catalytic Federal Government: A Report to Secretary Shaun Donovan* (Philadelphia, PA: Penn Institute for Urban Research, February 2009), 159. U.S. Department of Education and National Center for Education Statistics, *Digest of Education Statistics, 2008* (Washington, DC: NCES, 2009), chapter 3, http://nces.ed.gov/fastfacts/display.asp?id=98.

2. Harkavy et al., "Anchor Institutions as Partners," especially 148–149; Henry Taylor, personal correspondence, May 4, 2010.

3. Henry S. Webber and Mikael Karlstrom, *Why Community Investment is Good for Non-profit Anchor Institutions: Understanding Costs, Benefits, and the Range of Strategic Options* (Chicago: Chapin Hill at the University of Chicago, 2009), especially 4–6.

4. Ira Harkavy and Harmon Zuckerman, *Eds and Meds: Cities' Hidden Assets* (Washington, DC: Brookings Institution, 1999), 1.

5. Arloc Sherman and Chad Stone, *Income Gaps between Very Rich and Everyone Else More than Tripled in Last Three Decades New Data Show* (Washington, DC: Center on Budget and Policy Priorities, June 25, 2010), 3.

6. We had initially sought to assess the quantifiable impact university partnerships are having on poor and low-income residents, as a fourth purpose; however, we quickly realized that such data was not readily available and creating appropriate quantitative measures on our own was beyond the scope of this study. We continue to believe this is an important issue for the field, however, and include it in our discussion of recommendations of areas for future research.

7. We wish to recognize many leading community development efforts under way by colleges and universities that were not included in this study such as the University of

Wisconsin–Milwaukee, Duke University, University of Southern California, Trinity College, University of Akron, and Ohio State University. The experience of these universities would add much to the wealth of knowledge of anchor-based community development.

8. While the authors met with multiple community partners at each site, and efforts were made to reach out directly to such individuals, many of the organizations and opinions represented here are strongly connected to the higher education institutions' initiatives.

Chapter 1. Brief History of Universities, Community Partnerships, and Economic Development

1. James Collier, "Scripting the Radical Critique of Science: The Morrill Act and the American Land-Grant University," *Futures* 34, no. 2 (2002),182–191, especially 183. Steve Dubb and Ted Howard, *Linking Colleges to Communities: Engaging the University for Community Development* (College Park, MD: Democracy Collaborative at the University of Maryland, August 2007), 11–13.

2. Although university-community partnership work has deep historical roots, there are important differences between today's movement and the land-grant and settlement house movements of a century ago. In particular, today's movement puts less emphasis on provision of university expertise for communities and places greater emphasis on building mutually beneficial and reciprocal partnerships. (See, for example: Dubb and Howard, *Linking Colleges,* 57).

3. University of Wisconsin Extension, "Timeline: 1901–1918: The Van Hise/LaFollette Era," *History-UW-Extension,* 2010, http://www.uwex.edu/about/uw-extension-history.html#timeline (accessed April 2, 2011). Dubb and Howard, *Linking Colleges,* 13, 31.

4. Dwight E. Giles and Janet Eyler, "The Theoretical Roots of Service-Learning in John Dewey: Toward a Theory of Service-Learning," *Michigan Journal of Community Service Learning* 1 (1994), 77–85.

5. Michael Lounsbury and Seth Pollack, *Institutionalizing Civic Engagement: Shifting Logics and the Cultural Repackaging of Service-Learning in Higher Education* (Ithaca, NY: Cornell University, 2001), 17, www.ilr.cornell.edu/lounsbury/papers/pollack.pdf (accessed March 27, 2011).

6. Lounsbury and Pollack, *Institutionalizing Civic Engagement,* 20. Definition of service-learning is taken from Hollie Lund, Director of Service-Learning at Cal Poly Pomona; see Hollie Lund, "The Many Shapes of Service-Learning," California State University, Pomona, no date. Campus Compact, *5-Year Impact Summary* (Providence, RI: Campus Compact, 2004); Campus Compact, *2004 Service Statistics: The Engaged Campus—Highlights and Trends of Campus Compact's Annual Membership Survey* (Providence, RI: Campus Compact, 2005).

7. Dubb and Howard, *Linking Colleges,* 21–23.

8. Dubb and Howard, *Linking Colleges,* 30, 108 (note 77). As noted in chapter 11 below, these limited programs have recently seen their funding slashed. In fiscal year 2011, the Office of University Partnership programs and Learn and Serve America both received zero funding.

9. Bureau of Justice Statistics, *Crime—Large Local Agencies: Trends in One Variable, Murder and Non-negligent Manslaughter* (Washington, DC: DOJ, August 27, 2009), http://bjs.ojp.usdoj.gov/dataonline/Search/Crime/Local/TrendsInOneVarStepTwoLarge.cfm?NoCrimeCrossId=Yes&CFID=1380684&CFTOKEN=24221505 (accessed January 7, 2010). Pennsylvania Firearms Owners Association, *Philly Murder Rates before 1996?* (Philadelphia: PFOA, no date), http://forum.pafoa.org/pennsylvania-10/8238-philly-murder-rates-before-1996-a.html (accessed January 7, 2010). Alfred Bloumstein, Frederick P. Rivara, and Richard Rosenfeld, "The Rise and Decline of Homicide—And Why," *Annual Review of Public Health* 21 (2000), 505–541, especially 529.

10. Lee Benson, Ira Harkavy, and John Puckett, *Dewey's Dream: Universities and Democracies in an Age of Education Reform* (Philadelphia: Temple University Press, 2007), 79. Dubb and Howard, *Linking Colleges,* 56–61, 116.

11. Carol Morello and Dan Keating, "D.C. Population Soars Past 600,000 for First Time in Years," *Washington Post,* December 22, 2010, A-1, www.washingtonpost.com/wp-dyn/content/article/2010/12/21/AR2010122102609_pf.html (accessed June 12, 2011).

12. Initiative for a Competitive Inner City and CEOs for Cities, *Leveraging Colleges and Universities for Urban Economic Revitalization: An Action Agenda* (Boston: ICIC and CEOs for Cities, 2002), 2 and 9. David Perry and David Cox, Internal Submission to Anchor Institutions Task Force, December 2008. David Maurrasse, *City Anchors: Leveraging Anchor Institutions for Urban Success* (Chicago: CEOs for Cities, September 2007), 2.

13. Coalition of Urban Serving Universities, *A Vital Partnership: Great Cities, Great Universities* (Washington, DC: USU, 2008). Harkavy et al., "Anchor Institutions as Partners," 147–168, see especially 150 and 209.

14. American Association of State Colleges and Universities, *Muriel Howard* (Washington, DC: AASCU, no date), www.aascu.org/association/president/howardbio.htm (accessed May 31, 2010). Justin Wellner, personal correspondence, May 2010. Association of Public and Land-Grant Universities, "Shari O. Garmise, Ph.D. Appointed Vice President, APLU/USU Office of Urban Initiatives," *A Public Voice: A•P•L•U's Online Newsletter,* June 25, 2010, www.aplu.org/NetCommunity/Page.aspx?pld=1660 (accessed July 8, 2010).

15. Ernest Boyer, *Scholarship Reconsidered: Profiles of the Professoriate* (Princeton, NJ: Carnegie Foundation for the Advancement of Teaching, 1990).

16. Derek Bok, *Universities and the Future of America* (Durham, NC: Duke University Press, 1990), 120.

17. John Saltmarsh, Matt Hartley, and Patti Clayton, *Democratic Education White Paper* (Boston: New England Resource Center for Higher Education, February 2009), 6.

18. David Cox, telephone interview by Rita Axelroth Hodges, April 8, 2009.

19. Henry Taylor, telephone interview by Rita Axelroth Hodges, April 16, 2009.

20. Elizabeth Hollander, telephone interview by Rita Axelroth Hodges, April 23, 2009.

21. Community Partnership Summit Group, "Achieving the Promise of Community-Higher Education Partnerships: Community Partners Get Organized," in Hiram E. Fitzgerald, Cathy Burack, and Sarena D. Seifer, eds., *Engaged Scholarship: Contemporary Landscapes, Future Directions,* vol. 2: *Community Campus Partnerships* (East Lansing: Michigan State University Press, 2010), 199–221, especially 207. Michelle Sarche, Douglas

Novins, and Annie Belcourt-Dittloff, "Engaged Scholarship with Tribal Communities," in Hiram E. Fitzgerald, Cathy Burack, and Sarena D. Seifer, eds., *Engaged Scholarship: Contemporary Landscapes, Future Directions*, vol. 1: *Institutional Change* (East Lansing: Michigan State University Press, 2010), 215–228, especially 224–225.

Chapter 2. Three Strategies of Anchor-Based Community Development

1. Barry Checkoway, "*University for What?* Renewing the Civic Mission of the American Research University," *Journal of Higher Education*, March–April 2001, 125–147.

Chapter 3. Higher Education Approaches to Urban Issues

1. Eleanor Sharpe, *Anchor Institutions Toolkit: A Guide to Neighborhood Revitalization* (Philadelphia: Netter Center for Community Partnerships at the University of Pennsylvania, March 2008), 15–24.

2. Henry S. Webber and Mikael Karlstrom, *Why Community Investment is Good for Non-profit Anchor Institutions: Understanding Costs, Benefits, and the Range of Strategic Options* (Chicago: Chapin Hill at the University of Chicago, 2009), 6.

3. Initiative for a Competitive Inner City and CEOs for Cities, *Leveraging Colleges and Universities for Urban Economic Revitalization: An Action Agenda* (Boston: ICIC and CEOs for Cities, 2002), 21–22.

4. Ted Howard, telephone interview by Rita Axelroth Hodges, April 10, 2009.

5. David C. Perry and Wim Wiewel, eds., *The University as Urban Developer: Case Studies and Analysis* (London: Lincoln Institute of Land Policy and M.E. Sharpe, 2005), 304–314.

6. Allegra Calder, Gabriel Grant, and Holly Hart Muson, "No Such Thing as Vacant Land: Northeastern University and Davenport Commons," in Perry and Wiewel, *University as Urban Developer*, 256–257.

7. Ziona Austrian and Jill S. Norton, "An Overview of University Real Estate Investment Practices," in Perry and Wiewel, *University as Urban Developer*, 202.

8. Sharpe, *Anchor Institutions Toolkit*, 67.

9. Rensselaerville Institute, *Duke Durham Neighborhood Partnership: Results from the First Decade* (Durham, NC: Rensselaerville Institute, March 2008), 5 and 11.

10. Steve Dubb and Ted Howard, *Linking Colleges to Communities: Engaging the University for Community Development* (College Park, MD: Democracy Collaborative at the University of Maryland, August 2007), 65–66. Laura Dueñes, Michelle Ciurrea, Eliza Edelsberg, and Rhae Parkes, *Building Partnerships for Neighborhood Change: Promising Practices of the University-Community Partnership Initiative* (Washington, DC: Fannie Mae Foundation, December 2001).

11. Henry Taylor, telephone interview by Rita Axelroth Hodges, April 16, 2009. On support of community development financial institutions, for Yale, see chapter 6. On Duke, see Rensselaerville Institute, *Duke Durham Neighborhood Partnership*, 11. As of March 2008, Duke had a commitment to deposit $5 million in Latino Community Credit Union and also had $5.5 million already on deposit at various area minority-owned banks.

12. David Maurrasse, *Beyond the Campus: How Colleges and Universities Form Partnerships with Their Communities* (London: Routledge, 2001), 55.

13. Ira Harkavy et al., "Anchor Institutions as Partners in Building Successful Communities and Local Economies," in Paul Brophy and Rachel Godsil, eds., *Retooling HUD for a Catalytic Federal Government: A Report to Secretary Shaun Donovan* (Philadelphia: Penn Institute for Urban Research, February 2009), 147–168, especially 163. Alliance for Excellent Education, *The Nation's Path to Economic Growth: The Economic Benefits of Reducing the Dropout Rate* (Washington, DC: AEE, November 2009).

14. Coalition for Community Schools, *Community Schools Research Brief 09* (Washington, DC: Institute for Educational Leadership, 2009), www.communityschools.org (accessed March 17, 2009).

15. Harkavy et al., "Anchor Institutions as Partners," 162.

16. Community-Campus Partnerships for Health, *Community-Campus Partnerships for Health: Transforming Communities and Higher Education* (Seattle: CCPH, no date), www.ccph.info (accessed July 2, 2010).

17. Victor Rubin, telephone interview by Rita Axelroth Hodges, April 8, 2009.

18. For further discussion of scholarly engagement, as well as institutionalization of the work, see Lorilee R. Sandmann, Courtney H. Thornton, and Audrey J. Jaeger, eds., *Institutionalizing Community Engagement in Higher Education: The First Wave of Carnegie Classified Institutions* (San Francisco: Jossey Bass, 2009).

19. Perry and Wiewel, *University as Urban Developer*, 309–315.

Chapter 4. Addressing the Challenges

1. Michael Morand, personal correspondence, April 28, 2010.

2. Eleanor Sharpe, *Anchor Institutions Toolkit: A Guide to Neighborhood Revitalization* (Philadelphia: Netter Center for Community Partnerships at the University of Pennsylvania, March 2008), 104.

3. Carnegie Foundation for the Advancement of Teaching, *Carnegie Selects Colleges and Universities for New Elective Community Engagement Classification*, www.carnegie-foundation.org/news/sub.asp?key=51&subkey=2126 (accessed June 15, 2010).

4. Avis Vidal et al., *Lessons from the Community Outreach Partnership Center Program: Final Report* (Washington DC: Urban Institute, March 2002), 5–9. Richard Meister, telephone interview by Steve Dubb, October 15, 2004.

5. Steve Dubb and Ted Howard, *Linking Colleges to Communities: Engaging the University for Community Development* (College Park, MD: Democracy Collaborative at the University of Maryland, August 2007), 84.

6. Dubb and Howard, *Linking Colleges*, especially 80–82.

7. Dubb and Howard, *Linking Colleges*, 30–31, 51–56, 116. The now-defunct Campus Outreach Partnership Center program most commonly gave three-year, $400,000 grants. Minority-serving institution grants had a somewhat larger average at $700,000. Armand Carriére, personal correspondence, April 30, 2010.

8. David Dixon and Peter J. Roche, "Campus Partners and The Ohio State University: A Case Study in Enlightened Self-Interest," in David C. Perry and Wim Wiewel, eds., *The University as Urban Developer: Case Studies and Analysis* (London: Lincoln Institute of Land Policy and M.E. Sharpe, 2005), 272–3.

9. Dubb and Howard, *Linking Colleges*, 65.

10. Stephen Viederman, "Can Universities Contribute to Sustainable Development," in Robert Forrant and Linda Silka, eds., *Inside and Out: Universities and Education for Sustainable Development* (Amityville, NY: Baywood, 2006), 26.

11. Dubb and Howard, *Linking Colleges*, 98–99.

12. David Maurrasse, *Beyond the Campus: How Colleges and Universities Form Partnerships with Their Communities* (London: Routledge, 2001), 11–13.

13. Maurrasse, *Beyond the Campus*, 184.

14. Rachel Weber, Nik Theodore, and Charles Hoch, "Private Choices and Public Obligations: The Ethics of University Real Estate Development," in Perry and Wiewel, *University as Urban Developer*, 288.

15. Victor Rubin, telephone interview by Rita Axelroth Hodges, April 8, 2009.

16. Sharpe, *Anchor Institutions Toolkit*, 108.

17. Ziona Austrian and Jill S. Norton, "An Overview of University Real Estate Investment Practices," in Perry and Wiewel, *University as Urban Developer*, 212.

18. Rosalind Greenstein, telephone interview by Rita Axelroth Hodges, April 14, 2009.

19. Elizabeth Hollander, telephone interview by Rita Axelroth Hodges, April 23, 2009.

20. Maurrasse, *Beyond the Campus*, 186. For further discussion on asset-based community development, see Gord Cunningham and Alison Mathie, "Asset-Based Community Development—An Overview," 2002, www.synergos.org/knowledge/02/abcdoverview.htm (accessed June 7, 2010). See also the Asset-Based Community Development Institute at the School of Education and Social Policy, Northwestern University, www.abcdinstitute.org/ (accessed June 7, 2010).

21. Harry C. Boyte, "Repairing the Breech: Cultural Organizing and the Politics of Knowledge," *Partnerships: A Journal of Service-Learning & Civic Engagement* 1, no. 1 (2009), 1.

22. Victor Rubin, personal correspondence, June 9, 2010.

Chapter 5. University as Facilitator: IUPUI, Portland State, and Miami Dade College

1. Ziona Austrian and Jill S. Norton, "An Overview of University Real Estate Investment Practices," in David C. Perry and Wim Wiewel, eds., *The University as Urban Developer: Case Studies and Analysis* (London: Lincoln Institute of Land Policy and M.E. Sharpe, 2005), 205.

2. Robert Bringle, interview by Rita Axelroth Hodges, Indianapolis, IN, August 3, 2009. Starla Officer, interview by Rita Axelroth Hodges, Indianapolis, IN, August 3, 2009.

3. "Quality of Life Plan: Creating our Future Near Westside Neighborhood," 2007, www.greatindyneighborhoods.org/index.php (accessed July 22, 2009). Diane Arnold, interview by Rita Axelroth Hodges, Indianapolis, IN, August 3, 2009.

4. Bringle, interview. Patrice Duckett, interview by Rita Axelroth Hodges, Indianapolis, IN, August 3, 2009.

5. Anne-Marie Predovich Taylor, interview by Rita Axelroth Hodges, Indianapolis, IN, August 4, 2009. Arnold, interview.

6. Coalition for Community Schools, *Coalition for Community Schools*, www.communityschools.org (accessed February 17, 2010).

7. Officer, interview. George Washington Community High School, www.421.ips.k12.in.us/index.php?id=8107 (accessed April 1, 2010). Starla Officer, personal correspondence, April 29, 2010. Robert Bringle, personal correspondence, April 11, 2010.

8. Libby Laux, interview by Rita Axelroth Hodges, Indianapolis, IN, August 3, 2009.

9. Bringle, interview. Krista Hoffman-Longtin, interview by Rita Axelroth Hodges, Indianapolis, IN, August 3, 2009.

10. Laura Littlepage, interview by Rita Axelroth Hodges, Indianapolis, IN, August 4, 2009.

11. Kevin Kecskes, interview by Rita Axelroth Hodges, Portland, OR, July 14, 2009.

12. Wim Wiewel, telephone interview by Rita Axelroth Hodges, August 13, 2009.

13. Roy Koch, interview by Rita Axelroth Hodges, Portland, OR, July 15, 2009. Kecskes, interview. Lynn Knox, telephone interview by Rita Axelroth Hodges, July 16, 2009.

14. For more information on this topic, see Andrew Mott, *University Education for Community Change: A Vital Strategy for Progress on Poverty, Race and Community-Building* (Washington, DC: Community Learning Project, May 2005). Portland State's effort is discussed briefly on p. 20 of the report.

15. Stephanie Farquhar, telephone interview by Rita Axelroth Hodges, July 16, 2009.

16. Genny Nelson, interview by Rita Axelroth Hodges, Portland, OR, July 15, 2009.

17. Laurie Powers, telephone interview by Rita Axelroth Hodges, July 22, 2009.

18. Lara Damon, interview by Rita Axelroth Hodges, Portland, OR, July 13, 2009.

19. Knox, interview. Kecskes, interview. Wiewel, interview.

20. Mark Gregory, interview by Rita Axelroth Hodges, Portland, OR, July 13, 2009.

21. Lindsay Desrochers, interview by Rita Axelroth Hodges, Portland, OR, July 13, 2009. Desrochers served as vice president for finance and administration in the early 1990s and then again from 2005 through 2010. Monica Rimai (formerly at University of Cincinnati and State University of New York) took over this position in 2011.

22. Lew Bowers, interview by Rita Axelroth Hodges, Portland, OR, July 15, 2009. Koch, interview.

23. Miami Dade College, *Miami Dade College Highlights and Facts, 2009* (Miami: MDC, 2009). Daniella Levine, interview by Rita Axelroth Hodges, Miami, FL, May 11, 2009.

24. Theodore Levitt, interview by Rita Axelroth Hodges, Miami, FL, May 11, 2009.

25. H. Leigh Toney, interview by Rita Axelroth Hodges, Miami, FL, May 12, 2009.

26. Josh Young, interview by Rita Axelroth Hodges, Miami, FL, May 11, 2009.

27. Geoffrey Gathercole, interview by Rita Axelroth Hodges, Miami, FL, May 12, 2009.

28. Overtown Collaborative, *Chronology of Overtown History: University of Miami Oral History Project*, www.floridacdc.org/members/overtown/hist-his3.htm (accessed December 14, 2009).

29. Phil Bacon, interview by Rita Axelroth Hodges, Miami, FL, May 11, 2009.

30. Florida Campus Compact recognized this effort as the state's most outstanding campus-community partnership for 2009.

31. Marilyn Brummitt, interview by Rita Axelroth Hodges, Miami, FL, May 11, 2009.

32. Levine, interview.

33. Vivian Rodriguez, interview by Rita Axelroth Hodges, Miami, FL, May 11, 2009. Wim Wiewel, internal submission to Anchor Institutions Task Force, December 2008.

34. Sheldon Edwards, interview by Rita Axelroth Hodges, Miami, FL, May 12, 2009.

35. Alex Alvarez, interview by Rita Axelroth Hodges, Miami, FL: May 11, 2009.

36. Linda Scharf, interview by Rita Axelroth Hodges, Miami, FL, May 11, 2009. Levitt, interview.

37. Officer, interview.

38. Desrochers, interview.

39. Wiewel, interview.

40. Young, interview.

41. Alvarez, interview.

42. Dilafruz Williams, Partnership Institute Featured Session, "Sites of Knowledge, Service, and Research: How to Grow Long-Term Partnerships among Schools, Universities, and Communities," May 19, 2009.

43. Robert Bringle, Julie Hatcher, and Barbara Holland, "Conceptualizing Civic Engagement: Orchestrating Change at a Metropolitan University," *Metropolitan Universities 18, no.* 3 (2007), 57–74.

44. Bringle, interview. Darrell Nickolson, interview by Rita Axelroth Hodges, Indianapolis, IN, August 3, 2009.

45. Bacon, interview.

46. Eduardo Padrón, e-mail interview by Rita Axelroth Hodges, June 5, 2009. Gathercole, interview.

47. Wiewel, interview. Scott Gallagher, "News: Jonathan Fink Joins Portland State University Leadership as Vice President for Research and Strategic Partnerships," *University News,* http://www.pdx.edu/news/jonathan-fink-joins-portland-state-university-leadership-as-vice-president-for-research-and-strategi (accessed June 26, 2011).

48. Miami Dade College, "Saviors of Our Cities: Survey of Best College and University Civic Partnerships," draft submission, May 22, 2009.

49. Gregory, interview. Damon, interview.

50. Richard Bray, interview by Rita Axelroth Hodges, Indianapolis, IN, August 3, 2009.

51. Taylor, interview. Arnold, interview.

52. Ethan Seltzer, interview by Rita Axelroth Hodges, Portland, OR, July 13, 2009.

53. Padrón, e-mail interview.

54. Norma Goonen, interview by Rita Axelroth Hodges, Miami, FL, May 11, 2009. Toney, interview. Padrón, e-mail interview.

55. Bray, interview.

56. Edwards, interview.

57. Robert Halter, interview by Rita Axelroth Hodges, Indianapolis, IN, August 4, 2009.

58. Karen Preston, interview by Rita Axelroth Hodges, Portland, OR, July 14, 2009. The U.S. Green Building Council is the lead group that has developed the LEED (Leadership in Energy and Environmental Design) rating system. For more information on LEED, see

United States Green Building Council, *LEED* (Washington, DC: USGBC, 2011), http://www.usgbc.org/DisplayPage.aspx?CategoryID=19 (accessed June 14, 2011).

59. Desrochers, interview.

60. Levitt, interview.

61. Bringle, interview. Duckett, interview.

62. Kevin Kecskes, "Beyond the Rhetoric: Applying a Cultural Theory Lens to Community-Campus Partnership Development," *Michigan Journal of Community Service-Learning, Spring 2006*, 5–14. Kecskes, interview.

63. Lisa Abuaf, interview by Rita Axelroth Hodges, Portland, OR, August 15, 2009.

64. Brian Hoop, interview by Rita Axelroth Hodges, Portland, OR, July 14, 2009. Steve Trujillo, interview by Rita Axelroth Hodges, Portland, OR, July 14, 2009.

65. Farquhar, interview. Knox, interview.

66. Elizabeth Mejia, interview by Rita Axelroth Hodges, Miami, FL, May 12, 2009.

67. Denis Russ, interview by Rita Axelroth Hodges, Miami, FL, May 11, 2009. Levine, interview.

68. Paul Leistner, interview by Rita Axelroth Hodges, Portland, OR, July 14, 2009.

69. Aaron Laramore, interview by Rita Axelroth Hodges, Indianapolis, August 20, 2009.

70. Levitt, interview.

71. Wiewel, interview.

Chapter 6. University as Leader: Penn, Cincinnati, and Yale

1. National Association of College and University Business Officers, *All Institutions Listed by Fiscal Year 2008 Market Value of Endowment Assets with Percentage Change Between 2007 and 2008 Endowment Assets* (Washington, DC: NACUBO, 2009). National Association of College and University Business Officers and Commonfund, *U.S. and Canadian Institutions Listed by Fiscal Year 2009 Endowment Market Value and Percentage Change in Endowment Market Value from FY 2008 to FY 2009* (Washington, DC: NACUBO and Commonfund, 2010).

2. University of Pennsylvania, *Penn Facts and Figures*, 2009, www.upenn.edu/about/facts.php; University of Pennsylvania, *2008–2009 Financial Report*, 2009, 20; Yale University, *About Yale: Facts*, no date, http://yale.edu/about/facts.html; University of Cincinnati, *About UC*, no date, www.uc.edu/about/ucfactsheet.html (websites accessed May 23, 2010). In fiscal year 2009, Penn hospital revenues and expenses were roughly 56 percent of Penn's total budget; the $2.5 billion figure for Penn's budget without the Health System assumes a similar percentage in FY 2010 (since the FY 2010 financial report is not published as of press time). Since Yale New Haven Hospital, unlike Penn Health Systems, is a separate corporation and thus does not appear on the books of its parent university, the Penn Health numbers need to be subtracted to arrive at comparable numbers.

3. Although beyond the scope of this study, "town and gown" have interacted ever since the university was founded. An interesting parallel to the West Philadelphia Initiatives in Penn's history is the university's 1959 creation of the West Philadelphia Corporation, formed in response to a murder of a Penn graduate student the previous year. Generally,

this early effort is seen as much more "top down" than Penn's current efforts. The "top down" nature of the 1959 effort can be seen in the language of the partnership effort, which, according to Sharpe, was focused on the "need for elbow room and a more healthy campus environment." For more information, see Judith Rodin, *The University and Urban Revival: Out of the Ivory Tower and into the Streets* (Philadelphia: University of Pennsylvania Press, 2007), especially chapter 3; and Eleanor Sharpe, *Anchor Institutions Toolkit: A Guide for Neighborhood Revitalization* (Philadelphia: Netter Center for Community Partnerships, March 2008), especially 29–30 and 46. Eleanor Sharpe, personal correspondence, April 30, 2010.

4. Tom Burns, telephone interview by Steve Dubb, Philadelphia, PA, May 13, 2009. Ira Harkavy, telephone interview by Steve Dubb, September 15, 2005. See also Sharpe, *Anchor Institutions Toolkit*, 35–38. Ralph Maier, interview by Steve Dubb, Philadelphia, PA, May 5, 2009.

5. Burns, interview. Tony Sorrentino, interview by Steve Dubb, Philadelphia, PA, May 5, 2009.

6. John Kromer and Lucy Kerman, *West Philadelphia Initiatives: A Case Study in Urban Redevelopment* (Philadelphia: University of Pennsylvania, 2004), 36, 38, and 52.

7. Diane-Louise Wormley, interview by Steve Dubb, Philadelphia, PA, May 8, 2009. Richard Redding, interview by Steve Dubb, Philadelphia, PA, May 4, 2009.

8. Redding, interview. Ira Harkavy, interview by Steve Dubb, Philadelphia, PA, May 8, 2009. Harkavy, interview, September 15, 2005. Barbara and Edward Netter Center for Community Partnerships, *Annual Report 2008–2009*, 18.

9. Maier, interview.

10. Sorrentino, interview. Glenn Bryan, interview by Steve Dubb, Philadelphia, PA, May 5, 2009.

11. Sorrentino, interview. Kromer and Kerman, *West Philadelphia Initiatives*, 28 and 52.

12. Lewis Wendell, interview by Steve Dubb, Philadelphia, PA, May 4, 2009. Sorrentino, interview. University City District, "University City Report Card 2009," 50 and 58. Kromer and Kerman, *West Philadelphia Initiatives*, 22. Additional University City District programs include marketing, street cleaning, recycling promotion, summer jobs for community youth, a farmer's market, maintenance of two local parks, homeless outreach, and graffiti removal. Lewis Wendell, personal correspondence, April 2010; Tom Burns, personal correspondence, May 2010. Burns, interview.

13. David Grossman, interview by Steve Dubb, Philadelphia, PA, May 8, 2009. Hillary Kane, interview by Steve Dubb, Philadelphia, PA, May 8, 2009. Eleanor Sharpe, personal correspondence, April 30, 2010.

14. James Lytle, interview by Steve Dubb, Philadelphia, PA, May 5, 2009. School District of Philadelphia, *School Profile, Penn Alexander School: Ethnicity* (Philadelphia: School District of Philadelphia, 2010), https://webapps.philasd.org/school_profile/view/1280 (accessed May 31, 2010). For historical data, see Stephen Seplow, "Penn Neighborhood Blooms around a Top School," *Philadelphia Inquirer,* April 5, 2010, http://articles.philly.com/2010–04–05/news/25212784_1_catchment-area-neighborhood-blooms-philadelphia-school-district (accessed March 27, 2011).

15. Ann Kreidle, interview by Steve Dubb, Philadelphia, PA, May 5, 2009. Lytle, interview. Cory Bowman, interview by Steve Dubb, Philadelphia, PA, May 8, 2009. Netter Center for Community Partnerships, "University-Assisted Community Schools," report in possession of author, 2008.

16. Bowman, interview. Harkavy, interview, May 8, 2009.

17. Michael Romanos, David Edelman, and Mahyar Arefi, *Community Interactions and Collaborations: Study of Peer Institutions—Main Report* (Cincinnati, OH: University of Cincinnati, Office of the President, November 2006), especially 13–14. Gerald Siegert, personal correspondence, April 26, 2010.

18. Michael Romanos, *The University of Cincinnati's Community Involvement* (Curitiba, Brazil: Seminario Internacional de Curitiba, August–September 2007), 20. Gerald Siegert, interview by Rita Axelroth Hodges, Cincinnati, OH, September 10, 2009. Interview with Tony Brown, The Democracy Collaborative, College Park, MD, September 2007, 2, http://www. community-wealth.org/strategies/cw-interviews.html (accessed October 8, 2011). Mary Stagaman, interview by Rita Axelroth Hodges, Cincinnati, OH, September 10, 2009. In June 2010, Stagaman left her position at the University of Cincinnati to serve as executive director of Agenda 360, a regional economic action plan that includes the University as a partner.

19. Romanos, Edelman, and Arefi, *Community Interactions and Collaborations*, especially 16–24, 53, 102–103, 123. Tony Brown, presentation at CEOs for Cities, "*Leveraging Anchor Institutions for Urban Success*," San Jose, CA, May 1–2, 2007.

20. Stagaman, interview.

21. Kathy Dick and Michael Sharp, interview by Rita Axelroth Hodges, Cincinnati, OH, September 11, 2009. Monica Rimai, telephone interview by Rita Axelroth Hodges, October 5, 2009. Stagaman, interview.

22. Rimai, interview. Siegert, personal correspondence, April 26, 2010.

23. Stagaman, interview.

24. Not all of these redevelopment corporations are currently active. Siegert, interview.

25. Stagaman, interview.

26. Olivetree Research and UC Marketing Students, "Uptown Market Landscape," May 2009.

27. Romanos, Edelman, and Arefi, *Community Interactions and Collaborations*, 20–21. Rimai, interview.

28. Jeff Edmonson, interview by Rita Axelroth Hodges, Cincinnati, OH, September 10, 2009. Jennifer Blatz, interview by Rita Axelroth Hodges, Cincinnati, OH, September 10, 2009. Mary Stagaman, personal correspondence, May 6, 2010. Strive's 2010 annual report indicates improvement on forty of fifty-four key measures of success, including a 10 percent increase in Cincinnati Public School graduates enrolling in college since 2004, the majority of whom attend the University of Cincinnati. Coalition of Urban Serving Universities, *Urban Universities: Anchors Generating Prosperity for America's Cities* (Washington, DC: USU, July 2010), 13.

29. The Kalamazoo Promise is a pledge to provide all students who graduate from Kalamazoo Public Schools with a scholarship to any public university or community college in

the state of Michigan. As noted below in the discussion of Yale, the Kalamazoo Promise has already spawned additional imitators, including the University of Pittsburgh and Yale University.

30. Larry Johnson, interview by Rita Axelroth Hodges, Cincinnati, OH, September 11, 2009; Edmonson, interview.

31. Johnson, interview.

32. Scott Stiles, interview by Rita Axelroth Hodges, Cincinnati, OH, September 11, 2009. Bill Fischer, interview by Rita Axelroth Hodges, Cincinnati, OH, September 11, 2009.

33. Stagaman, interview. Myrita Craig, interview by Rita Axelroth Hodges, Cincinnati, OH, September 10, 2009.

34. Cliff Peale, "Health Alliance Future Clouded," *Cincinnati Enquirer,* July 12, 2009, http://news.cincinnati.com/article/20090712/COL/907120347/Health-Alliance-future-clouded (accessed December 29, 2009). Anonymous, "Health Alliance to become UC Health," *Business Courier,* September 2, 2010, http://www.bizjournals.com/cincinnati/stories/2010/08/30/daily47.html?s=print (accessed April 3, 2011). Gregory Williams, "Address by President Gregory H. Williams to All-University Faculty Meeting, University of Cincinnati," November 18, 2009, http://www.uc.edu/president/communications/speech_11_18_09.html (accessed March 27, 2011); Tony Brown, telephone interview by Rita Axelroth Hodges, October 27, 2009. In June 2010, the Uptown Consortium board of trustees selected Beth Robinson as its new president and CEO; Robinson formerly served as the University of Cincinnati's director of real estate development.

35. Although not a focus of this report, Yale's involvement with the community evidently did not begin in 1991. For example, Michael Morand, associate vice president of Yale's Office of New Haven and State Affairs, notes that in 1987, Yale committed to invest $50 million over five years in housing and commercial and industrial development in New Haven. Michael Morand, personal correspondence, April 28, 2010.

36. Sheila Masterson, interview by Steve Dubb, New Haven, CT, October 6, 2009. Linda Thompson-Maier, interview by Steve Dubb, New Haven, CT, October 6, 2009.

37. Yale Office of Public Affairs, "Yale's Office of New Haven and State Affairs," *Yale Bulletin and Calendar,* Spring–Summer 2002, www.yale.edu/opa/arc-ybc/ybc_alumni/story104.html (accessed March 27, 2011). Yale Office of Public Affairs, "Yale Names Urban Revitalization Leader to Head University's New Haven and State Affairs," August 28, 1997, http://opa.yale.edu/news/article.aspx?id=5793 (accessed December 24, 2009). Morand, personal correspondence, April 28, 2010.

38. U.S. Census Bureau, "New Haven (City) Connecticut," *State and County Quick Facts,* data derived from Population Estimates, 2000 Census of Population and Housing, 1990 Census of Population and Housing, Small Area Income and Poverty Estimates, County Business Patterns, 2002 Economic Census, Minority- and Women-Owned Business, Building Permits, Consolidated Federal Funds Report, Census of Governments (Washington, DC: Dept. of Commerce, Nov. 17, 2009), http://quickfacts.census.gov/qfd/states/09/0952000.html (accessed December 24, 2009). Sheila Shanklin, interview by Steve Dubb, New Haven, October 7, 2009.

39. Richard C. Levin, "Universities and Cities: The View from New Haven," inaugural colloquium, Case Western Reserve University, January 30, 2003, http://opa.yale.edu/president/message.aspx?id=36 (accessed December 24, 2009).

40. Jon Soderstrom, interview by Steve Dubb, New Haven, CT, October 7, 2009. Shana Schneider, interview by Steve Dubb, New Haven, CT, October 8, 2009. Morand, personal correspondence, April 28, 2010.

41. Reggie Solomon, *New Haven Investments—Summary 1990–2009* (New Haven, CT: Yale University, Office of New Haven and State Affairs, November 23, 2009). Masterson, interview. Thompson-Maier, interview.

42. Reggie Solomon, interview by Steve Dubb, New Haven, CT: October 8, 2009. Michael Morand, interview by Steve Dubb, New Haven, CT, October 6, 2009. Solomon, *New Haven Investments.* Morand, personal correspondence, April 28, 2010.

43. Solomon, *New Haven Investments.*

44. Claudia Merson, interview by Steve Dubb, New Haven, CT, October 7, 2009. Suzannah Holsenbeck, interview by Steve Dubb, New Haven, CT, October 8, 2009.

45. Colleen Murphy-Dunning, interview by Steve Dubb, New Haven, CT, October 6, 2009.

46. Solomon, *New Haven Investments.*

47. Solomon, *New Haven Investments*

48. Abigail Rider, interview by Steve Dubb, New Haven, CT, October 8, 2009. Morand, personal correspondence, April 28, 2010.

49. Rider, interview.

50. Office of New Haven and State Affairs, *Welcome to ONHSA* (New Haven: Yale University, 2008). Yale Office of Public Affairs and Communications, "New Haven Promise Program to Provide Scholarships for City Youth," November 9, 2010, http://opac.yale.edu/news/article.aspx?id=7989 (accessed April 3, 2011).

51. University of Pennsylvania, "West Philadelphia Data & Information Resources," no date, http://westphillydata.library.upenn.edu (accessed December 29, 2009). Redding, interview.

52. Olivetree Research and UC Marketing Students, *Uptown Market Landscape* (Cincinnati, OH: UC, May 2009).

53. Nelson Bregon, General Deputy Assistant Secretary, Community Planning and Development, United States Department of Housing and Urban Development, *Testimony Before the Subcommittee on Select Revenue Measures of the House Committee on Ways and Means,* U.S. House of Representatives, October 7, 2009, Attachment 1, http://waysandmeans.house.gov/hearings.asp?formmode=view&id=8080 (accessed December 29, 2009).

54. Seplow, "Penn Neighborhood Blooms." Lucy Kerman, interview by Steve Dubb, Philadelphia, PA, May 4, 2009. Wormley, interview.

55. Morand, personal correspondence, April 28, 2010.

56. Ira Harkavy, Carol de Fries, Joann Weeks, Cory Bowman, Glenn Bryan, and Dawn Maglicco, "Strategy for Taking Penn's Local Engagement Effort from Excellence to Eminence," submitted to Van McMurtry, Vice President, Office of Government and Community Affairs, University of Pennsylvania, January 9, 2006.

57. Bowman, interview.

58. Sharpe, *Anchor Institutions Toolkit*, 93–94. Randy Belin, interview by Steve Dubb, Philadelphia, PA, May 4, 2009. Wendell, personal correspondence, April 2010.

59. Michael Sharp, interview by Rita Axelroth Hodges, Cincinnati, OH, September 11, 2009.

60. Stagaman, interview.

61. Solomon, interview.

62. Jeanette Ickovics, interview by Steve Dubb, New Haven, CT, October 6, 2009. Bill Placke, interview by Steve Dubb, New Haven, CT, October 7, 2009.

63. Anonymous, "University Trustees' November Meeting Coverage," *University of Pennsylvania Almanac*, November 10, 2009, www.upenn.edu/almanac/volumes/v56/n11/trustees.html (accessed March 27, 2011). Steve Dubb and Ted Howard, *Linking Colleges to Communities: Engaging the University for Community Development* (College Park, MD: Democracy Collaborative at the University of Maryland, August 2007), 63–64. Ira Harkavy, personal correspondence, April 27, 2010.

64. Kathy Merchant, telephone interview by Rita Axelroth Hodges, October 14, 2009. Siegert, personal correspondence, April 26, 2010. Sharp, interview. Michael Romanos, telephone interview by Rita Axelroth Hodges, October 1, 2009.

65. Stagaman, interview. University of Cincinnati, Office of the President, *"Biography,"* no date, www.uc.edu/president/biography.html (accessed July 2, 2010).

66. Soderstrom, interview.

67. Morand, interview.

68. University of Nevada, Reno, "Case Study #4: University of Pennsylvania-Philadelphia, Pennsylvania," *University and College Community Partnerships: University of Nevada, Reno Comprehensive Master Plan* (Reno: University of Nevada, Reno, March 11, 2004), 2, www.unr.edu/masterplan/worktodate.html (accessed December 30, 2009). Barbara and Edward Netter Center for Community Partnerships, *Annual Report 2007–2008*, 39.

69. Stagaman, interview. Siegert, interview. Siegert, personal correspondence, April 26, 2010. Thomas Croft, personal correspondence, May 17, 2010.

70. Merchant, interview.

71. Solomon, *New Haven Investments*. Note: the Office of New Haven and State Affairs includes "uncompensated medical care" among its community partnership expenditures. We have elected to exclude this category, in part because this is not strictly a "voluntary contribution" and recalculated Yale's contribution totals accordingly (i.e., nonprofit hospitals are legally obliged to provide charity care and, moreover, the amount a nonprofit hospital "contributes" for charity care depends on how many uninsured patients need medical care, a factor that is largely beyond the nonprofit hospital's control).

72. Maier, interview. Natalie Kostelni, "UCD Adds New Jobs Initiative," *Philadelphia Business Journal*, June 25, 2010, http://philadelphia.bizjournals.com/philadelphia/stories/2010/06/28/story1.html (accessed July 12, 2010).

73. Tom Guerin, interview by Rita Axelroth Hodges, Cincinnati, OH, September 11, 2009.

74. Stiles, interview. Fischer, interview.

75. Morand, interview.

76. Kromer and Kerman, *West Philadelphia Initiatives*, 12.

77. Romanos, Edelman, and Arefi, *Community Interactions and Collaborations*, 14.

78. Romanos, interview. Romanos, Edelman, and Arefi, *Community Interactions and Collaborations*, especially 23–25. Stagaman, personal correspondence, May 6, 2010.

79. Matt Bourgeois, interview by Rita Axelroth Hodges, Cincinnati, OH, September 11, 2009. Rob Neel, interview by Rita Axelroth Hodges, Cincinnati, OH, September 10, 2009.

80. Masterson, interview. Thompson-Maier, interview. Florita Gonzalez, interview by Steve Dubb, New Haven, CT, October 6, 2009.

81. Wormley, interview. Kerman, interview.

82. TCC Group, "Netter Center for Community Partnerships: Strategic Plan," February 2008, 5, 18, 29. Harkavy, interview, May 8, 2009.

83. Burns, interview.

84. Stagaman, interview.

85. Rimai, interview.

86. Merson, interview. Michael Morand, quoted in Mark Alden Branch, "Then . . . and Now: How a City Came Back from the Brink," *Yale Alumni Magazine*, May–June 2009, 45.

87. Paul Grogan and Tony Proscio, *Comeback Cities: A Blueprint for Urban Neighborhood Renewal* (Boulder, CO: Westview, 2000), 13. Branch, "Then . . . and now," 46.

88. Harkavy et al., *Strategy for Penn's Local Engagement*. Sorrentino, interview. Burns, interview.

89. Olivetree Research and UC Marketing Students, "Uptown Market Landscape," May 2009.

90. Brown, interview, October 27, 2009.

91. On Cincinnati's formal commitment to poverty reduction: see Nancy Zimpher, "State of the University Address," University of Cincinnati, 2007, http://www.uc.edu/president25/2007_State_of_the_University_Address.html (accessed March 27, 2011), where Zimpher says, "These are a set of neighborhoods that face some very daunting challenges—high poverty, high unemployment, low literacy, low home ownership, and safety and transportation issues. And that's why the Uptown Consortium is committed to a five-pronged strategy focused on housing, retail, safety, transportation and neighborhood amenities." On Penn's formal commitment, see Harkavy et al., "Strategy." See especially p. 8, where the authors write, "Penn is not, nor should it be, a social service agency. However, the University can make a significant difference by harnessing and marshalling our academic and institutional resources to solve universal problems (such as poverty, unequal healthcare, substandard housing, and inadequate, unequal education) that are manifested locally in West Philadelphia."

92. Yale Office of Public Affairs, "Yale Reduces Greenhouse Gas Emissions by 17%," 2008, http://environment.yale.edu/news/5565 (accessed December 28, 2009). Holly Parker, interview by Steve Dubb, New Haven, CT: October 7, 2009. Rafi Taherian, interview by Steve Dubb, New Haven, CT, November 23, 2009.

Chapter 7. University as Convener: Syracuse, Minnesota, LeMoyne-Owen, and Emory

1. Nancy Cantor, interview by Rita Axelroth Hodges, May 29, 2009.

2. Marilyn Higgins, interview by Rita Axelroth Hodges, Syracuse, NY, May 28, 2009. Kevin Morrow, "State Approves Syracuse University Investing $13.8 Million Loan Repayment

in Near Westside Initiative," September 21, 2007, www.syr.edu/news/archives/story. php?id=4341 (accessed May 30, 2009).

3. Higgins, interview. Marilyn Higgins, personal correspondence, March 23, 2010. Kathy Goldfarb-Findling, interview by Rita Axelroth Hodges, Syracuse, NY, May 29, 2009.

4. Ed Bogucz, interview by Rita Axelroth Hodges, Syracuse, NY, May 28, 2009. Higgins, personal correspondence, March 31, 2010.

5. Linda Littlejohn, interview by Rita Axelroth Hodges, Syracuse, NY, May 28, 2009.

6. Eric Persons, interview by Rita Axelroth Hodges, Syracuse, NY, May 29, 2009. Benjamin Sio, interview by Rita Axelroth Hodges, Syracuse, NY, May 29, 2009.

7. Douglas Freeman, interview by Rita Axelroth Hodges, Syracuse, NY, May 29, 2009. "Guaranteed Mortgage Program," http://realestate.syr.edu/RealEstate/display.cfm?content_ ID=%23%288I-%0A; "Home Ownership Grant Program," http://realestate.syr.edu/ RealEstate/display.cfm?content_ID=%23%28%28-%28%0A (accessed May 25, 2009).

8. Louis Marcoccia, Douglas Freeman, Eric Beattie, and Allan Breese, interview by Rita Axelroth Hodges, Syracuse, NY, May 29, 2009. Louis Marcoccia, personal correspondence, June 22, 2009.

9. Cantor, interview.

10. Higgins, personal correspondence, March 31, 2010.

11. Harry Boyte, telephone interview by Steve Dubb, September 9, 2005. For details, see Edwin Fogelman, "Civic Engagement at the University of Minnesota," *Journal of Public Affairs* 6, Supplemental Issue 1 (2002), 103–117.

12. W. K. Kellogg Foundation, "Engaged Institutions Cluster Evaluation—Case Study: The University of Minnesota," draft report in possession of author, 2009.

13. Craig Taylor, interview by Rita Axelroth Hodges, Minneapolis, MN, August 24, 2009; Office for Business and Community Economic Development, University of Minnesota, "About Us," no date, www.ced.umn.edu/About_Us.html (accessed June 4, 2010).

14. "UROC Development Surpasses Contracting and Hiring Goals," *InsightNews.com*, January 22, 2010, www.insightnews.com/news/5487-uroc-development-surpasses-contracting-and-hiring-goals (accessed June 4, 2010).

15. Taylor, interview. Robert Jones, interview by Rita Axelroth Hodges, Minneapolis, MN, August 24, 2009.

16. Sherrie Pugh, interview by Rita Axelroth Hodges, Minneapolis, MN, August 24, 2009.

17. University Northside Partnership, "Welcome," 2008, www.unpmn.org (accessed March 27, 2011).

18. Martha Coventry, "McClaurin Helps Forge New Partnerships: Engaging with the Northside," UMN News, July 22, 2008, http://www1.umn.edu/news/features/2008f/ UR_192846_REGION1.html (accessed June 4, 2010).

19. Jones, interview.

20. Jones, interview. Reynolds-Anthony Harris, telephone interview by Rita Axelroth Hodges, Minneapolis, MN, August 24, 2009. Erik Hansen, interview by Rita Axelroth Hodges, Minneapolis, MN, August 25, 2009.

21. Erline Belton and Reynolds-Anthony Harris, *Strategic Planning Process Phase One: Report on Interviews, Findings, & Preparation for the Futures Conference* (Pittsburgh,

PA: Lyceum Group. 2008). Sara Axtell, interview by Rita Axelroth Hodges, Minneapolis, MN, August 24, 2009.

22. Eric Robertson, interview by Rita Axelroth Hodges, Memphis, TN, October 13, 2009.

23. Jeffrey Higgs, interview by Rita Axelroth Hodges, Memphis, TN, October 12, 2009.

24. For a detailed history of the LeMoyne-Owen College Community Development Corporation, including its internal organizational structure, external oversight, relationship to the college, specific program initiatives, and the college's participation in the HUD HBCU grant program, see Nina Liou, Laurel Davis, and Sheila Ards, *Historically Black Colleges and Universities: Three Case Studies of Experiences in Community Development*, vol. 2, *Case Study Reports*, prepared for the U.S. Department of Housing and Urban Development Office of Policy Development & Research (Baltimore, MD: Optimal Solutions Group LLC, October 2007), 37–72.

25. Higgs, interview. Liou, Davis, and Ards, *Historically Black Colleges and Universities*, 64. LeMoyne-Owen College, "Accepting Tenants," *The Beacon*, fall 2010, page 7. On the struggle to find a grocery store tenant in a recessionary economy, see: Hannah Sayle, "Unjust Deserts, Finding Quality Food is a Daunting Task for Thousands of Memphians," *Memphis Flyer*, September 2, 2010, http://memphisfoodpolicy.blogspot.com/2010/09/from-memphis-flyer.html (accessed October 14, 2011).

26. Higgs, interview. Liou, Davis, and Ards, *Historically Black Colleges and Universities*, 68.

27. Higgs, interview. Austin Emeagwai, interview by Rita Axelroth Hodges, Memphis, TN, October 13, 2009. Liou, Davis, and Ards, *Historically Black Colleges and Universities*, 55.

28. Higgs, interview. "Students Prepare to Graduate from Recovery Act Funded Highway Worker Training Program," http://news.tennesseeanytime.org/node/5227 (accessed June 14, 2010).

29. Michael Powell, "Blacks in Memphis Lose Decades of Economic Gains," *New York Times*, May 30, 2010, www.nytimes.com/2010/05/31/business/economy/31memphis.html (accessed June 14, 2010). Higgs, interview. Liou, Davis, and Ards, *Historically Black Colleges and Universities*, 43–44 and 68–69.

30. Femi Ajanaku, interview by Rita Axelroth Hodges, Memphis, TN, October 12, 2009.

31. LeMoyne-Owen College, *Transformation Plan* (Memphis, TN: LeMoyne Owen College, 2008).

32. National Association of College and University Business Officers and Commonfund, *All Institutions Listed by Fiscal Year 2009 Market Value of Endowment Assets with Percentage Change Between 2008 and 2009 Endowment Assets* (Washington, DC: NACUBO and Commonfund, 2010). Jane Roberts, "Alumna leaves LeMoyne-Owen College Gift of San Francisco Real Estate," *Commercial Appeal* (Memphis, TN), May 7, 2010, www.commercialappeal.com/news/2010/may/07/alumna-leaves-lemoyne-owen-college-gift-san-franci/(accessed March 27, 2011). David Cox, interview by Rita Axelroth Hodges, Memphis, TN, October 13, 2009. Alicia Philip, interview by Steve Dubb, Atlanta, GA, June 18, 2009.

33. National Association of College and University Business Officers, *All Institutions Listed by Fiscal Year 2008 Market Value of Endowment Assets with Percentage Change Between 2007 and 2008 Endowment Assets* (Washington, DC: NACUBO, 2009). National

Association of College and University Business Officers and Commonfund, *U.S. and Canadian Institutions Listed by Fiscal Year 2009 Endowment Market Value and Percentage Change in Endowment Market Value from FY 2008 to FY 2009* (Washington, DC: NACUBO and Commonfund, 2010).

34. Craig Schneider and Andy Miller, "Emory Cuts Grady Debt $20 million," *Atlanta Journal-Constitution,* December 19, 2008, www.ajc.com/hotjobs/content/printedition/2008/12/19/grady.html (accessed March 27, 2011). Robert Lee, interview by Steve Dubb, Atlanta, GA, June 18, 2009; Emory University, "*Grady Facts,*" 2011, www.emory.edu/grady/emory-at-grady/facts.html (accessed March 27, 2011).

35. David Jenkins, interview by Steve Dubb, Atlanta, GA, June 18, 2009.

36. Madge Donnellan, interview by Steve Dubb, Atlanta, GA, June 17, 2009. Crystal McLaughlin, interview by Steve Dubb, Atlanta, GA, June 17, 2009. Emory University, *Transformations: A Blueprint for Engaging Emory in Scholarship and Learning in Science and Community,* Report of the Emory: Engaging Community Advisory Board, June 7, 2007, 6.

37. Alicia Franck, interview by Steve Dubb, Atlanta, GA, June 17, 2009.

38. David Hanson, interview by Steve Dubb, Atlanta, GA, June 17, 2009. Betty Willis and Denise Walker, interview by Steve Dubb, Atlanta, GA, June 17, 2009. J. Lynn Zimmerman, interview by Steve Dubb, Atlanta, GA, June 17, 2009. Emory University, "*About the Clifton Community Partnership,*" 2008, http://cliftoncommunitypartnership.org/about/index.html (accessed November 20, 2009). "Emory's Clifton Partnership Aids Business, Community, and the Environment," *Knowledge @Emory,* October 9, 2008, http://knowledge.emory.edu/article.cfm?articleid=1188 (accessed November 20, 2009).

39. Of course, if one factors in the housing allowance and tuition waiver, the effective wage rate is much higher than nine dollars an hour. Kate Grace, interview by Steve Dubb, Atlanta, GA, June 17, 2009.

40. Grace, interview. Nathaniel Smith, interview by Steve Dubb, Atlanta, GA, June 17, 2009. Philip, interview.

41. Sam Marie Engle, interview by Steve Dubb, Atlanta, GA, June 17, 2009. Beverly Clark, "Community Partnership Programs Boosted by University Investment," *Emory Report* 59, no. 11 (November 13, 2006), www.community-wealth.org/_pdfs/articles-publications/universities/article-clark.pdf.

42. Smith, interview. Moshe Haspel, interview by Steve Dubb, Atlanta, GA, June 17, 2009.

43. Michael J. Rich, interview by Steve Dubb, Atlanta, GA, June 17, 2009.

44. The letter *V*—not the Roman numeral for the number five. For planning purposes, the City of Atlanta has chosen to group neighborhoods into "neighborhood planning units," each designated by a separate alphabet letter.

45. Rich, interview. Hanson, interview. Michael Rich and Sam Emory, "Connecting Campus to Community: A Place-Based Strategy for Preparing Engaged Scholars," Emory University, 2009, photocopy.

46. Andrew Furco, telephone interview by Rita Axelroth Hodges, September 8, 2009.

47. Freeman, interview. Jan Morlock, telephone interview by Rita Axelroth Hodges, September 16, 2009. Irma McClaurin, personal correspondence, June 4, 2010.

48. Bob Fockler, interview by Rita Axelroth Hodges, Memphis, TN, October 13, 2009.

49. Higgins, interview. Goldfarb-Findling, interview.

50. Rachel Gazdick, interview by Rita Axelroth Hodges, Syracuse, NY, May 29, 2009. "Syracuse Say Yes to Education and Economic Development," www.sayyestoeducation.org/syte/content/view/83/32/ (accessed May 25, 2009).

51. Thomas Scott and Kris Nelson, "Engaging the Northside Community: CURA and the Northside Partnership," *CURA Reporter*, Spring 2007.

52. For example, the Minnesota Youth Community Learning Initiative (MYCL) is a university-community partnership that has been associated directly with the Konopka Institute rather than the overall university. The Konopka Institute has a long history and deep ties in North Minneapolis but has not been directly involved with the Northside Partnership. W. K. Kellogg Foundation, "Engaged Institutions Cluster Evaluation," 9–10.

53. Belton and Harris, *Strategic Planning Process*.

54. Andy Schneggenburger, interview by Steve Dubb, Atlanta, June 17, 2009.

55. Cheryl Golden, Femi Ajanaku, and Damita Dandridge, interview by Rita Axelroth Hodges, Memphis, TN, October 12, 2009. "Hollis F. Price Middle College," www.loc.edu/hollis%20f%20price/about.htm (accessed December 18, 2009).

56. Louis Marcoccia, interview by Rita Axelroth Hodges, Syracuse, NY, May 29, 2009. Higgins, personal correspondence, March 31, 2010.

57. Eric Kaler, who comes from Stony Brook University in New York, was named the sixteenth president of the University of Minnesota on July 1, 2011, replacing Bruininks (who returned to teaching). In an op-ed for the local newspaper, Kaler indicated his support for continued university engagement. See: Eric Kaler, "Principles of a Great University," *Minneapolis Star-Tribune*, October 7, 2011, www.startribune.com/opinion/otherviews/131361643.html (accessed October 31, 2011).

58. Taylor, interview. Jones, interview. "University of Minnesota, Promotion and Tenure: Key Changes to the Faculty Tenure Policy," 2007, www.academic.umn.edu/provost/faculty/tenure/changes.html (accessed March 27, 2011).

59. Higgs, interview. Johnnie B. Watson, interview by Rita Axelroth Hodges, Memphis, TN, October 13, 2009. Liou, Davis, and Ards, *Historically Black Colleges and Universities*, 40–42.

60. Cantor, interview. Gazdick, interview.

61. Urban Research and Outreach/Engagement Center, "Broadband Access Project," www.uroc.umn.edu/programs/bap.html (accessed June 24, 2010). Irma McClaurin, personal correspondence, June 4, 2010. Minnesota's associate vice president for public engagement, Andy Furco, notes that the university also continues to make substantial investments in non-urban-focused public engagement initiatives, supporting more than 200 units, centers, and programs that conduct community-engaged work across the state, nationally, and internationally. Andy Furco, personal correspondence, June 30, 2010.

62. Emeagwai, interview. Robert Lipscomb, interview by Rita Axelroth Hodges, Memphis, TN, October 13, 2009. Liou, Davis, and Ards, *Historically Black Colleges and Universities*, 40–42. Pamela Perkins, "Towne Center at Soulsville set to go up in South Memphis," May 10, 2008, http://www.commercialappeal.com/news/2008/may/10/towne-center-set-to-go-up/ (accessed October 1, 2011).

63. Marcoccia, interview.

64. Ciannat Howett, telephone interview by Steve Dubb, Atlanta, GA, June 19, 2009. Ozzie Harris, interview by Steve Dubb, Atlanta, GA, November 3, 2009.

65. Higgs, interview. Minister Suhkara A. Yahweh, interview by Rita Axelroth Hodges, Memphis, TN, October 13, 2009.

66. Bogucz, interview.

67. Frank Caliva and Kevin Schwab, telephone interview by Rita Axelroth Hodges, July 10, 2009.

68. Irma McClaurin, personal correspondence, June 4, 2010.

69. Minister Suhkara, interview.

70. Nicci Brown, "Downtown Warehouse to Be a Focal Point for Syracuse University and Community Programs," March 24, 2005, www.syr.edu/news/archives/story.php?id=1643 (accessed June 2, 2009). Higgins, personal correspondence, March 31, 2010.

71. Higgs, interview. Tk Buchanan, personal correspondence, June 14, 2010. Sources include IRS income data, 2000–2007, and Geolytics Population estimates from 2009. Minister Suhkara, interview.

72. Reynolds-Anthony Harris, interview, August 24, 2009. Taylor, interview.

73. Caliva and Schwab, telephone interview. Tim Carroll, interview by Rita Axelroth Hodges, Syracuse, May 28, 2009. Daniel Queri, interview by Rita Axelroth Hodges, Syracuse, May 29, 2009.

74. Earl Lewis, interview by Steve Dubb, Atlanta, GA, June 17, 2009.

Chapter 8. Promising Practices and Lessons Learned

1. Dwight E. Giles Jr., Lorilee R. Sandmann, and John Saltmarsh, "Engagement and the Carnegie Classification System," in Hiram E. Fitzgerald, Cathy Burack, and Sarena D. Seifer, eds., *Engaged Scholarship: Contemporary Landscapes, Future Directions*, vol. 2, *Community Campus Partnerships* (East Lansing: Michigan State University Press, 2010), 161–176, especially 164–165.

2. Randy Stoecker, Mary Beckman, and Bo Hee Min, "Evaluating the Community Impact of Higher Education Civic Engagement," in Fitzgerald, Burack, and Seifer, *Engaged Scholarship*, vol. 2, 180. Carol Coletta, "CEOs for Cities: Engaged Scholarship for Urban Development," in Fitzgerald, Burack, and Seifer, *Engaged Scholarship*, vol. 2, 375.

3. For more on this theme, see Community Partnership Summit Group, "Achieving the Promise of Community-Higher Education Partnerships: Community Partners Get Organized," in Fitzgerald, Burack, and Seifer, *Engaged Scholarship*, vol. 2, 199–221, especially 205 and 214.

4. Penny A. Pasque, "Collaborative Approaches to Community Change," in Fitzgerald, Burack, and Seifer, *Engaged Scholarship*, vol. 2, 295–310, especially 306.

5. Lou Anna Kimsey Simon, "Engaged Scholarship in Land-Grant and Research Universities," in Fitzgerald, Burack, and Seifer, *Engaged Scholarship*, vol. 1, 99–118, especially 107.

6. Nancy E. Franklin and Timothy V. Franklin, "Engaged Scholarship and Transformative Regional Engagement," in Fitzgerald, Burack, and Seifer, *Engaged Scholarship*, vol. 1, 75–97, especially 92.

7. Eleanor Sharpe, *Anchor Institutions Toolkit: A Guide to Neighborhood Revitalization* (Philadelphia: Netter Center for Community Partnerships at the University of Pennsylvania, March 2008), 24.

8. Ira Harkavy, personal correspondence, April 27, 2010.

9. Lee Benson, Ira Harkavy, and John Puckett, *Dewey's Dream: Universities and Democracies in an Age of Education Reform* (Philadelphia: Temple University Press, 2007), 84. Cory Bowman, interview by Steve Dubb, Philadelphia, May 8, 2009.

10. Lewis Wendell, interview by Steve Dubb, Philadelphia, PA, May 4, 2009. Tony Sorrentino, interview by Steve Dubb, Philadelphia, PA, May 5, 2009. University City District, "University City Report Card 2009," 50 and 58. John Kromer and Lucy Kerman, *West Philadelphia Initiatives: A Case Study in Urban Revitalization* (Philadelphia: University of Pennsylvania, 2004), 22. Sharpe, *Anchor Institutions Toolkit*, especially 54, 69–72, and 91; Nicole Contosta, "Lewis Wendell, UCD's Third Executive Director, to Leave in June," *UC Review*, November 26, 2008, www.ucreview.com/default.asp?sourceid=&smenu=1& twindow=&mad=&sdetail=1114&wpage=&skeyword=&sidate=&ccat=&ccatm=&restate =&restatus=&reoption=&retype=&repmin=&repmax=&rebed=&rebath=&subname=&pf orm=&sc=2320&hn=ucreview&he=.com (accessed May 31, 2010). Lewis Wendell, personal correspondence, April 2010

11. Nancy Cantor, "A New Morrill Act: Higher Education Anchors the 'Remaking of America," *The Presidency*, Fall 2009, http://findarticles.com/p/articles/mi_qa3839/is_200910/ai_ n39234189 (accessed January 11, 2010).

12. Kathy Goldfarb-Findling, interview by Rita Axelroth Hodges, Syracuse, NY, May 29, 2009.

13. Marilyn Higgins, interview by Rita Axelroth Hodges, Syracuse, NY, May 28, 2009.

14. Connective Corridor, "Project Overview," no date, http://connectivecorridor.syr.edu/ project-overview/ (accessed February 8, 2010).

15. Jan Cohen-Cruz, interview by Rita Axelroth Hodges, Syracuse, NY, May 29, 2009. Eric Persons, interview by Rita Axelroth Hodges, Syracuse, NY, May 29, 2009.

16. Craig Taylor, interview by Rita Axelroth Hodges, Minneapolis, August 24, 2009. OBCED also runs a Community Workers Mentoring Initiative designed to match entry-level construction workers with experienced craftsman who will guide them to success on the job. Office for Business & Community Economic Development website, www.bced. umn.edu/Community_Program.html (accessed January 11, 2010).

17. Taylor, interview. Irma McClaurin, personal correspondence, April 26, 2010.

18. Ralph Maier, interview by Steve Dubb, Philadelphia, PA, May 5, 2009. Purchasing Services, "Local Community Supplier Spend," no date, www.purchasing.upenn.edu/sup ply-chain/local-community-supplier-spend.php (accessed June 12, 2011); Purchasing Services, "Purchase Order Spend," no date, http://www.purchasing.upenn.edu/supply- chain/purchase-order-spend.php; and Purchasing Services, "Diversity Supplier Spend," http://www.purchasing.upenn.edu/supply-chain/diversity-supplier-spend.php (accessed June 12, 2011). In fiscal year 2010 alone, Penn purchased approximately $100.5 million (approximately 11 percent of its total purchase order spending) from West Philadelphia suppliers; when Penn began its effort in 1986, its local spending was only $1.3 million. Determining economic impact is an inexact science, but given that

Penn has shifted more than $100 million of its spending to West Philadelphia, a rough estimate would suggest that Penn's effort has generated close to 190 additional local jobs and $6 million more in local wages than if old spending patterns had stayed in place. This estimate for local purchasing effect is extrapolated from a study of Grand Rapids and surrounding Kent County in 2008, which found that if residents shifted 10 percent of their retail purchases to local stores ($840 million), this would generate 1,614 new jobs, $53.3 million in wages, and $137.3 million in economic activity. Penn's shift of $100.5 million is one-eighth of this amount; see Civic Economics, *Local Works: Examining the Impact of Local Business on the West Michigan Economy* (Grand Rapids, MI: Civic Economics and Local First, September 2008). For further information on the Penn model, see research of Professor John Kromer, cited in Radhika K. Fox and Sarah Treuhaft, with Regan Douglass, *Shared Prosperity, Stronger Regions: An Agenda for Rebuilding America's Older Core Cities* (Oakland, CA: PolicyLink; Denver, CO: Community Development Practitioners' Network, 2006), 70–72. This estimate was originally configured by Steve Dubb in Ira Harkavy et al., "Anchor Institutions as Partners in Building Successful Communities and Local Economies," in Paul C. Brophy and Rachel D. Godsil, eds., *Rethinking HUD for a Catalytic Federal Government: A Report to Secretary Shaun Donovan* (Philadelphia: Penn Institute for Urban Research, University of Pennsylvania, February 2009), 147–168, especially 159.

19. Maier, interview.

20. Maier, interview.

21. Diane-Louise Wormley, interview by Steve Dubb, Philadelphia, PA, May 8, 2009. Maier, interview.

22. Maier, interview. Speaking to Penn's continued commitment to economic inclusion through three presidencies, Assistant Vice President of Community Relations Glenn Bryan, notes, "Resources aren't the answer to success as much as it's the commitment to think outside the box. You need strong senior management support for the initiative. This work is part of the Penn Compact, coming out of the Office of the President." Glenn Bryan, interview by Steve Dubb, Philadelphia, PA, May 5, 2009.

23. Michael J. Rich, interview by Steve Dubb, Atlanta, GA, June 17, 2009. Kate Grace, interview by Steve Dubb, Atlanta, GA, June 17, 2009. Young Hughley, executive director of RRC, a community development corporation in Reynoldstown, hosted Emory fellows during the program's first year and vouches for its impact: "We had five to six kids, really bright kids. They worked with my CDC and three other community-based organizations to do an assessment of our services, our service area, and our capacity . . . What really came out of that was a matrix that talked about duplication of services, strengths of our organization, and what we could leverage." Young Hughley, interview by Steve Dubb, Atlanta, GA, June 18, 2009.

24. Steve Dubb, Emory Community Building & Social Change Fellows Program meeting notes: Discussion led by Michael J. Rich and Kate Grace, Atlanta, GA, June 17, 2009.

25. Steve Dubb, Emory Community Building & Social Change Fellows Program meeting notes.

26. Emory University, Office of University-Community Partnerships, "OUCP Staff," no date, http://oucp.emory.edu/pages/oucp/staff.html (accessed June 9, 2010).

27. Richard Bray, Darrell Nickolson, and Starla Officer, "CHANGE—Campuses Helping to Address Neighborhood & Grassroots Efforts," presented at the Twenty-second Annual National Conference on Race and Ethnicity in American Higher Education (NCORE), San Diego, 2009. Jim Grim, Monica Medina, and Starla Officer, "GWCHS and IUPUI—Partners in the Community," presentation at the National Conference on University-Assisted Community Schools as an Effective Strategy for Education Reform K-16+, University of Pennsylvania, June 3, 2009.

28. Diane Arnold, interview by Rita Axelroth Hodges, Indianapolis, IN, August 3, 2009. Indiana University–Purdue University Indianapolis (IUPUI), *Community Outreach Partnership Center New Directions: Grant Agreement #COPC-IN-03–045, Final Report*, July 2007–June 2008. Another public health initiative led by the Office of Neighborhood Partnerships resulted from a five-year community health plan developed in partnership with Near Westside leadership as part of a COPC grant. This plan was used by Clarian Health to secure a $720,000 grant from the U.S. Department of Health and Human Services to address health disparities in the Westside, which is now being coordinated through a local community center. Starla Officer, personal correspondence, April 29, 2010.

29. Lana Coleman, interview by Rita Axelroth Hodges, Indianapolis, IN, August 3, 2009. Officer, personal correspondence, April 29, 2010. Starla Officer, interview by Rita Axelroth Hodges, Indianapolis, IN, August 3, 2009. IUPUI News Center, "New IUPUI Center to Support Regional University-Community-School Partnerships," October 5, 2011, http://newscenter.iupui.edu/5361/New-IUPUI-Center-to-Support-Regional-UniversityCommunity-School-Partnerships (accessed October 27, 2011).

30. Jim Grim, personal correspondence, May 18, 2009.

31. Ceraso also notes, "Some on the university side thought we were going to think that the university was going to provide all kinds of financial backup. We worked out this mutual agreement—we were really more interested in the university's educational and human resources." Michael Ceraso, interview by Steve Dubb, New Haven, CT, October 8, 2009.

32. Ceraso, interview.

33. Merson also emphasizes building sustainable partnerships: "Twice a month the high school students come to the university to work with first-year medical students and do dissections at the Medical School. That uses university resources in a way that is completely sustainable and is not grant dependent." Claudia Merson, interview by Steve Dubb, New Haven, CT, October 7, 2009. Abby Benitez, interview by Steve Dubb, New Haven, CT, October 8, 2009.

34. Yale also aims to design its interventions to minimize the potentially disruptive impact of principal turnover. According to Merson, "Usually you don't go from a great principal to a terrible one, but it happens from time to time. Schools are not known for managing their boundaries. We'll leave if necessary. It has not happened often. Most of the things that we provide in the schools are so well managed that [they're seen as] bringing an asset to the school. We aim for user-friendly resources." Merson, interview. Joanna Price, interview by Steve Dubb, New Haven, CT, October 8, 2009. David Heiser, interview by Steve Dubb, New Haven, CT, October 7, 2009.

35. "Quality of Life Plan: Creating Our Future Near Westside Neighborhood," 2007, www. greatindyneighborhoods.org/index.php (accessed July 22, 2009). Robert Bringle, interview by Rita Axelroth Hodges, Indianapolis, IN, August 3, 2009.

36. Office of Neighborhood Partnerships, "Faculty Community Fellows," IUPUI, no date, http://csl.iupui.edu/onp/1b3.asp (accessed August 30, 2009).

37. Bringle, interview. Indiana University–Purdue University Indianapolis (IUPUI), *Community Outreach Partnership Center New Directions: Grant Agreement #COPC-IN-03-045, Final Report*, July 2007–June 2008.

38. Darrell Nickolson, interview by Rita Axelroth Hodges, Indianapolis, IN, August 3, 2009.

39. Portland State University, "Economic Development Strategy: A 10 Year Plan for Strengthening PSU's Contribution to Regional Economic Growth," 2009. University relationships with the city have not always been this strong, according to Lindsay Desrochers, former vice president for finance and administration at Portland State: "Since the 1960s, it's been a gradual progression: relationships waxed and waned with intensity of involvement, but we've always been on the positive side of the ledger . . . In the early1990s, Portland State did not have as much connection to the city. But we [also] didn't have much state money, so we *had* to partner with the city to get our development done. . . . And in today's recession, we are really the only ones providing construction jobs in Portland." Lindsay Desrochers, interview by Rita Axelroth Hodges, Portland, OR, July 13, 2009.

40. Bowers adds, "Their plan is good; we pushed them as far as we could. Of course, it's not as audacious as we'd like. I would like to see them have a little more focused, targeted partnership . . . But again, they are grossly underfunded; they have done a lot with very little." Lew Bowers, interview by Rita Axelroth Hodges, Portland, OR, July 15, 2009. Lisa Abuaf, interview by Rita Axelroth Hodges, Portland, OR, July 15, 2009.

41. Mark Gregory, interview by Rita Axelroth Hodges, Portland, OR, July 13, 2009.

42. Wim Wiewel, telephone interview by Rita Axelroth Hodges, August 13, 2009.

43. Portland State University, "Economic Development Strategy," 2009.

44. According to the Uptown Cincinnati website (an identity created by the Consortium), Consortium members alone employ nearly 52,000 people and have a payroll of $1.4 billion, http://uptowncincinnati.com/ (accessed December 10, 2009).

45. Michael Romanos, David Edelman, and Mahyar Arefi, *Community Interactions and Collaborations: Study of Peer Institutions—Main Report* (Cincinnati: University of Cincinnati, Office of the President, November 2006), 17.

46. Tony Brown, telephone interview by Steve Dubb, September 2007. Mary Stagaman, personal correspondence, May 6, 2010. Of course collaboration between the Consortium and the City of Cincinnati does not always go smoothly. "In a public-private partnership, what comes first—the plan, the subsidy, or site control?" asks Brown in a 2009 interview. "If you start with the plan, from a community development finance standpoint, any project requires 20–30 percent subsidy. So we would acquire a block and have it assembled, and often times the city wasn't ready with the subsidy. We tried to get a commitment for the subsidy while we were planning the project, but the city pushed back and said, 'No. Create the project first.' So how do you balance the financial risk

before you get public commitment?" Perhaps just as important, this deliberation can cause unmet expectations, particularly among neighborhood organizations involved in the planning phases. Tony Brown, telephone interview by Rita Axelroth Hodges, Cincinnati, OH, October 27, 2009.

47. Gerald Siegert, interview by Rita Axelroth Hodges, Cincinnati, OH, September 10, 2009. Gerald Siegert, personal correspondence, April 26, 2010. The Consortium initially held three community planning "Uptown Summits" that were held in 2004 and 2005. The consultant who helped the CEOs initially collaborate also conducted a general study of the community, which led to the development of a preliminary plan focused on public safety, transportation, housing, economic development, and integrated social services. As a result of resident input during the first summit, education became an additional focus area for the Consortium. Although many of these areas have yet to be fully addressed, in 2009–2010 the Consortium Board reaffirmed its broader socioeconomic mission. Romanos, Edelman, and Arefi, *Community Interactions and Collaborations*; Mary Stagaman, personal correspondence, May 6, 2010.

48. Scott Stiles, interview by Rita Axelroth Hodges, Cincinnati, OH: September 11, 2009. Mary Stagaman, interview by Rita Axelroth Hodges, Cincinnati, OH, September 10, 2009.

49. Syracuse University, "Our Vision," no date, www.syr.edu/about/vision.html (accessed Feb. 1, 2010)

50. Ed Bogucz, interview by Rita Axelroth Hodges, Syracuse, NY, May 28, 2009.

51. Marion Wilson, interview by Rita Axelroth Hodges, Syracuse, NY, May 28, 2009.

52. Higgins, interview. Higgins also brings with her experience as a former economic development executive for the regional utility company National Grid, a corporate partner of Syracuse University.

53. Nancy Cantor, interview by Rita Axelroth Hodges, Syracuse, NY, May 29, 2009. Louis Marcoccia, Douglas Freeman, Eric Beattie, and Allan Breese, interview by Rita Axelroth Hodges, Syracuse, NY, May 29, 2009.

54. Cantor, interview.

55. Monica Rimai, telephone interview by Rita Axelroth Hodges, October 5, 2009.

56. Gerald Siegert and William L. Doering, "Implementing Community Development at the University of Cincinnati," presented at the Treasury Symposium, Jan. 26, 2009. Rimai, interview. In addition, the university established reserves of approximately 20 percent of principal and a portion of accrued interest "because of the extended periods over which we expect to be able to recover those investments," says Siegert. Siegert, personal correspondence, April 26, 2010.

57. Bourgeois also comments that with the university's name on the planning document and a very open planning process through CHCURC, property owners realized that "UC's checkbook" was behind the efforts. "Basically, we paid a huge premium [for property] because of our transparency." Matt Bourgeois, interview by Rita Axelroth Hodges, Cincinnati, OH, September 11, 2009.

58. Bourgeois, interview. Matt Bourgeois, "Clifton Heights Community Urban Redevelopment Corp.," Cincinnati, OH: September 14, 2009, document in possession of author.

Mary Stagaman, interview by Rita Axelroth Hodges, Cincinnati, OH, September 10, 2009.

59. Rimai, interview. Dan Monk and Lucy May, "Tax Credits Could Catalyze Cincinnati Projects," *Business Courier of Cincinnati,* August 28, 2009, http://cincinnati.bizjournals. com/cincinnati/stories/2009/08/31/story1.html (accessed October 20, 2009); "CDFI Awards for Uptown Consortium, Inc. NMTC (2009)—$45,000,000," www.topgovern-mentgrants.com/cdfi.php?State=OH&cdfi_id=1634 (accessed July 7, 2010). "Uptown Cincinnati: Key Accomplishments, Investments, and Redevelopment Efforts," Cincinnati, OH: August 25, 2011, document in possession of author.

60. Rimai, interview.

61. For more information on LeMoyne-Owen College's and the LeMoyne-Owen CDC's participation in the HUD HBCU grant program, see Nina Liou, Laurel Davis, and Sheila Ards, *Historically Black Colleges and Universities: Three Case Studies of Experiences in Community Development, vol. 2, Case Study Reports,* prepared for the U.S. Department of Housing and Urban Development Office of Policy Development & Research (Baltimore: Optimal Solutions Group LLC, October 2007), 37–72 and 111–124.

62. The senator also had previous relationships with Soulsville's STAX museum and had secured $2 million for its reconstruction a few years earlier. Jeffrey Higgs, interview by Rita Axelroth Hodges, Memphis, TN, October 12, 2009.

63. Higgs, interview. Liou, Davis, and Ards, *Historically Black Colleges and Universities,* especially 69–70. Pamela Perkins, "Towne Center at Soulsville Set to Go Up in South Memphis," May 10, 2008, http://www.commercialappeal.com/news/2008/may/10/ towne-center-set-to-go-up/ (accessed October 1, 2011). Daniel Connolly, "Soulsville Rising in South Memphis," August 15, 2009, http://www.commercialappeal.com/ news/2009/aug/15/soulsville-rising/ (accessed October 1, 2011).

64. Community Development Financial Institutions Fund of the US Department of the Treasury, "New Markets Tax Credit Program Overview," www.cdfifund.gov/what_we_ do/programs_id.asp?programID=5 (accessed Jan. 18, 2009). Higgs, interview. Romanos, Edelman, and Arefi, *Community Interactions and Collaborations,* especially 125–127.

65. Higgs, interview.

66. Miami Dade College, *Miami Dade College Highlights and Facts* (Miami: MDC, 2009).

67. "MDC's Hospitality Institute to Offer Customer Service Training and Job Opportunities to Inner City Residents," *Miami Dade College News and Events,* April 27, 2009, www. mdc.edu/main/news/articles/2009/05/h_i_job_opportunities.asp (accessed March 27, 2011). Geoffrey Gathercole, interview by Rita Axelroth Hodges, Miami, FL, May 12, 2009. "The Hospitality Institute," http://egov.ci.miami.fl.us/Legistarweb/Attachments/57266. pdf (accessed March 27, 2011).

68. H. Leigh Toney, interview by Rita Axelroth Hodges, Miami, FL, May 12, 2009. Eduardo Padrón, e-mail interview by Rita Axelroth Hodges, June 5, 2009.

69. Padrón, e-mail interview. *Miami Dade College Highlights and Facts, 2009.* Miami Dade College, "Saviors of Our Cities: Survey of Best College and University Civic Partnerships," draft revised May 22, 2009.

70. Sherrie Pugh, interview by Rita Axelroth Hodges, Minneapolis, MN, August 24, 2009.

71. Tom Moran, "Some North Side Residents Wary of U Partnership," *Minnesota Daily*, May 1, 2008.

72. University Northside Partnership, *Community Affairs Committee*, www.unpmn.org/cac/index.html (accessed Aug. 30, 2009).

73. Makeda Zulu-Gillespie, interview by Rita Axelroth Hodges, Minneapolis, MN, August 25, 2009. CAC members consist of resident, community and faith-based organizations, local businesses, and city representatives, as well as university faculty, staff and students.

74. Geoff Maruyama, interview by Rita Axelroth Hodges, Minneapolis, MN, August 24, 2009. Mary Fitzpatrick, interview by Rita Axelroth Hodges, Minneapolis, MN, August 24, 2009.

75. Zulu-Gillespie, interview. UROC's consultants have also recommended that they develop guiding principles—such as community participation in planning and implementation phases—for all university research projects proposed for the Northside community. Erline Belton and Reynolds-Anthony Harris, *Strategic Planning Process Phase One: Report on Interviews, Findings, & Preparation for the Futures Conference* (Pittsburgh: Lyceum Group, 2008).

76. The building, which was named a finalist for the Best in Real Estate Award, has space that is available for community and organizational meetings. Since opening its doors in October 2009 up until its official grand opening and ribbon cutting on May 12, 2010, almost 9,000 people visited the Center. Irma McClaurin, personal correspondence, June 4, 2010.

77. Irma McClaurin, interview by Rita Axelroth Hodges, Minneapolis, MN, August 24, 2009; Raymond Dehn, interview by Rita Axelroth Hodges, Minneapolis, MN, August 25, 2009.

Chapter 9. Building Internal Constituencies for Partnership Work

1. Nancy Cantor, "A New Morrill Act: Higher Education Anchors the 'Remaking of America," *The Presidency*, Fall 2009, http://findarticles.com/p/articles/mi_qa3839/is_200910/ai_n39234189 (accessed Jan. 11, 2010).

2. Cantor, "A New Morrill Act."

3. Cantor, "A New Morrill Act."

4. Harry Boyte, "Civic Mission Work, Report on Overall Lessons, 1997–2005," *Report to Kettering Foundation*, August 31, 2005, 1.

5. Boyte, "Civic Mission Work," 1 and 6. Lee Benson, Ira Harkavy, and John Puckett, *Dewey's Dream: Universities and Democracies in an Age of Education Reform* (Philadelphia: Temple University Press, 2007), 33 and 126.

6. Maggie Astor and Betsy Morais, "Court Rejects Eminent Domain in Manhattanville," *Columbia Spectator*, December 4, 2009, http://www.columbiaspectator.com/2009/12/04/court-rejects-eminent-domain-manhattanville (accessed March 27, 2011). Kate Tighe, "Allston Residents Feel 'Steamrolled' by Harvard Development," *The Citizen: The Student Newspaper of the Kennedy School*, November 14, 2007, http://harvardcitizen.com/2007/11/14/allston-residents-feel-%E2%80%9Csteamrolled%E2%80%9D-by-harvard-development (accessed February 10, 2010).

7. Victor Rubin, personal correspondence, June 9, 2010.

8. Ira Harkavy et al., "Anchor Institutions as Partners in Building Successful Communities and Local Economies," in Paul C. Brophy and Rachel D. Godsil, eds., *Rethinking HUD for a Catalytic Federal Government: A Report to Secretary Shaun Donovan* (Philadelphia: Penn Institute for Urban Research, University of Pennsylvania, February 2009), 147–168, especially 153.

9. David Perry, Wim Wiewel, and Carrie Menendez, *The City, Communities, and Universities: 360 Degrees of Planning and Development* (Cambridge, MA: Lincoln Institute of Land Policy, 2009), 4.

10. Rosalind Greenstein, interview by Rita Axelroth Hodges, April 14, 2009.

11. Andrew Hahn with Casey Coonerty and Lili Peaslee, *Colleges and Universities as Economic Anchors: Profiles of Promising Practices* (Waltham, MA: Heller Graduate School of Social Policy and Management and Institute for Sustainable Development/Center for Youth and Communities, Brandeis University; Oakland, CA: PolicyLink, 2002).

12. The National Review Board for the Scholarship of Engagement, led by Amy Driscoll and Lorilee Sandmann, represents one significant effort to ensure that the same level of strong peer review exists for anchor institution mission or engagement work as exists for research and teaching. For more on this topic, see Steve Dubb and Ted Howard, *Linking Colleges to Communities: Engaging the University for Community Development* (College Park, MD: Democracy Collaborative, August 2007), 80–82.

13. Carnegie Foundation for the Advancement of Teaching, "2008 Community Engagement Classification," http://classifications.carnegiefoundation.org/descriptions/ce_2008.php (accessed June 17, 2010).

Chapter 10. Catalyzing Change with Philanthropy

1. Barbara and Edward Netter Center for Community Partnerships, *Annual Report 2007–2008*, 39.

2. Cory Bowman, interview by Steve Dubb, Philadelphia, PA, May 8, 2009.

3. Steve Dubb and Ted Howard, *Linking Colleges to Communities: Engaging the University for Community Development* (College Park, MD: Democracy Collaborative, August 2007), 91–94, see especially 92.

4. Elizabeth Hollander, telephone interview by Steve Dubb, September 2, 2005.

5. Harry Boyte, telephone interview by Steve Dubb, September 9, 2005.

6. John Burkhardt, telephone interview by Steve Dubb, September 12, 2005.

7. Justin Wellner, personal correspondence, May 2010. Coalition of Urban Serving Universities, *Initiatives: Annie E. Casey Foundation* (Washington, DC: USU, 2010), www.usu-coalition.org/initiatives/annieecasey.html (accessed May 31, 2010). Strive—Cincinnati/Northern Kentucky, "Strive Model Spreading to Other Cities," April 29, 2009. The Casey Foundation has also been a critical supporter of the Anchor Institutions Task Force.

8. On the Social Innovation Fund, see: Corporation for National and Community Service, *Social Innovation Fund*, Washington, DC, March 2, 2010, www.nationalservice.gov/about/programs/innovation.asp (accessed March 27, 2011).

9. The Foundation Center's Statistical Information Service, *Distribution of Foundation Grants by Subject Categories, circa 2009* (New York: Foundation Center, 2011), http://

foundationcenter.org/findfunders/statistics/gs_subject.html (accessed October 31, 2011).

10. "Engaged Institutions: Enriching Communities & Strengthening Families," www. engagedinstitutions.org (accessed January 25, 2010).

11. Ted Howard, personal correspondence, September 28, 2009. These ideas are also described in Gar Alperovitz, Ted Howard, and Thad Williamson, "The Cleveland Model," *The Nation,* March 1, 2010.

Chapter 11. Policy Support for the Anchor Institution Mission

1. Henry Taylor, telephone interview by Rita Axelroth Hodges, April 16, 2009.

2. In fiscal year 2010, NIH's total budget was $31.246 billion. National Institutes of Health, *Enacted Appropriations for FY 2008–FY 2010* (Bethesda, MD: NIH, 2010). On its website, the NIH notes that "more than 80% of the NIH's funding is awarded through almost 50,000 competitive grants to more than 325,000 researchers at over 3,000 universities." "NIH Budget: Research for the People," May 18, 2010, www.nih.gov/about/budget.htm (accessed March 27, 2011). For NSF grants to universities in FY 2010, see National Science Foundation, "NSF FY 2011 Budget Request to Congress," Arlington, VA, 2010, 12. On funding of the land-grant program, see The Cornerstone Team, "NIFA Programs Spared Cuts in President's FY 2011 Budget Request; AFRI Funding Proposed at $429M," *The Cornerstone Report,* February 1, 2010, www.land-grant.org/reports/2010/02–01.htm (accessed March 27, 2011). Figure for the Office of University Partnerships from Gar Alperovitz, Steve Dubb, and Ted Howard, *Rebuilding America's Communities: A Comprehensive Community Wealth Building Federal Policy Proposal* (College Park, MD: Democracy Collaborative at the University of Maryland, April 2010), 28. NSF budget in FY 2011 was $6.806 billion (versus $6.872 billion in FY 2010, effectively a 1 percent cut. (The lower number cited for FY 2010 reflects the amount regranted to universities, not the entire NSF budget.) The NIH budget also received a 1 percent cut. The NIFA budget was cut more deeply. On NIH, see American Society of Hematology, "NIH Funding Update: NIH to Receive About 1 Percent Cut In FY 2011," Washington, DC, April 12, 2011, http://www.hematology.org/News/2011/6566.aspx (accessed October 7, 2011). On NSF, see Bethany Johns, "NSF Funding for FY 2011," *AAS Policy Blog,* American Astronomical Society, April 13, 2011, http://blog.aas.org/2011/04/13/nsf-funding-for-fy2011 (accessed June 2, 2011). On NIFA, budget was cut by $128 million, more than 9 percent, for a FY 2011 total of $1.23 billion. See National Coalition for Food and Agricultural Research, "Letter to the Honorable Jack Kingston, Chair and Ranking Member Farr, Re Support for Restoring Funds to Top-Line Budgets of ARS and NIFA," May 13, 2011. OUP data based on telephone conversation with Kinnard Wright, grant specialist at the HUD Office of University Partnerships, June 2, 2011.

3. On the elimination of Learn and Serve America funding for FY 2011, see Patrick Covington, *Update on the 2011 National Service Budget* (Washington, DC: Office of the CEO, Corporation for National and Community Service, April 18, 2011), http://www. nationalservice.gov/about/newsroom/statements_detail.asp?tbl_pr_id=1960 (accessed June 27, 2011). The Obama administration has proposed restoring funding in FY 2012.

See Office of Management and the Budget, *Fiscal Year Budget of the United States Government* (Washington, DC: White House, 2011), 167–168.

4. United Neighborhood Centers of America, *$65 Million for Choice Neighborhoods* (Washington, DC: UNCA, December 10, 2009), http://unca-acf.org/?p=643 (accessed March 3, 2010). Hayling Price, *Promise Neighborhoods: A Planning How-To Guide* (Washington, DC: Alliance for Children and Families and United Neighborhood Centers of America, September 30, 2009). American Planning Association, *APA's Overview of Federal Interagency Partnership for Sustainable Communities Programs in the FY 2011 Budget Proposal* (Washington, DC: APA, February 2, 2010). US Department of Health and Human Services, *Obama Administration Details Healthy Food Financing Initiative* (Philadelphia, PA: HHS, February 19, 2010), www.hhs.gov/news/press/2010pres/02/20100219a.html (accessed March 27, 2011). Radhika Fox and Sarah Treuhaft, *The President's 2011 Budget: Creating Communities of Opportunity*, (Oakland, CA: PolicyLink, 2010). Robin Shulman, "Harlem Program Singled Out as Model," *Washington Post*, August 2, 2009, www.washingtonpost.com/wp-dyn/content/article/2009/08/01/AR2009080102297.html (accessed March 27, 2011). American Humane Association, *Federal Fiscal Year (FY) 2011 Budget* (Washington, DC: AHA, April 14, 2011). National Low Income Housing Coalition, *FY11 and FY12 Budget Chart for Selected HUD Programs* (Washington, DC: NLIHC, April 27, 2011).

5. Office of University Partnerships, *Grantee Database* (Washington, DC: HUD, June 6, 2009), http://oup.org/grantee/map_search.asp (accessed February 21, 2010).

6. Avis Vidal, Nancy Nye, Christopher Walker, Carlos Manjarrez, Clare Romanik, *Lessons from the Community Outreach Partnership Center Program* (Washington, DC: Urban Institute, 2002), prepared for the U.S. Department of Housing and Urban Development Office of Policy Development and Research, chapter 1, 11.

7. Ira Harkavy et al., "Anchor Institutions as Partners in Building Successful Communities and Local Economies," in Paul C. Brophy and Rachel D. Godsil, eds., *Rethinking HUD for a Catalytic Federal Government: A Report to Secretary Shaun Donovan* (Philadelphia: Penn Institute for Urban Research, University of Pennsylvania, February 2009), 147–168; Ira Harkavy et al., "Anchor Institutions as Partners in Building Successful Communities and Local Economies: Recommendations for HUD Action: Budget Documents," Jan. 2009, unpublished addendum in possession of authors. For more policy recommendations from the Coalition of Urban Serving Universities, see "Summary of the Urban University Renaissance Act of the 21st Century," July 2010, www.usucoalition.org/advocacy/uura.html (accessed July 26, 2010).

8. On the federal government sustainability office (established in 2009) and its developing program, see U.S. Environmental Protection Agency, *HUD-DOT-EPA Interagency Partnership for Sustainable Communities* (Washington DC: EPA, May 7, 2010), www.epa.gov/dced/partnership/index.html, (accessed March 27, 2011).

9. Ira Harkavy et al., "Anchor Institutions as Partners," especially 154 and 159–161.

10. Victor Rubin, telephone interview by Rita Axelroth Hodges, April 8, 2009. Note that Rubin's comment does not directly apply to HUD funding provided for Minority-Serving Institutions, which has served as substantially more than "seed funding." Armand Carriére, personal correspondence, April 27, 2010.

11. PolicyLink, "Equitable Development Toolkit," Oakland, CA, http://policylink.com/ (accessed January 25, 2010).

12. David Cox, telephone interview by Rita Axelroth Hodges, April 8, 2009.

13. Ira Harkavy et al., "Anchor Institutions as Partners," see especially 154 and 156.

14. Rosalind Greenstein, telephone interview by Rita Axelroth Hodges, April 14, 2009.

15. Taylor, interview. Ira Harkavy et al., "Anchor Institutions as Partners," especially 160.

16. Cox, interview. Taylor, interview. Irma McClaurin, interview by Rita Axelroth Hodges, Minneapolis, MN, August 24, 2009.

Conclusion. Thinking Forward

1. Derek Bok, *Universities and the Future of America* (Durham, NC: Duke University Press, 1990), 21 and inside book flap.

2. Steve Dubb, personal notes, Anchor Institutions Task Force Meeting, Philadelphia, PA, June 10, 2010. Coalition of Urban Serving Universities, *Urban Universities as Anchor Institutions: A Report of National Data and Survey Findings* (Washington, DC: USU, July 2010). For more detailed data from this survey by school, see Coalition of Urban Serving Universities, *Urban Universities: Anchors Generating Prosperity for America's Cities* (Washington, DC: USU, July 2010). Armand Carriére, visiting fellow at the New England Resource Center for Higher Education, notes that there is also a need for the field to collect more outcome measurements in addition to process measurements—e.g., what percentage of local residents secured a job after participating in a workforce training program, not merely how many completed the training. Armand Carriére, personal correspondence, April 27, 2010. A few promising examples of outcomes measurements were presented in this report.

3. Steve Dubb, personal notes.

4. Lee Benson, Ira Harkavy, and John Puckett, *Dewey's Dream: Universities and Democracies in an Age of Education Reform* (Philadelphia: Temple University Press, 2007), 84.

Index